Westminster Shorter Catechism

Bible Study and Commentary

Paula Rodriguez

Tanglewood Publishing

Tanglewood Publishing

800-241-4016

Fortressbk@aol.com

Grateful acknowledgement is made to:

Dean and Chapter of Westminster for permission to use the Jerusalem Chamber
picture in works on the Westminster Confession of Faith and Catechisms; and to
Crossway/Goodnews publishers for quotations from the English Standard Version
of the Bible.

ISBN-13: 978-0-9852897-7-5

Layout and Design by

Wendy C. Potzgo

Printed in the United States of America

Very Special Thanks

The doctrines of God are serious things, and I wanted to make sure that this study was as useful and theologically sound as possible, so I asked for two separate groups of opinions.

For theological guidance, I turned to my many pastor and elder friends. Each one read at least one lesson (several read many more than one) and gave me valuable advice and encouragement. I would like to thank my husband, Charlie Rodriguez, and also John Allen, Roger Collins, John Currid, Charles Dunahoo, Ken Elliott, Tim Fortner, Matt Giesman, Brian Kinney, Simon Kistemaker, Alan Kolodny, Lou Lavallee, Paul Lipe, Paul Long, Don Malin, Mike Milton, Elias Medeiros, "Buck" Mosal, Gordon Reed, John Reeves, David Sinclair, David Wakeland, Guy Waters, and Richard Wiman for helping me to make sure the comments in this study are theologically valid and in accordance with Scripture and the Westminster Standards.

The second group was asked to do the lessons and to critique the questions and answers. I would like to thank Barb Martin, Emily Prince, Andrea Perkins, and Emily Reeves for their help with this. One friend in particular went above and beyond, and she became my editor for this project. I first met Amy Carter when she was twelve or thirteen years old, and I was a friend of her mother. Amy has since earned a master's degree in English and is now a friend in her own right. She has been through every lesson, and she has not only answered all of the questions, but she has also edited all of the written work. Amy, I could not have done this without you.

Above all, I thank my Father in Heaven, Jesus Christ His Son, and the Holy Spirit in guiding me through this process. I have learned a lot, and realized that I still have a lot to learn.

TABLE OF CONTENTS

Section THREE: Communion with Our God

INTRODUCTION

The *Westminster Confession of Faith* and the Shorter Catechism which grew out of it are statements of doctrine, of what many people believe are the teachings of the Bible. We who were involving in writing this study believe that they contain the best summary of what God has revealed to us through His Word. We also believe that if a person understands these teachings, they will bring much peace and comfort to his or her life in Christ. But we do not believe that understanding all of this doctrine is necessary to salvation.

The truths contained in the Shorter Catechism cannot be understood unless a person first has come to a saving knowledge of Jesus Christ. These truths are spiritually understood; they do not make sense to the human mind without the guidance of the Holy Spirit. If you have not yet established a personal relationship with Jesus Christ, this might not be the right time for this study. If you choose to continue with it, please remember that salvation comes first, then very slowly, the understanding of the knowledge of God.

The Shorter Catechism or the *Westminster Confession of Faith* is NOT the gospel. The Gospel is very simple: "Believe in the Lord Jesus Christ, and you will be saved." This means that we must understand that we are sinners and have broken the law of God, and that therefore we deserve to be punished. But Christ, in His mercy, took on our sins and died in our place. If we accept His death as punishment for our sins and agree to live in obedience to Him, out of our love and gratitude to Him, we will live forever with Him in eternity. That is the Gospel. The Shorter Catechism seeks to teach believers the doctrine of what we call the Reformed faith.

That is where this study comes in. Our goal is that by entering into this study, you will gain a better understanding of the teaching that is called the Reformed faith, which is contained in the *Westminster Confession of Faith* and the Larger and Shorter Catechisms.

There are some parts of the Shorter Catechism that are easy to understand and others that are very difficult. God leads each of us into understanding of this doctrine in our own time; so if there are things that seem too hard to take in, we encourage you to pray, search the Scripture, and then let God lead you in your own time as He directs. We also encourage you to be patient with others as they take their own individual journey through the mysteries of God's plan. Let God be God. He is much better at it than we are.

The Westminster Confession and Catechisms

On May 13, 1643, the British Parliament organized an assembly of ministers (or "divines") to create standards for a Church of England that would be reformed in worship, government, and doctrine. The Assembly comprised 151 members, including 30 laymen, chosen by Parliament to represent the counties, the universities, the House of Lords, and the House of Commons. Three were ministers of the Reformed Church of France, serving congregations in Canterbury and London. Twenty-eight did not attend, and twenty-one were appointed later to replace members who did not attend or who died during the proceedings.

The Westminster divines, mostly teachers and pastors of churches, were described by the Parliament as "learned, godly, and judicious." And they were. The Assembly's members were all Calvinists in theology; the main difference among them was in their views of church government and discipline. This resulted in a number of groups or parties—moderate Episcopalians (most of whom declined to attend out of loyalty to the king), Presbyterians (much the largest group), and Congregationalists.

The Assembly met at first in Westminster Abbey's imposing Henry VII Chapel. As the weather turned cooler, the divines were glad to move to the more comfortable Jerusalem Chamber. Every member took a vow to "maintain nothing in point of doctrine but what I believe to be most agreeable to the Word of God; nor in point of discipline, but what may make most for God's glory and the peace and good of his Church." The Assembly met every day except Saturday and Sunday, from nine o'clock until one or two. In the afternoons, the divines worked in committees. One of the rules guiding the deliberations required that "what any man undertakes to prove as necessary, he shall make good out of Scripture." The minutes and other reports of the Assembly's work reveal a strong commitment to this rule.

Much of the time of the Westminster divines was taken up with preaching and hearing sermons. Many hours were spent in corporate prayer and discussion concerning the lessons of God's providence. There were 1163 numbered sessions of the Westminster Assembly, the last coming on February 22, 1649.

Over the course of five and a half years, during a time of political and religious chaos, the Westminster Assembly created five great documents of theological orthodoxy and ecclesiastical stability for the church in England, Ireland, and Scotland.

The Westminster Confession of Faith is the Assembly's most important work. Drawing on the richness of the creeds and confessions of church history, the Westminster divines summed up in thirty-three chapters "what man is to believe concerning God, and what duty God requires of man." The Westminster Assembly also produced two catechisms—"one more exact and comprehensive, another more easy and short for new beginners." The Larger Catechism was completed in October 1647, and The Shorter Catechism a month later.

The Westminster Confession has been translated into many languages and has shaped Reformed churches and thought throughout the world. Its biblical faithfulness has helped many to know "how we may glorify and enjoy" God.

--excerpted from David B. Calhoun. "The Westminster Assembly." *The Confessions of Our Faith*. The Fortress Edition. 2007.

Used with permission.

How to Use This Study

As a teacher, I always want my students to be prepared when they come to class. I want them to be familiar with the material before they hear what I have to say about it.

That is the way I have approached this study. First, I want you to be familiar with the material. I want you to see for yourself what Scripture has to say about these doctrines. I have done that by giving you questions to answer related to each of the Catechism questions. After you have answered the questions, then read what I have to say. Test what I say against what you have read. Your discussions will be much richer if you have prepared each lesson.

Finally, many people like to memorize the Catechism questions and answers. That is not my purpose, but I am not opposed to it. It is much more important, however, to understand the truths of the words than to memorize the words themselves.

The Shorter Catechism questions and answers used in this study are from the Fortress Edition, which is a standard English edition. This edition seeks to maintain the original wording of the Confession and Catechisms as often as possible, while updating archaic or obsolete language to make it more understandable to the modern reader.

If you have questions about the doctrines contained in these studies, please ask your pastor about them. I would also be happy to discuss these things with you via email. My address is paula.catechism@gmail.com.

SECTION ONE

Created by God/Purchased by Christ

LESSON ONE
What are we here for?

Question 1:

What is the chief end of man?

Answer: Man's chief end is to glorify God and to enjoy him forever.

1. What does it mean that this is our <u>end</u>?

   Read Proverbs 16:4a; Isaiah 43:7

2. When should we glorify God?

   Read I Corinthians 10:31.

3. What does it mean to glorify God?

   Read I Thessalonians 5:16-18; Acts 17:11; 2 John 6; I John 4:21

4. How long should we glorify God?

   Read Psalm 86:12

5. How can your life be more glorifying to God?

6. What does it mean to enjoy God?

   Read Psalm 73:25; Philippians 4:4-7

7. How long will we be able to enjoy Him?

   Read John 6:51; Revelation 22:3-5

8. What are some things in your life that are keeping you from truly enjoying God?

9. How can you change things in your life to be able to enjoy God more fully?

Question 2:

What rule has God given to direct us how we may glorify and enjoy him?

Answer: The Word of God which is contained in the Scriptures of the Old and New Testaments is the only rule to direct us how we may glorify and enjoy him.

10. Where do the Scriptures come from?

    Read 2 Timothy 3:16

11. What about other books that have been written after the Bible or in addition to the Bible?

Read Galatians 1:8; Revelation 22:18-19

12. How do we know the Old Testament is still valid?

Read Matthew 13:10-17 What is Jesus quoting in this passage?

Question 3: What do the Scriptures principally teach?

Answer: The Scriptures principally teach what man is to believe concerning God, and what duty God requires of man.

13. What can you learn from the Scriptures?

Read II Timothy 3:16

14. What truths have you learned from the Scriptures recently that can be helpful to you in glorifying or enjoying God?

Commentary
Lesson 1

What are we here for?
Catechism Questions 1, 2, and 3

Have you ever wondered why you were put on this earth? Especially when you are afraid that your purpose might be to stare at a computer or to take care of children or to hammer nails for all eternity? Fortunately, God has a higher calling for all of us.

There is a popular poem by Langston Hughes called "The Creation" which portrays God as creating man because He is lonely; but let's be very clear about this—as good as Langston Hughes's poetry is, and it is very good, God has never been lonely. There is nothing that God needs that He does not already possess. God does not need us in the same way that we need Him or that we need other people.

So why did He create us? The Bible tells us that He created us for His own purposes. He made us because He wanted to. Okay, but what does that tell us about <u>our</u> purpose? Simply that we have one. As the old saying goes, "God don't make no junk." Everything God makes has a purpose. So why were we created? God tells us through His Word that He created us for His glory, and therefore, that our purpose is first of all to glorify Him.

Great. If you are like a lot of folks, you see the word glorify and it might as well be written in a foreign language. How in the world do you glorify someone? Do you walk around all day with your hands raised up saying, "I glorify you, O Lord!" You could, but that's probably not what God expects. It really wouldn't even get the job done, because in saying the words, you would be missing opportunities to do the deed. Fortunately, the Bible does give us answers, so we are not left without any direction. (Actually, I have found that God very seldom leaves us without any direction, if we look for it. Often, we just don't want to look.)

There are many Scriptures that point to what it means to glorify God; but to condense it all down to one word, that word would be **obedience**. When we obey God, we glorify Him, because we are giving Him first priority in our lives. This becomes especially important when our obedience to Him conflicts with what the rest of the world considers important. When we are faced with a choice between doing what our friends or co-workers think is the reasonable thing to do, and doing what we know God would want us to do—what choice do we make? If we choose God's way, that is glorifying God.

If no one knows about our choice, if we are faced with a temptation to sin, but we call on God and ask Him to help us resist it—that is glorifying God.

If we make a habit of reading the Bible and praying—that is glorifying God.

If we teach our children, grandchildren, nieces, nephews, etc. about God—that is glorifying God.

If we thank God for everything that He gives us, even the little things that we might often take for granted—that is glorifying God.

And if we tell other people about the things that God has done for us—that is glorifying God.

What other examples can you think of?

As Pastor Rick Warren has said in his book *The Purpose Driven Life*, it's not about you. He is right, it's about God. But God cares about you, because another purpose God has for you is for you to enjoy Him. Have you ever thought about enjoying God? We talk about worshipping God, praying to God, serving God, extolling God, loving God, trusting God, believing God, thanking God, etc., but hardly ever does anyone talk about enjoying God. Why not? We enjoy our spouses, we enjoy our children, we enjoy our friends, we enjoy our co-workers, we enjoy our fellow church members, why should we not enjoy God?

Marriage counselors tell us that we should enjoy our marriage partner because no one else knows us on such a deep and intimate level. But there are things that even our spouse does not know. For instance, my husband Charlie does not know that when he puts the dishes away, I sometimes re-stack them because I do not like the way he does it. I will not ever criticize him for this because I am eternally grateful that he is so handy around the house, but I am also a really picky woman. Okay, he knows now because he has read this. But there are lots of other things he does not know. However, there is nothing that God does not know. If someone were to tell you that he did not read the Bible this morning, but not to tell God because he didn't want Him to find out, you would be justifiably concerned about his sanity. So if our relationship with God is the most intimate relationship we have, does it not follow that we should get the most enjoyment out of that relationship?

So how do we do that? First of all, to thoroughly enjoy God, He must be first in our hearts; He must take first place on our priority list. It is easy to put something or someone else in that place, but if we do that, then we can slip into the sin of worshipping that thing or that person instead of God. And we can see God as "interfering" with our plans for our lives with that thing or person.

We have three daughters, and we love them dearly. Our idea of the perfect life could be that they all buy homes within a few minutes of mine and come over every evening with supper. (Notice that I did not say for supper. They all know that I am not fond of cooking.) However, God had other plans for them. None of them lives closer than a six hour drive from us. One lives in a different country.

We could really resent that. We have to plan and pack and drive (or even fly) if we want to see them. We have friends who probably feel sorry for us. But God has given our family so much fun and a wonderful son-in-law from a country we would never even have thought to visit. If God has first place, then we can enjoy Him and whatever plans He has for us.

Second, we need to not only accept what God has for us, but rejoice in it. As Paul tells us in his letter to the Philippians, we should present our requests to God, because He wants us to communicate with Him, and part of that communication is telling Him what we want. But part of that communication should also be thanksgiving for what He has already done for us and given us. By reminding ourselves of what He has already given us, it will be easier to rejoice and enjoy Him in the future.

We should rejoice always, but we need to be careful not to confuse joy with happiness. Happiness is a fleeting feeling of having what we want. Joy is a permanent feeling of knowing that everything is under control, even when we are not happy. It is possible to have joy even in the midst of deep sorrow, when we know that even though we don't understand the reason for our distress, there is a God who has everything under control. It is this underlying joy that makes our suffering bearable. I write this with great trepidation, because I have not even begun to master this. I will not set myself up as an example. I only know of others who have been examples to me. I know of a friend who faced her imminent death from ovarian cancer with a grace and serenity that could only have come from a deep and abiding joy in the Lord. I know of acquaintances who lost a newborn daughter they were never supposed to have been able to have in the first place, who managed to survive and raise other children to love the Lord only because of what must have been their deep faith and joy in the love of their God. And I know that in the deaths of two people who were very precious to me, of whose salvation I was not at all certain, I was kept from utter despair only because of the certainty that there is a God who knows the end from the beginning and who has everything under control and keeps us close in His sovereign hand.

Not only do we glorify God and get to enjoy Him, but it lasts forever! We will live forever! Think of it. Of course, if forever weren't any better than the life we have now, there are times we wouldn't want it. But our forever will be perfect. Forever begins now and continues into the next life, without sin, sickness, or sorrow. That's the kind of forever we can look forward to. And that's the kind of forever God promises us we will have. And all we have to do in return is glorify and enjoy Him.

How do we know that this is all true? The answer comes from one of the most basic of all Christian hymns, one that every one of us probably learned when we were children, "The Bible tells me so." The

Bible is the literal Word of God, meaning that God the Holy Spirit guided and directed what the men who wrote it were to write. One of the most amazing things about the Bible is that even though it was written over many centuries, by many different people, it is consistent in its teaching and its story. Through the Scriptures in the Bible, we can learn about God and how we can best serve and glorify Him [teaching]. We can also learn what we are doing that does not glorify Him [reproof], and how we can change that [correction]. And we can learn how to be the person that God has intended us to be [training in righteousness].

There are other books that claim to be messages from God, or divinely inspired books, but isn't it astounding! Even before any of those other books were written, God knew about them and warned us against them. Everything we need to know about God, and everything that is true about God, has been given to us in His Word. We can turn to others to help us understand His Word, but we must be very cautious whenever anyone adds to or takes away from what is written there.

Finally, let me say a word about the Old Testament. How do we know that it is still valid? There are some churches which call themselves "New Testament" churches, and do not consider the Old Testament to be relevant to our lives today. However, there are many, many examples of instances where an Old Testament passage is quoted in the New Testament. In many cases, these passages are quoted by Christ Himself. It is safe to assume that if Christ considered the Old Testament as valid, we can as well. The entire Bible, from beginning to end, is a picture of God's relationship with His people. We cannot ignore anything that God wants to tell us, no matter where in His Word it is located.

LESSON TWO
What is God like?

Question 4:

What is God?

Answer: God is a Spirit, infinite, eternal, and unchangeable, in his being, wisdom, power, holiness, justice, goodness, and truth.

1. What does it mean that God is infinite?

   Read Job 11:7-9; I Kings 8:27;

2. What does it mean that God is eternal?

   Read Psalm 90:2,10:16

3. What does it mean that God is unchangeable?

   Read James 1:17; Hebrews 13:8

4. How is God infinite, eternal, and unchangeable in His being?

   Read Psalm 139:7-10; Revelation 22:13; Hebrews 13:8

5. How is God infinite, eternal, and unchangeable in His wisdom and power?

Read Jeremiah 51:15; Psalm 147:5; Daniel 7:14

6. How is God infinite, eternal, and unchangeable in his holiness?

Read Psalm 111:9; Isaiah 6:3; Revelation 4:8; Numbers 23:19

7. How is God infinite, eternal, and unchangeable in his justice?

Read Psalm 33:5-6, Zephaniah 3:5

8. How is God infinite, eternal, and unchangeable in his goodness?

Read Psalm 100:5; Malachi 3:6

9. How is God infinite, eternal, and unchangeable in his truth?

Read John 14:16-17; I Peter 1:23-25

Question 5:

Are there more Gods than one?

Answer: There is but one only, the living and true God.

10. What does it mean that God is a living God?

Read Jeremiah 10:9-11; 2 Corinthians 6:16

11. What does it mean that God is the true God?

Read Deuteronomy 4:39

Question 6:

How many Persons are there in the Godhead?

Answer: There are three Persons in the Godhead: the Father, the Son, and the Holy Spirit; and these three are one God, the same in substance, equal in power and glory.

12. Where in Scripture do we see the three persons of the Godhead referred to together?

Read Matthew 3:16-17; 28:19; 2 Corinthians 13:14

Commentary
Lesson 2

What Is God Like?

Catechism Questions 4, 5, and 6

It is hard to fathom what or who God is. My daughter Lael has heard many different descriptions of God while working with a campus ministry in Europe. The students at the university where she worked prided themselves on their knowledge, openness to all ideas, and ability to think "critically;" so when asked the question "Who is God?" the campus workers got a wide range of, umm, "critical-ly-thought-through" answers. One answer was that God is a woman in the sky who does not judge anyone. Another said God is someone who helps us when we need it. Some believed that we create God our-selves according to our own personal beliefs. All of the answers were only half-hearted attempts to describe something that the students had never really considered because they were afraid of facing the truth and exploring something unknown. People are afraid to face the idea of God, because if there is a God, then they are subject to Him.

What is God like? To begin with, God is a Spirit; He does not have a body--not a man's body or a woman's body. He is not an old man or an old woman sitting in the sky looking down on us.

No one has ever seen the Spirit (unless there are some who may have seen Him in visions), but all of us have seen the effects of the Spirit. Jesus compared the work of the Spirit to the effects of the wind[1], and Billy Graham likes to expand on this idea. We cannot see the wind when it blows, but we can see what the wind does. We see the leaves blowing and we know that the wind is there because of the effects we see. God is everywhere, and we can know He is there by the things He does in the world and in our lives. God's Spirit is too wonderful and terrifying for us to see; it would be too overwhelming for our human eyes to bear. However, we can see the wonders that He

---

1   John 3:8

performs. God's Spirit is with us everywhere; He has no limits.

Although there is only one God, that God exists in three distinct persons. This is an aspect of the nature of God that all other religions have failed to recognize. Many people like to believe that everyone basically worships the same god regardless of the precise religion they follow, but that is simply not true. (Of course I am talking about major world religions here, not various Christian denominations.) All other religions either acknowledge more than one god or fail to acknowledge all three persons of the Godhead, which we call the Trinity. To do either of these things is to fail to worship the true God.

How do we know that God exists in three persons? Because Christ Himself told us so. In Matthew 28:19, He specifically instructed us to baptize believers in the name of the Father and of the Son and of the Holy Spirit. He told us that He and the Father are one[2] and that He would send us the Holy Spirit, who proceeds from the Father.[3] John also tells us in his first letter "For there are three that bear witness in heaven: the Father, the Word, and the Holy Spirit; and these three are one." (I John 5: 7) Because of what he wrote in his Gospel, we know that by "the Word" John is referring to Christ.

So how does that work, exactly? How can there be one God in three persons? I have absolutely no idea. Rumor has it that in our presbytery, when men were being examined for ordination, a particular seminary professor used to like to ask the question, "Can you explain the Trinity?" This was actually a trick question because the correct answer is "No." We cannot explain the Trinity. Every time we try, we not only fall far short of a good explanation, we usually end up committing one or more serious doctrinal errors. The problem is that our minds are too small to understand the ways of God. But rather than being upset by this, we should be comforted. I will probably say this many times during this study, but I am extremely glad that I cannot understand everything about God. I want God to know much more than I know and to understand things that I can-not possibly understand. If God's abilities were limited only to the things I can understand, He would be a very weak and limited God,

---

2   John 10:30

3   John 15:26

and that is not the kind of God I need or want. And fortunately, that is not the kind of God He is. God is not limited by what I know, by what I understand, or even by the things that limit me.

For example, God is not limited by time as I am because He has always existed in the past and will exist forever in the future. He is never in a hurry to get things done because He is afraid He will run out of time. Why? Because He created time! Look at Jesus' own words, "Before Abraham was, I am!" (John 8:58) Jesus did not say "I was" for a reason; God exists in the past, present, and future all at the same time. This is hard for us to understand because we exist within the time that God created. We have no understanding of something without a beginning or an end. When Lael was little, she would lie in her bed at night and think about how God did not have an end, and how, when we are with Him, we also do not have an end. This was so big for her little mind to understand that she would literally start crying and run to Mom and Dad for comfort. Our human minds simply cannot wrap around ideas of infinity and eternity because we had a definite beginning and we see so many endings.

God had no beginning and He has no end, and throughout all time God has never changed. His nature is exactly the same today as it was thousands of years ago. The God who spoke to Moses is the same God who is with us today. His attributes have not changed. God never gets any wiser or more powerful because He has always been as wise and as powerful as anything could ever be. His holiness has not decreased; He is still holy, holy, holy. God is still a just God, and in His wisdom He reigns with justice. We live in a world where people like to take situations into their own hands and do what they think is best, but God is the only pure and wise judge. We know that His justice will continue through all eternity and that He is the one who will right all wrongs.

God's goodness is so beautiful. His goodness has never changed; He wants the best for his children. He will never stop being a good God. Isn't that wonderful? Sometimes I have trouble remembering God's complete goodness. I see all the destruction in the world and it is easy to forget that we have a loving and good God who is there in the midst of it all. But because God's truth never changes and never diminishes, we know that we can trust that no aspect of God will ever change and that all of His words are forever true. He will always be there to love us unconditionally, to be with us in times of trouble, and to keep us on the right path.

Lael and I wish that the students she talked to could understand who God truly is. Instead they are limited by the fear of giving up control of their lives. We understand how frightening it is to give up control, but if we recognize who God truly is, then it is not frightening at all—because God is the one person we can totally and completely trust in and count on.

LESSON THREE

How big is your God?

Question 7:

What are the decrees of God?

Answer: The decrees of God are His eternal purpose, according to the counsel of His will, by which, for His own glory, He has foreordained whatever comes to pass.

1. How much control does God have?

    Read Daniel 4:35

2. Is God impulsive in what He does?

    Read Isaiah 46:10; 55:11; Proverbs 19:21

3. Does God have purposes for people?

    Read Exodus 9:16; Jeremiah 29:11

4. What does it mean that God has foreordained things?

    Read Isaiah 55:11; Jeremiah 1:5

5. What things has God foreordained?

    Read Proverbs 16:4

6. What difference does it make to know that God has a purpose for your life?

Question 8:

How does God execute His decrees?

Answer: God executes His decrees in the works of creation and providence.

7. What things did God create?

   Read Psalm 104:5-24

8. How did He create everything?

   Read Psalm 33:6-9

9. How does creation glorify God?

   Read Psalm 19:1; Psalm 104:12-13, 27-28, 31

10. How does God exercise His providence over us?

   Read Psalm 73: 24

11. How does this glorify God?

   Read John 16:13-14

12. In what ways have you been aware of the guidance of the Holy Spirit in your own life?

Commentary
Lesson 3:

How big is your God?
Catechism Questions 7 and 8

When our children were little, my husband and I used to teach classes in the Children's Catechism. The first question is "Who made you?" and the answer is "God." Really easy. And everybody got it right on the first day, even the very young ones. But the second question—oh my!

It sounds simple enough—"What else did God make?" The answer is "God made all things." Still pretty simple, right? For grown ups. But children are so literal. Almost every child we ever taught answered that question with a list—"God made flowers and trees and bunnies and penguins and oatmeal and mommies and butterflies and sandwiches and cars and milk …" You get the idea. But how do you correct them? They aren't wrong. God did make those things. We want them to understand that God made <u>all</u> things (we just don't want them to try to list them!)

Why did God do this? Simply because He wanted to. He had, and still has, a purpose for creating everything that He has created. (There are a few things that I am still wondering about, like those creatures that I sometimes have to exterminate out of my house, but I will have to trust that there is some kind of eternal purpose for them too.) The important thing here is purpose. Nothing, I repeat, NOTHING, on this earth exists here by chance, by accident. Everything is here to fulfill a purpose of God.

That can be hard to imagine in light of some of the horrible things that happen in today's world. But those same horrible things have happened ever since the beginning of time. Think of the first crime ever committed—a man killed his own brother because of jealousy. Not long after that and we have rape, incest, child sacrifice, and everything else that you can imagine. As Solomon says in Ecclesiastes,

"There is nothing new under the sun."

God knows about these things, and He can use these things for His purposes too. We may not be able to see how, but that is one reason that I am glad He is God and I am not. I am not smart enough to take these horrible events and make any good at all come out of them, but God can. God can see the end from the beginning, and He can orchestrate events so that good can triumph over evil, even if we never see it happen.

Have you ever stopped to think about what this means in your own life? You were created for a purpose. Before you were born, or even formed in your mother's womb, God had a purpose for you. God knew who you would be, what your name would be, where you would grow up, and under what circumstances. Some of us would have preferred to grow up in circumstances other than the ones we had. But we have to remember that God had a purpose in everything that happened to us. And His purpose is for our ultimate good. In Jeremiah 29:11 God tells us that His plans are to give us a hope and a future. Those are good plans. If you have been through hard times, I do not in any way want to minimize the pain and suffering you have been through. I would not pretend to try to explain what God's purpose was in allowing those things to happen. I am not nearly as wise as God. I will only tell you that I am absolutely positive that God's ultimate plan for you is good.

I also know that God created you for that good plan. Romans 9: 23-24 tells us that we who believe in Christ are not just allowed to share in Christ's glory, but we were actually created for that very purpose! Does that make you proud? It shouldn't. We had absolutely nothing to do with it. Just like you had nothing to do with your skin color or hair color (your <u>original</u> hair color ☺) or eye color, you had nothing to do with being created to share in Christ's glory. God did it all. It's nothing to brag about. It is something to thank God for.

Let's think about creation for a minute. There are those who want to leave God out of the picture, who want to leave it all up to chance. I don't want to dwell on the details of creation too much because we will take that up in the next lesson, but honestly, it takes much more faith to believe this all just "bloomed" into being. As a former pastor used to explain, if you were driving along the road and saw a random pile of boards, nails, and shingles, would you assume that was a house coming into being or a house falling down? Most of us would assume the house was falling down. Houses come into being in a more orderly manner. Usually the lumber is neatly stacked, the nails are in boxes, and the shingles are in boxes or stacks as well. Admittedly, there are messy contractors, but you get my point. Things come into being in an orderly way. First, you build the foundation, then the support beams, etc. You don't just mix up the boards and wait for a house to grow.

Most people who want to take God out of the picture of the formation of the world do so because they want to take God out of the picture of their lives. If God was there at creation, then He is probably still there. And if He is still there, He might expect something from them, and that might make them uncomfortable. So if they can explain God away from the beginning of things, then maybe they can make him cease to exist altogether.

If only logic really worked that way! If only I could make things cease to exist just because I don't want them to! Then my friend who died of cancer would not have died because I could have refused to believe the cancer existed, and it would have been gone. And my nephew whose wife left him could have refused to believe there was a problem in his marriage, and everything would have been fine. We could all live according to the motto on a dish towel my sister gave me: "Better living through denial."

Please don't read this and think I don't want God to exist. I am simply pointing out the absurdity of thinking that if I don't believe in Him, I can make Him go away. But as the title of one of Dr. Francis Schaeffer's books reads, "God is there and He is not silent." Refusing to believe in Him will not make Him go away. And there is not one shred of scientific evidence that disproves the existence of God and the "miraculous" appearance of life without intelligent interference, i.e. evolution. I do not have space to go into this argument here, but I will give a list of books at the end of this study that you can consult if you would like to do further reading.

God exists. He created everything simply by speaking it into being. And all of creation exists to glorify God, which it does, although imperfectly, because we live in an imperfect, fallen world. Which leads to the question—as part of His creation, are you doing your part to glorify Him?

But amazingly, that is not the only purpose God had in creating us. He also created each one of us to allow us to share in His glory. Wow! I can't believe I just wrote that. But it is absolutely true.

That would be enough, but God's providence means that He doesn't leave us alone to figure things out on our own. He guides us through this mess we call life. Have you ever thought about how messy life really is? People do not behave the way they are supposed to. I was talking with some friends the other night, and we were discussing how much better life would be if everyone would just obey the Golden Rule (Do to others as you would have them do to you). But we can't even get that right. So life gets messy. We have to deal with those people. And sometimes we are those people.

But God is still there with us in all the mess.

Have you ever smelled a skunk? Many of you know what skunks look, and more importantly, smell like. If you don't, imagine the worst thing you have ever smelled in your life. Now mix that with vinegar. That's skunk. When my youngest daughter was in college, she told me about a time when a skunk wandered onto the campus. One young man decided to try to catch it. He was not successful, but he got close. You can imagine the results. His roommate, in fact his whole dorm, was not amused. He smelled for days. He was pretty unpopular for a while.

Now imagine that was your four-year-old son. What would you do? You would have to help him. You couldn't stay away, because he wouldn't be able to take care of himself. So you would have to face the smell and deal with it. That's what God does. He can't stay away, because we can't take care of ourselves. We are like little children, and He cares too much for us to let us flounder about on our own. So He deals with the smells and the muck and whatever else we get ourselves into and cleans us up and puts us back on the right track until we mess up again.

Now if that guy had asked for advice, such as, "Do you think I should try to catch that skunk?" I'm sure someone would have given him some much-needed wisdom. Some of those students had undoubtedly smelled skunk before and didn't want to smell it again. And if we ask God for wisdom, He also promises to give it. We just have to remember to take time to ask. But too often we are so attracted by the pretty white stripe that we forget to ask if it's really good for us. And we end up suffering the consequences. But we never suffer alone. God is always with us.

So if we want to ask for advice, where do we find the counsel of God? We must always find His counsel in a way that is glorifying to Him. So first, we should look to His own Word in the Scriptures. We should be reading the Bible every day. We can often find the exact answer to the very question we have in our reading for that day. Or a good concordance can help us to find Bible verses which contain specific words. Other Bible study aids can help us to find passages on particular subjects.

Second, we can pray and ask God to direct us, but we need to be careful with this. We must be sure that the answer we think is from God is not in conflict with what is revealed in His Word. We must also be sure that we are ready to hear what God has to say. I had two dear aunts who are now with Jesus. They both loved the Lord, and on one visit to my family in Louisiana, they had a conflict. Aunt Sarah had driven there from Oklahoma and Aunt Jane had taken the bus from Arkansas. Aunt Jane wanted Aunt Sarah to take her home, but Aunt Sarah didn't want to. They decided to go into separate rooms to pray about it and see how God led them. After prayer, they came out and Aunt Jane said that God had revealed to her that Aunt Sarah should indeed drive her home. Aunt Sarah said that God had told her that Aunt Jane should take the bus. If you are going to pray, you have to be prepared to listen to God, not your own selfish desires. Sometimes our selfishness can yell so loud we don't allow ourselves to hear the clear, authoritative voice of God.

In addition to prayer, you can ask Christian friends. But again, we must be careful that they have our best interests and the truth of God at heart and not their own agenda. Cultivate godly friends who search the Scriptures for answers for their own lives, and they will do the same for you. And be certain you are asking Christian friends. People who are living to glorify God do not see the world in the same way that others do. We need advice from people who understand our purpose in the world and who know and love the God who created and sustains us.

God has a purpose for this world, and that purpose has not changed since the beginning of time. Part of that purpose was to create you to share in His glory. And having created you, He is still with you every step of the way. Listen to His voice and follow his guidance. He will lead you to your hope and your future, for His glory.

LESSON FOUR
Who made you?

Question 9:

What is the work of creation?

Answer: The work of creation is God's making all things from nothing, by the word of His power, in the space of six days, and all very good.

1. What does it mean that God made all things from nothing?

   Read Genesis 1:2; Hebrews 11:3

2. How did God create all things except man?

   Read Genesis 1: 3, 6, 9, 11, 14, 20, 24

3. How is a day defined in the Creation passage?

   Read Genesis 1: 5, 8, 13, 19, 23, 31

4. In what order did God create the world?

   Read Genesis 1: 3, 6, 9, 11, 14, 20, 24, 26

5. Why was everything good?

   Read Genesis 1:4, 10, 12, 18, 21, 25, 31; Psalm 19:1; Psalm 104:16-28

6. How was the Holy Spirit involved in creation?

   Read Genesis 1:2

7. How was Christ involved in creation?

   Read John 1:1-3, 14

8. How is the Triune God made evident in the Creation story?

   Read Genesis 1:26

9. How did God create man?

   Read Genesis 2:7

10. How did God create woman?

    Read Genesis 2:21-22

11. If you are a creation of God, and not a product of evolutionary chance, what difference does that make in your life?

Commentary
Lesson 4

Who made you?
Catechism Question 9

There are few issues in the Christian faith that can stir up as much controversy between believers and non-believers, and even among Christians, as the issue of Creation. Did God really create the earth? What about evolution? Hasn't science proved that all of life evolved from primitive organisms? And couldn't God have used evolution to create what now exists on earth?

I cannot possibly answer these questions in detail. Whole books have been written by men and women who are far more knowledgeable than I about such matters, and you can find a list of such books at the end of this study guide. However, I will touch on some of the basics.

First of all, since Scripture is to be our guide for all of life, then we must look to Scripture first; and Scripture tells us that God did indeed create everything in six days. There was absolutely nothing in existence other than God before Creation; there was an entire universe in existence afterward. We are given a fairly brief but detailed account of how it was done. God spoke, and things sprang into being. That is a miracle. But since God is in the business of miracles, we shouldn't be surprised.

Let's consider the alternative for a moment. First of all, let's define the term evolution. There are two major types of "evolution" to consider. Number one is something that most scientists, even creationists, agree on. Plants and animals do change over time. For example, in England there was a species of moth that came in black and white varieties. Since the white variety blended in better with the tree bark, the birds could see more of the black ones. More of the black ones got eaten, so there were more white ones. When the industrial revolution came along, the factories put out so much smoke that the trees were covered with black soot. All of a sudden the black moths were hidden and the white moths were easier for the birds to see. Now there were more black moths. That is a version of evolution called natural selection. Aspects of a creature that make it better able to adapt to its environment get carried on in its gene pool, and more and more of the creature have that characteristic. But the key is that the basic creature does not change into another creature. A moth is still a moth, a snail is still a snail, etc.

The second type of evolution is the problem. According to this theory, at one time there was a mass of something (matter, energy?) which suddenly exploded. This begs the question of where the mass of something came from, but let's proceed anyway. Eventually some of this stuff cooled off and formed spheres and some of it remained hot and formed stars. Or maybe the hot stuff spun off matter that then cooled off. Anyway, because of gravitational pull, the cool stuff began to rotate around the hot stuff, and we had solar systems. And also because of gravity, these solar systems were attracted to one another, and grouped together to form galaxies.

On some of these cool places (or maybe just one of them), where conditions were just exactly right, the exact right combination of hydrogen and oxygen formed in sufficient quantities to produce water. A little while later, the exact right combination of other elements combined to produce small cell-like structures, which then mutated to become living cells, which then combined and mutated until they became primitive organisms. These primitive organisms then mutated over and over again until they became more advanced organisms, and finally, primitive man developed. Man became more and more advanced until we are what we are today.

This is where creation science and evolutionary science part company. And yes, there are many reputable scientists who believe in Creation. In fact there are many scientists who find that true science provides much more evidence for the concept of Creation than for the idea of evolution.

Consider the odds of something like this actually happening. Let's look at the possibility of the formation of just one tiny part of a living cell--amino acids. The chance of the random generation of even one amino acid capable of existing in a living cell is 10 to the 123rd power. In other words 1 chance in 10 followed by 123 zeros. i.e. 1 in 1,000,000,000,000,000,000,000,000,000,000,000,000, 000,00 0,000,000,000,000,000,000,000,000,000,000,000,000, 000,00 0,000,000,000,000,000,000,000,000,000,000,000,000. The odds of winning the lottery are 1 in 80,000,000. And to sustain a living cell, this would need to happen 500 times.[4] What a miracle! But wait— this is science. Evolutionary science has no room for miracles. And these are the odds for just one of the millions of building blocks of life.

This sounds highly unlikely to me. But let's assume, for the sake of argument, that we hit the cosmic jackpot and actually got enough amino acids to create a living cell. There are still a lot of major road-blocks standing in the way of creating a human being, or anything remotely close.

First, there is the problem of going from the single cell to the multi-cellular, extremely complex organism called man. This would require that single cell to differentiate itself over and over again to form different organs and systems of the body. Many evolutionists want to explain this differentiation using the concept of mutation. The problem is that according to science, beneficial mutations do not occur. Mutations produce genetic abnormalities which are harmful, or even fatal, to an organism. But for random processes to have caused man to come into existence, such beneficial mutations would have had to occur thousands, if not millions, of times.

Second, there is a pesky little thing called the Second Law of Thermodynamics. It sounds complicated, but it's really not. To begin with, a Law is something that we really do know is true—like the Law of Gravity. We know that if we throw something into the air, it will fall down. Always. Every time. That's why it's called a Law.

The Second Law of Thermodynamics basically tells us that in a closed system (one that is not acted on by an outside force), there will be more and more disorder and less and less ability to do work

---

until there is no more ability to do any work at all. In other words, things wind down until they stop. For the universe and all it contains to have come into being through random processes, the universe must have had less disorder and more order, or in other words, the universe would have had to wind up and go faster and faster. That just doesn't happen. Not ever.

If the universe were created by God, however, the Second Law of Thermodynamics would not even apply. The universe would no longer be a closed system, since it would be acted upon by an outside force [God] and given the extra energy needed to do the job of creating and sustaining life.

So let's accept the fact that God did create the universe and everything in it, including us. How did He do it? He simply spoke, and it came into being. I was going to say we can only imagine—but I don't think we really can. In his book *The Magician's Nephew*, C. S. Lewis gives us a beautiful allegorical picture of what that might have looked like. Read Job 38:4-11 for God's own description of His work of creation. And He proclaimed that it was good.

How do you define good? Too often I consider something good if it's good for me—if I like it or want it or it makes me happy. But I don't think that's God's definition. I don't think that when the Bible says that God saw that something was good, it means that it made God happy. I do think it means that it pleased Him.

So what pleases God? According to I Samuel 12:23-24, it would be fearing the Lord and serving Him faithfully; in other words, obedience. When God created each thing, He gave it a purpose and told each thing what to do. And everything did as it was told; everything in all creation was perfectly obedient to God's command. So everything was perfectly good.

I have not yet touched on another tricky part of this whole story—the six days bit. Did God really create the entire universe in six days? Let me ask you a question—Could God have created the universe in six days?

If your answer is no, or even, I'm not sure, then you are

not giving God enough credit. Of course He could. He is God. He is all-powerful. He can do anything He desires to do. Nothing is impossible for God. Whether He could do it should not be up for discussion. But there is some question among godly and intelligent Bible scholars about whether He did.

I am not going to try to pretend that I know more than my brothers and sisters in Christ who have studied this far more than I have. I would just ask us all to be careful as we consider this issue and be sure we are letting our study of the Bible guide our study of "science" and not the other way around. In my own humble opinion, if God could do it, and the Bible says He did do it, there is no reason to believe He did not do it.

Throughout this discussion I have been talking about God creating the universe. What does the term God bring to your mind? God the Father? Sometimes we forget that the entire Trinity has always existed and will always exist. God—Father, Son, and Holy Spirit—created us. John makes it crystal clear that we are created by Christ, that He existed in the beginning and was and is God the Creator. Genesis refers to the Spirit of God being involved in the act of Creation.

I am a teacher of communication, and one of the basics of communication is that human beings have an innate need to communicate. John McCain is quoted as saying that when he was a prisoner of war, the men would risk torture and even death to communicate with one another. Most women have an innate need to communicate; we find particular pleasure in the act of communicating. Anyway, as a communication teacher, I find Genesis 1:26 fascinating. God said, "Let us make man in our image." Who was He talking to? To Himself. God has perfect fellowship with Himself. He doesn't need anyone else to communicate with because He has Himself.

I am not saying that I understand this. I absolutely do not. How the Trinity exists and operates is totally beyond the ability of my tiny brain to comprehend. But that actually gives me a great deal of comfort. The fact that I cannot understand God means that God is infinitely more wise and knowledgeable than I am, and that is the kind of God I want and need.

And this God, who did not and still does not need anyone or anything, chose to create you in His image. Of all of the millions of creatures He created, you are the one He created in a unique and special way. You are the one he formed from the dust of the ground, or from the rib of man, and into whom He breathed the breath of life. You are the one He created in His likeness. You are the one with whom He has a special bond.

What is your response to His creation? Do you understand how special this makes you? Does this humble you to know that the God who created the entire universe in six days, merely by speaking, loves you and desires fellowship with you? Can you respond to this awesome knowledge with the obedience that God desires and that He will call good?

LESSON FIVE
What's a person to do?

Question 10:

How did God create man?

Answer: God created man male and female, after His own image, in knowledge, righteousness, and holiness, with dominion over the creatures.

1. Is either man or woman more important to God?

    Read Genesis 1:27-28; Galatians 3:28

2. Describe the godly widow in I Timothy 5:9-10.

3. Describe the godly woman in Proverbs 31:13-25.

4. How do each of these women reflect the image of God?

    Read Nahum 1:7; Isaiah 61:10; Psalm 104:14

5. How are we to exercise dominion over the creatures?

    Read I Timothy 5:18; Genesis 9:3; Proverbs 12:10

6. How does your life reflect the image of God?

Question 11:

What are God's works of providence?

Answer: God's works of providence are His most holy, wise, and powerful preserving and governing all His creatures, and all their actions.

7. How does God preserve His creation?

   Read Hebrews 1:3; Job 39-41; Matthew 6:26-28

8. How does God govern His creation?

   Read Job 38:8-11, 35; 39:5-8, 26-29; Mark 4:35-41

9. How does God preserve His people?

   Read Psalm 121:8; Psalm 1:1-3

10. Does God preserve only His chosen people, or all people?

    Read Matthew 5:45, 6:31-33

11. How does God govern His people?

    Read Exodus 20:1-17; Job 12:23; Proverbs 3:6; Psalm 92:9

12. What is your response to the knowledge that God governs His creation?

Commentary
Lesson 5

What's a person to do?
Catechism Questions 10 and 11

I had a student a few years ago who was in her mid-thirties. She explained to me that she was going to college at this time in her life because her father had not let her go when she was younger. His opinion was that a girl only needed a high school education. After that, her role was to get married, have babies, and let her husband take care of her. I was stunned. I associated that kind of thinking with Jane Austen novels. I had no idea it still existed.

How does God view the role of women? Let's look at a few Scriptures. In Genesis, we have the examples of Sarah, Rebekah, Leah, and Rachel, who worked at home caring for their families. In the New Testament, we see the same types of examples in the lives of Mary the mother of Jesus, Elizabeth, and Martha. On the other hand, Proverbs 31 paints a picture of a wife and mother who takes care of her household and at the same time works as a very successful merchant. One of the judges of Israel was Deborah.[5] In Acts 16, we are told that the first Christian convert in Macedonia was Lydia, a seller of purple goods. We are never told that she was admonished to stop selling her wares. In Acts 18, we are introduced to Aquila and Priscilla, and we are told that they were tentmakers by trade. Later in that same chapter, we read that both Priscilla and Aquila instructed Apollo in the ways of God more accurately. Interestingly, Priscilla is mentioned first here.

Why then does Peter refer to women as the "weaker vessel"?[6] I think because it's the truth. Generally speaking, women are not as physically strong as men. That's why there are separate events for women and men in sporting events such as the Olympics. Women are also more emotional, as a rule. For example, we cry more easily.

---

5   Judges 4-5
6   I Peter 3:7

Women are generally more tender-hearted, which can make them more vulnerable to the deception of others. Peter is telling men to be understanding of this because that is the way God created us. Notice that Peter does not say "less intelligent vessel" or "less deserving vessel" or "less capable vessel." Please do not extrapolate meanings from the term "weaker" that God did not intend it to have. If He had meant less intelligent, etc., He would have said so.

So what about the idea that a woman's place is in the home? Where did that come from? Well, first of all, for most of history, everyone's place was in the home. All of the work, whatever it was, was done in the home. Somewhere along the way, men realized that they could leave the home, not being tied down with nursing babies, so they established places of business elsewhere. So it is basically a tradition that has come down to us from fairly recent history. I can find nothing in Scripture that commands that it is the mother who must do the majority of the child-rearing in the family. In fact, almost all of the Scriptures dealing with the raising of children are directed to the fathers.

In the country of Sweden, where Lael lives, they are trying to create a balance in child-rearing. When a couple has a child, both parents get seven months of child-care leave at 80% of their salary, with guaranteed re-employment at the end of the leave. Fathers must take at least two months of that leave and are encouraged to take their full seven months. This means that in Sweden, no child is away from a parent for at least the first year of life. Now there are many things about Swedish parenting laws that I have questions about, but this is something I can really support, especially when I see six-week-old babies in day-care because their mothers have no choice but to return to work if they are going to be able to financially make ends meet.

I suppose the point I am trying to make, in a very roundabout way, is that God created both male and female, and neither is less valuable to Him, nor less capable of serving Him. Nor has He limited what either gender can do in their service of Him, other than in certain roles in the church. Every once in a while I hear well-meaning Christians admonishing others, especially women, about life choices they have made. I think we need to be very careful about this. There are no instructions in Scripture about exactly what roles a woman is to take in society at large. There are examples of women who worked outside the home and women who worked in the home. Both can be valid and godly choices. Some women remain single and have fulfilling careers. Some women choose to stay at home and devote themselves full-time to the care of their families. Some choose to divide their time between family and career. Some even work full-time outside the home while their husbands stay home full-time and care for their children. It is up to each family to prayerfully consider what God would have them do, and it is up to other individuals and families to stay out of each others' business, unless they are specifically asked for advice. God does not give us the knowledge to judge each other's activities; in fact, He admonishes us against it.[7]

God may not have given us the knowledge to meddle in each other's lives, but He does give us knowledge of Himself and His Word. And if both male and female are created in God's image in knowledge, with no distinction, does it not follow that both are capable of understanding the things of God? Not as many women as men have formal seminary training, but women can read. And women need to study doctrine, formally or not. Not to do so is to be without necessary knowledge. That is part of the purpose of this study—to encourage both men and women in the understanding of the truths of our faith. There are lots of other good books out there, and we are all capable of understanding them.

Now if anyone has not become a new creature in Christ, then that's a different story. Godly knowledge is for God's people. If a person does not have the Spirit of God as his guide, he cannot understand the knowledge of God. It is incomprehensible and sometimes offensive to him. So in our evangelistic efforts, let's keep this in mind. Unsaved people need Jesus; they do not need the five points of Calvinism. My husband and I once met with a group of young Christians who were trying to start a Presbyterian church in their small town. They were very sincere in their beliefs, but perhaps a little over-zealous. One young woman confided in me that she had been witnessing to some-

---

7   Luke 6:41-42

one at work and was trying to explain to her the doctrine of limited atonement. I believe with all my heart in this doctrine, but that is not what this co-worker needed. She simply needed to hear that Jesus died for her sins. All of that other information is secondary; it does not lead to salvation. And in this case, I am very much afraid it was getting in the way of salvation. We cannot understand the things of God until we have the Spirit of God.

Along with understanding, which is a gradual process, we receive righteousness, which is immediate. When we receive Christ, His righteousness is counted as our righteousness. That is why His sinless life was so important. As sinful creatures, it is impossible for us to live the sinless life that God requires, so Christ did it for us. Then mysteriously, when God looks at our "sin account," He sees Christ's and sees no sin. It is as though we took a clean credit score and messed it all up. Instead of a perfect score of 850, we have reduced our score to 0. Whether through ignorance or greed, we have done everything wrong. Then Christ comes in and pays all of our debts and settles all of our accounts. And when God looks at our credit score, it's 850. Perfect. Okay, this analogy doesn't even come close really. A bad credit score in no way matches an entire life full of sin, but you get the point. If we would be grateful for a change in credit score, how much more grateful should we be for a change in the condition of our lives—from desperately sinful to perfectly righteous in God's eyes!

We are viewed as righteous, and we are also holy. This gets a little confusing, because we are told in Scripture that we are holy, and that we should work to be holy. In one sense, we are already holy—the moment we receive God's Holy Spirit, we are set apart from all of creation as one of God's chosen people. But in another sense, we must still strive to show that holiness in all of our daily activities. Can people look at your life and tell that God has set you apart for Himself? Do they see something different about you? A friend was telling me about a young girl she knows who was in tears one day because her friends were not as holy as she is. I think this young girl is missing the point. (Sort of like the man who won a medal for humility, only to have it taken away because he wore it.) Our holiness needs to be seen in our actions and in our words, but not by our proclaiming our holiness. The more we act in obedience to God's Word, the more others can see our holiness and desire it for themselves.

Please remember what holiness means—it is not "better than you." It is not sanctimonious, making a show of our piety. It is not judgmental of others. It is being set apart by God as His own and then choosing to obey God and His Word and to put Him in first place in our lives, in a quiet and humble manner. We can only begin in the smallest of ways to obey God in this life, but everyone who is born of God will begin to obey Him.

Holiness involves how we interact with all of God's creation. Regarding people, there is basically one rule and it is very simple: "Do to others what you would have them do to you." (Matthew 7:12) If everyone would just obey this one rule, the world would be a wonderful place. But of course we don't, so sometimes it isn't. Most major world religions have a version of this rule. In graduate school, I was assigned a paper on Jean Paul Sartre, an existentialist atheist philosopher and playwright. As Sartre thought about the world, even he came up with a version of this same rule. It just makes sense. Of course God thought of it first. Even more reason to follow it.

But how are we to treat the rest of creation? As just that—as something created by God. Man and woman's first job was to take care of creation. We are to preserve, conserve, and not waste what God has given us. We are to treat animals kindly, giving those in our care what they need to survive and thrive. If you choose a vegetarian lifestyle, that is your choice and I would support you in that choice, but let's not make the mistake of equating animals with human beings. God did give man and woman all kinds of animals as well as plants for food. He created man and woman differently from the way He created animals. Animals are wonderful creations, but they are not people.

Having created everything, God did not leave the world to take care of itself, but He is still involved in all of His creation. In fact, I understand from my scientific friends that when we consider the atom, everything in science would argue that the atom should fly apart. You and I should not exist. We should be in a billion tiny pieces. So what holds us together? God. Read Hebrews 1:3 again with that in mind. If God stopped for one minute, we would all literally fall apart. But we don't because God sustains and preserves us.

He also preserves us by providing for us. Some things He provides for everyone whether they believe in Him or not. Everyone is still held together. Everyone has food, shelter, clothing, etc. [Okay, most people.] But in some ways He particularly provides for His own people. There are special blessings that come from being a child of God. We know that He cares for us and will never leave us. We know that He is involved in our day to day activities and is concerned about the tiniest problems we might have. We know that He enjoys giving good gifts to those He loves. These are things reserved for His people. We also know that we will have an eternity with Him. Those who do not know Him have received their reward in full in this life. How sad that must be. This is it. This is all you get. This is the best it will ever be. There is only pain and suffering after this. In contrast, God's children know that pain and suffering is the temporary part, that this is worst it will ever be, and that after this, there is only joy and gladness.

Not only does God preserve us, He also governs us. Obviously, He has given us laws to live by, most notably the Ten Commandments. But He not only gives us laws to obey, He also guides and directs all of His creation. There are laws of physics that the entire universe follows. Where do you think those came from? Sometimes it seems that nature does a better job of obeying God than mankind does.

We must remember that God is always governing what happens on earth. We may not understand what's going on, but God always knows what is happening, and more importantly, He knows why it is happening. We should not be discouraged when things do not go the way we think they should, or when elections or politics fail to produce the results that we desire. We must always put our trust in God and not in man or in government. Human beings and human institutions will fail us and fall short of our expectations, but God will never fail us.

God has a perfect plan. We do not always [ever?] know exactly what that plan is. But God is always, let me repeat ALWAYS, in control of EVERYTHING. Things do not get out of His control. Whenever I feel that I don't understand what is happening in the world or in my life, I try to remember to be grateful that I have a God that I can't completely understand. That means that His wisdom and knowledge are so vastly superior to mine that He can know and understand things that I cannot begin to know and understand. So He is capable of knowing and understanding what is happening, and making it all turn out for the good of those who love Him.[8]

God made you in His image in knowledge, righteousness, and holiness. He is preserving and governing all of your life. Take a moment to consider how that will affect your day to day living of that life from now on.

---

8   Romans 8:28.

LESSON SIX

Who is your God?

Question 12:

What special act of providence did God exercise toward man, in the estate in which he was created?

Answer: When God created man, He entered into a covenant of life with him, on condition of perfect obedience, forbidding him to eat of Tree of the Knowledge of Good and Evil, on the pain of death.

1. Genesis 2:17 gives us the penalty for breaking the covenant of life that God established with Adam and Eve. From what you read in that verse, what was the covenant of life that God made with Adam and Eve?

Read Genesis 2:17

2. What was the one law that Adam and Eve were asked to obey to keep the covenant of life?

Read Genesis 2:17

Question 13:

Did our first parents continue in the estate in which they were created?

Answer: Our first parents, being left to the freedom of their own will, fell from the estate in which they were created, by sinning against God.

3. In the beginning, what was the only sin that Adam and Eve could possibly have committed?

Read Genesis 2:17

Question 14:

What is sin?

Answer: Sin is any lack of conformity to, or transgression of, the law of God.

4. How does a person sin by lack of conformity to the law of God?

Read James 4:17

5. How does a person sin by transgression of the law of God?

Read Daniel 9:11; Colossians 3:5

6. How have you sinned by lack of conformity to the law of God?

7. How have you sinned by transgression of the law of God?

Question: 15:

What was the sin by which our first parents fell from the estate in which they were created.

Answer: The sin by which our first parents fell from the estate in which they were created was their eating of the forbidden fruit.

8. How did Eve quote the law that she and Adam had been given?

   Read Genesis 3:3

9. How did the serpent finally tempt Eve to eat the fruit?

   Read Genesis 3:4-5

10. What kind of fruit was it?

   Read Genesis 3:1-12

11. What does Scripture tell us about how Eve convinced Adam to eat the fruit?

   Read Genesis 3:6

12. What happened immediately after they ate the fruit?

   Read Genesis 3:7

Commentary
Lesson 6

Who is your God?
Catechism Questions 12, 13, 14, and 15

Suppose in all of your life there was only one law. No traffic laws, no tax laws, no state laws, no federal laws—just one law: DON'T EAT THAT. You can eat anything else you want to. You can go anywhere you want to. You can do anything you want to. Just don't eat that one thing.

If you obey this one law, you will live in a perfect world forever. If you don't, you will die. Sounds like a good deal, doesn't it? I think I could live with that. The problem is, there would be that one thing, day after day, year after year. Always there. Staring at you. And you would start to wonder—what does it taste like? What does it feel like in your mouth? What is there about it that makes it so special? Why can't I have it?!

Have you ever been on a diet? All of a sudden, things you never even really wanted to eat seem incredibly important. I am thankful that I never started smoking because I'm not sure I would have the willpower to quit.

My husband once had a job teaching at a Christian college, and one part of his contract was that we both had to agree to two things: to attend a certain church and to not drink any alcohol, not even in our own home. The church was a good church and we didn't drink anyway, so we were not uncomfortable with signing this contract. But after a few months, those two stipulations became incredibly irritating. What if we wanted to go to a different church?! What right did they have to tell us what church to go to! And what if I wanted a glass of wine with dinner? I was an adult. How dare they tell us what to do in our own home! (Remember, we didn't have to sign that contract. He was free to refuse that job.)

So this is the situation Adam and Eve were faced with. One simple rule. One tree staring at them day after day, until Eve finally broke. We can understand it. We would have broken too. I can tell from what happened at that college that I certainly would have. But does that excuse her? Of course not. Because what her choice says about her is that she valued her own curiosity, her own "needs," above her love for God. She didn't love Him enough to obey one simple rule.

She had even added to the rule, possibly to help herself obey it. She had decided that she wouldn't even touch the tree, probably to keep herself from touching the fruit, to keep herself from eating the fruit. (God had never said not to touch the fruit, just not to eat it.) Now if that had helped Eve, I suppose it might have been okay. If something helps us avoid temptation, that can be a good thing. But we can't make those extra rules that we make for ourselves apply to everybody. Suppose Adam had touched the tree. Would she have yelled at him that he was breaking the rules? Jesus later on condemned the Pharisees for such behavior, for adding rules and regulations to the commands of God and then priding themselves on obeying their own rules rather than God's rules.[9]

So Eve's first problem was that she had really forgotten what the rule was. But her second problem was worse. She wanted to be like God. This was the temptation that got to her, the final straw. After she heard that, she could no longer resist. She took a bite; and she found that she did know something God knew. She knew what evil was. And not wanting to be alone in this knowledge, she gave some of the fruit to Adam. According to the passage in Genesis, it doesn't sound like he put up too much of a fight. There isn't any argument described there. She gave it to him and he ate it. So the deed was done.

As a side note, let's not blame the poor apple for this any longer. We are never told what kind of fruit this was. In my humble opinion, I think it was probably a fruit that we don't have any more. I do not know of any Knowledge of Good and Evil orchards around, so I suspect there are no such fruits anymore. You can picture that fruit any way you wish, but it did not look like anything you can get anywhere on earth today. I personally like apples and feel that they

---

9   Matthew 23:1-36

have suffered this indignity long enough.

But let's get back to this first sin—wanting to be like God. How is that manifest in our world today? How is it NOT manifest? There are some pretty blatant examples of this. Amazingly, there are people who have actually called themselves gods or Messiahs, such as David Koresh, who set himself up as the Messiah and leader of the Branch Davidians; Sun Myung Moon, the founder of the Unification Church, who sees his mission as completing what Christ left undone[10]; or the Maharishi Mahesh Yogi, the founder of Transcendental Meditation, who wanted to be seen as a Messiah.[11]

Then there are those who, though not calling themselves god, saw their role in society as that of a savior. Men like Napoleon, Adolf Hitler, Idi Amin, Pol Pot, and others have declared that they alone could save their nations from disaster. Ironically, all they managed to achieve was even greater disaster.

Even in our poetry, our wanting to be like God, or to be our own god, is evident. One of the most famous poems along this line is "Invictus" by William Ernest Henley, who died in 1903. The final stanza of that poem reads:

It matters not how strait the gate,
How charged with punishments the scroll,
I am the master of my fate:
I am the captain of my soul.

Interestingly, Timothy McVeigh, the man convicted of the Oklahoma City bombing, chose this poem to be his final statement. He gave a hand-written copy of it to the prison warden just before he was executed for his crime.

Does that surprise you? Horrify you? How could anyone claim that he is the captain of his own soul? Yet don't we all do that every single day?

---

10   The Unification Church, www.unification.org
11   "Maharishi Mahesh Yogi, Spiritual Leader, Dies," N Y Times, 02/06/08.

Suppose I have a particularly difficult friend, and she has said something particularly difficult to me. I know I should respond in love, but it's been a long day, and I'm tired, and besides, she has done this one too many times. So I tell her what I really think. And I probably hurt her in the process. But putting that aside for the moment, what am I saying to God? Basically I have told Him that I know what He wants me to do, but I don't care. I am the captain of my ship, and I will make the decisions for my life.

Every time we sin, we are declaring ourselves to be our own god. We are saying, in effect, "I will make the rules this time, no matter what God or anyone else thinks." We may not be as blatant or as vocal about it as some have been, but we are just as guilty. That is why every sin is equal in the eyes of God. Every sin is rebellion against His authority; every sin is setting ourselves up as our own god.

There are basically two kinds of sins, or two kinds of rebellion, if you will. The first is to do what we are commanded not to do. This is what Adam and Eve did. They had only one rule, and they refused to obey it. They were told not to eat the fruit, and they ate it anyway. We all commit this kind of sin every day because we choose to do things we are told not to do. Probably not the big things. You have probably never murdered anyone in your life. You have probably never stolen anything—or have you? Have you ever "borrowed" supplies from work?

Anyway, we may not have committed sins that would send us to jail, but Jesus made it very clear that we can sin in thought as well as in action. In Matthew 5:21-22, He tells us that even being angry with our brother is a sin like murder. Further on, in verses 27-28, He says that to even think about committing adultery is a sin, even if we do not actually do the deed. So let's not be too quick to acquit ourselves of even the "big sins."

There is another kind of sin, and that is when we fail to do what we know we ought to do. Have you ever seen the bedroom of a teen-age girl? I have had three. Now there are admittedly exceptions to this, but most teen-age girls have mysteriously forgotten the use of a clothes hanger. Their floor is carpeted with the day's rejects, or with yesterday's latest fashion. Have you ever tried to get one of those girls to clean that mess up? Their response usually runs something like, "It's my room, so I should be allowed to live like I want to. Just close the door." (Ever say that to your mother?)

And we, in turn, reply with something truly profound, such as, "This is my house, and you will do as I say. When you get your own house you can live in any kind of mess you want to." (Honestly, is that the best we can come up with?)

We want the room clean because the disorder affects the entire family. But the disobedience affects the entire family as well. We want the rules of household obeyed. But what is the disobedience? The daughter didn't do something she was told not to do; she was in her room, minding her own business. However, she did not do something she was specifically told to do.

That is the second kind of sin. We know what we should do, but we are too lazy, or busy, or self-absorbed to do it. Who knows how many times that happens in a day, much less a lifetime. We can always make excuses and rationalize our choices, but in the end, the excuses are just that—excuses. Whenever there is a good act that should be done, and we don't do it, we have also told God that we are now in control. We are the captains of our own little ships, and we aren't interested in what He thinks.

So we are all sinful. We can blame Adam and Eve for letting sin into the world, but we know in our hearts that we would have done exactly what they did. And we still do it every day. We want to be in control of our own lives, to be our own gods. Fortunately, God works in spite of our attitudes and does not leave us to our own devices, mistakes, and failures. Even though we are so often unfaithful to Him, He is constantly faithful to us.

LESSON SEVEN
Where did we go wrong?

Question 16:

Did all mankind fall in Adam's first transgression?

Answer: The covenant being made with Adam, not only for himself, but for his descendants, all mankind, descending from him by ordinary generation, sinned in him and fell with him, in his first transgression.

1. Who was included in the covenant of life that God made with Adam and Eve?

   Read I Corinthians 15:21-22; Romans 5:19

2. How did the results of the Fall apply to the descendants of Adam and Eve?

   Read Romans 5:12; Genesis 3:22

Question 17:

Into what estate did the Fall bring mankind?

Answer: The Fall brought mankind into an estate of sin and misery.

3. How was all mankind affected by Adam and Eve's first sin?

   Read Romans 5:12; Genesis 3:16-19

Question 18:

What is the sinfulness of that estate into which man fell?

Answer: The sinfulness of that estate into which man fell consists of: the guilt of Adam's first sin, the lack of original righteousness, and the corruption of his whole nature, which is commonly called original sin, together with all actual transgressions that proceed from it.

4. What does "original sin" mean?

   Read Psalm 14:2-3; Romans 3:23

5. What is the result of original sin?

   Read Matthew 15:19; Ephesians 2:1-3

Question 19:

What is the misery of that estate into which man fell?

Answer: All mankind, by their fall, lost communion with God, are under His wrath and curse, and so made liable to all miseries of this life, to death itself, and to the pains of hell forever.

6. What does it mean to be under God's wrath and curse?

   Read Psalm 88:14-18

7. Why are the miseries of this life worse for those without God?

   Read Romans 1:18, 28-32; Philippians 4:6-7

8. What is different about death for the believer than for the unbeliever?

Read Matthew 25:34, 41

9. How did Jesus describe Hell?

Read Mark 9:48

10. Who was hell primarily created to punish? Where is the devil now?

Read Matthew 25:41; I Peter 5:8; I John 4:4

Commentary
Lesson 7

Where did we go wrong?
Catechism Questions 16, 17, 18, and 19

Have you ever signed a contract that involved your entire family? Have you bought a house, opened a business, or borrowed money for any other reason? What would happen if you broke the contract? Would you be the only one affected? Unfortunately, the answer is usually no.

If a mother and father are unable to pay their mortgage or rent, the entire family is left without a place to live. If a small business goes bankrupt, often an entire family or several families are left without an income. What we do often affects others. Parents represent their children in paying the household bills. Business owners represent their employees in making business decisions. And so it was with Adam and Eve; they were our representatives in mankind's first dealings with God. I used to think that it was terribly unfair of God to punish everyone for the sins of these first two people, but now that I think about it logically, there was really no other choice.

What happened when Adam and Eve sinned? Evil entered the world. And along with evil came death. The first death recorded in the Bible was God's killing of an animal to make clothing for Adam and Eve. And since evil and death were in the world, obviously any children born to Adam and Eve would also be affected. They would know both good and evil, and they would be subject to death. There was no going back.

The punishment inflicted on Adam and Eve would also be inflicted on their children. Eve and all women who followed her would have pain in childbearing. If you have had a child, you know that this is no small thing. For some women, it is easier than others, but for every woman, there is pain involved. There is pain before the birth, during the birth, and even after the birth.

For Adam, and also for Eve, there was the difficulty of life on earth. Providing for our families would no longer be as easy as picking fruit off of trees. Adam and Eve, and all of their descendants, would have to work hard for their food. There would be drought, and floods, and insects, and harsh winds, and diseases that would destroy crops. None of this would have happened before the Fall.

Whatever problems you are facing today, you can blame them on Adam and Eve, at least a little. But not entirely, because much of the responsibility still falls on you. Although sin entered the world through Adam and Eve, we each choose to continue to sin on our own. If we are truly honest with ourselves, we will find that much of the misery and chaos in our lives is of our own making. We make choices based on our own selfish desires and find that they are not good for us at all. Some of the misery and chaos that we have to deal with is due to the choices of others. What we do affects others, and what they do affects us. All the way back to Adam and Eve. And on and on into the future.

Sounds pretty hopeless, doesn't it? And without Christ, it would be. Without Christ, this world wouldn't stand a chance. We would all just continue to sin and be sinned against as long as we were forced to live. That's basically what the term "original sin" means. Without Christ, we cannot do anything good. Without Christ, everyone sins. Everyone in the world is born with the tendency to sin.

But what about a sweet little newborn baby? She can't possibly sin, can she? She's so sweet and tiny and delicate. Just wait until that sweet little tiny baby is about four months old and then take something away from her that she wants. See how delicately she screams at you. Little babies can have a real temper! I know; I raised three girls. They were the three cutest little girls on the planet at the time, but they were still sinful little creatures.

My friend Cara's second child was a darling little boy. One morning when he was six weeks old, she put him in his car seat to go to the grocery store. He screamed. Cara knew something must be terribly wrong, so she took him out to see what was the matter. She checked his diaper, burped him, rearranged his clothing, and everything seemed fine. He seemed happy. She put him back in the car seat and he screamed again. So she took him out and checked him over, and again he seemed fine. She put him back in the car seat, and you guessed it, he screamed. Cara finally realized that she had a very smart little baby boy. At the age of six weeks, he had figured out how to get out of that car seat—scream really loud. Now I don't know if that's exactly sinful, but it is at least manipulative. And that was at six weeks old.

We humans are sinful. We are born sinful. And we continue to be sinful for our entire lives. That is original sin. We cannot change it. Actually, we don't want to change it. We are very happy with our sin. We are not always happy with the consequences, but we like doing what we want and thinking of our needs and desires first. We don't want to think about God, and we don't want to try to please Him. We don't even much like the idea of God at all. Left to ourselves, apart from His grace, we pretty much reject Him altogether.

And when we reject Him, we have no relationship with Him. We don't want one, so we don't think we miss it; but there is something in everyone that yearns for God. Deep in our hearts, everyone knows that there is a God who created him or her. When they are facing real trouble, they want God to be there. How many people all of a sudden began to pray on September 11, 2001?

But Christ does not want lukewarm believers.[12] We cannot love Him only when it suits us. Either believe or don't believe, but there is no middle ground. If we do not truly believe, then we are under His wrath and curse. So when we are afraid, there is really no one to turn to; we are alone with our fears.

Scripture even tells us that if we persist in our unbelief, God will give us over to our sins.[13] God will leave us alone to suffer the full brunt of the consequences of what we are doing. If we truly desire a life of sin, then He will allow us to live that life, with everything that it entails. He will allow us to have what we think we want. He will allow us to associate with the type of people who also want that lifestyle. He

12   Revelation 3:16
13   Romans 1:24-25

will not intervene to make our life easier. There will be sin in all of its debauchery and wickedness, with all of its accompanying misery. We will be not only the perpetrators but also the victims of a totally sinful lifestyle.

Contrast that with the promises made to those who trust in God. In our salvation, Christ, rather than Adam, becomes our representative with God. He promises to be near to us always, and to hear us when we call. He tells us to cast our cares on Him, and He promises to give us peace even in the midst of frightening circumstances because He will never leave us. And not only that, when this life is over, He promises us a place in His eternal kingdom forever.

What is the promise for those who continue to reject God? There is a promise for them as well, but it's not very attractive. God promises that they will be cast into the lake of fire, or Hell.

I don't like writing about Hell, and I'm pretty sure you don't like reading about it. In fact, I would prefer to skip this part of the lesson completely. But if Jesus talked about it, I don't have the liberty of ignoring it. Jesus warned against Hell, describing it as a place where the worm never dies and the fire is not quenched. It is a terrible place. And it is real. It is not something someone in church made up to scare people into coming forward and getting saved. Jesus warned people about it to scare them into taking their relationship with God seriously. And if it causes some people to recognize their need for a Savior and accept God's plan of salvation, then I have no problem with it.

I want to put to rest a myth about Hell that has circulated for years, perhaps for centuries. Maybe you could call this a "pet peeve" of mine, but I have heard so many people, even some preachers, get this wrong, and so many Christian songs get this wrong, that it is really starting to bother me. So let's set the record straight right now—Satan is not in charge of Hell. Hell is a place that God created to punish Satan and his followers. God is in charge of Hell, not Satan. Satan is not in Hell now; He is on earth, roaming around, creating havoc, tempting people to sin, causing destruction, etc. Satan will have no control over Hell, and it is not somewhere that he wants to be. I don't know where we got the idea that Satan is the King of Hell, except perhaps from Satan himself. The idea is nowhere in Scripture. Satan is referred to as the prince of the power of the air or the prince of this world, which confirm the idea that He is on earth seeking people to do his bidding. Hell is a real place, and it is terrifying. We don't want to be there and neither does Satan.

So far this is a pretty depressing picture; man without God is hopeless, doomed to a life of sin and misery on earth and an eternity in the lake of fire. Thankfully, the picture isn't finished. In the next lesson we will get to see things from a happier vantage point, our redemption in Christ.

LESSON EIGHT
Who is this Man?

Question 20:

Did God leave all mankind to perish in the estate of sin and misery?

Answer: God, having out of his mere good pleasure, from all eternity, elected some to everlasting life, did enter into a covenant of grace, to deliver them out of the estate of sin and misery, and to bring them into an estate of salvation by a Redeemer.

1. When did God decide on His plan of salvation?

   Read Ephesians 1:4

2. Why did God elect some people to everlasting life?

   Read Ephesians 1:4-5

3. Why do people need a Redeemer?

   Read Psalm 143:2; Romans 3:11-12

4. Why do you personally need a Redeemer?

5. Romans 3:23 and I Corinthians 15 15:3-4 describe what is called the Covenant of Grace. From what you read in these verses, what is the covenant of grace?

Read Romans3:23; I Corinthians 15:3-4

Question 21:

Who is the Redeemer of God's elect?

Answer: The only Redeemer of God's elect is the Lord Jesus Christ, who, being the eternal Son of God, became man, and so was, and continues to be, God and man, in two distinct natures, and one Person forever.

6. When did Christ begin to exist?

Read John 1:1, 17:5

7. What does it mean that Christ is the Son of God?

Read John 3:16; John 10:30; Matthew 3:17

Question 22:

How did Christ, being the Son of God, become man?

Answer: Christ, the Son of God, became man, by taking to Himself a true body, and a reasonable soul, being conceived by the power of the Holy Spirit, in the womb of the Virgin Mary, and born of her, yet without sin.

8. How was Jesus conceived?

Read Luke 1:35

9. Why is the virgin birth important?

Read Isaiah 7:14; Luke 1:35

10. How do we know that Christ had a real body, that he was fully man?

Read Luke 2:25-28, 8:45, 15:2, 22:63, 23:46

11. How do we know that Christ was really God?

Read Mark 2:10, 4:39, 5:35-42, 6:48, 16:1-7

12. Why is Christ's sinless life important?

Read Hebrews 4:15; Romans 5:19

Commentary

Lesson 8

Who is this Man?
Catechism Questions 20, 21, and 22

I mentioned in an earlier lesson that my husband and I taught a class for young children. He used to explain the problem of sin to them in this way: "We like to go outside and play, and sometimes we get really dirty. So then our mothers make us go in and take a bath and wash all the dirt off. They don't want us getting the dirt on the sofa or even the carpet, so they are happier when we are all clean. Sin is like invisible dirt. When we do something wrong, then we get invisible sin dirt on us. We can't see it, but God can. But we can't wash off the sin dirt with soap and water. We could scrub and scrub, but we could never get it off. But God's heaven is a holy place, and He can't let anyone in if they have sin dirt on them. So He sent Jesus to die for us. Jesus died to pay the penalty for our sins. Then when we believe in Jesus, all that sin dirt just goes away. It is washed off by Jesus. We can't wash it off, but Jesus can."

Admittedly, this is very simplistic, but we were working with three- and four-year-olds. But they got the message. One mother told me that her son was watching television when a commercial came on for laundry detergent. He piped up and said, "That stuff can't wash off sin dirt." How exciting! He was only four, but he got it.

We all have "sin dirt." And we can't get rid of it. But for some inexplicable reason, God wants us in His heaven, and He wants fellowship with us while we are still on earth. You know, there are days when I am in such a bad mood, I don't even want fellowship with myself, but God still cares for me and wants to be with me. God likes me better than I like myself.

God knew before He created the universe that we would have this problem. Long before He created them, He knew that Adam and

Eve would sin, and He had a plan to fix things. The Bible simply tells us that He did this for His purposes. Remember, the mind of God is vastly superior to ours, so we just have to accept that and let it be.

We do have some obligations, however. We are told to walk in good works and to treat others as we would want to be treated, etc. But that is not why God chose to save us. He didn't need this world or anything in it. He didn't look at the future and say, "There are going to be some real problems there that I am not going to be able to handle by myself, so I guess I'll have to save some people so they can help me straighten things up." He could have wiped out the whole place the moment Adam and Eve took that first bite of fruit, but for His own purposes, He didn't.

Adam and Eve, and therefore all of the rest of us, broke the Covenant of Life, which is also sometimes called the Covenant of Works. We all sin. No one is righteous or seeks God on his or her own. So God instituted what we call the Covenant of Grace. Basically, that is the Gospel. Since we needed a Savior, God provided one—Himself, in the form of God the Son.

God the Son, Christ, has always existed. He did not begin to exist when He was born in that stable. He was part of the Trinity that created the universe and that created you. He was part of the Trinity that created the plan of salvation. Christ created the men who would crucify Him and the tree that would provide the wood for His cross. He was totally and intimately involved with the plan of salvation. Of course, He was obeying His Father, but He also created the instructions.

That does not mean that the instructions were not unpleasant. Christ was also fully man. He suffered just as we suffer. It is important that we understand what the Bible teaches us about Christ's birth as well as His death. The Bible is a unit. We are not allowed to pick and choose what to believe. I have well-meaning friends who have said that they believe in the resurrection, but they don't think the Virgin Birth is really all that important. They can believe in Christ without having to believe in the Virgin Birth. But can they really? Can they fully understand and accept all that Christ is and all that He has done without acknowledging His miraculous birth?

First of all, the Virgin Birth was one of the signs given to us by God that would confirm the coming of the Messiah. Isaiah prophesied roughly 600 years before Christ's birth that He would be born of a virgin and born in Bethlehem. Refusing to believe in the Virgin Birth is refusing to acknowledge the prophecy and confirmation regarding Christ that God has given us.

Second, the Virgin Birth seems to me to have been necessary for Christ to have lived the sinless life that He did. Now this is just my opinion, but in my field of study, the use of logic is critical. I teach logical reasoning in most of my classes. Now, I don't believe that our sin nature is in our DNA. If scientists are able to figure out what every single part of our DNA is for, I don't think they will find a sin part. In my opinion, our inheritance of sin is spiritual, not physical. But my argument is this:

•The only way to live a sinless life is to avoid inheriting the sinfulness of Adam and Eve.

•In order to avoid inheriting that sinfulness, a person would have to have a sinless parent.

•The only sinless being in the universe is God Himself.

•Therefore, in order to live a sinless life, God Himself would have to be your parent.

BINGO. That is exactly what happened. Christ had a completely human mother, but a completely perfect Father. Therefore, He could live a sinless life. In order for Christ to be both fully human and fully divine, He would have to have a fully human parent and a fully divine parent. And that's what He had.

Now I don't think for one minute that God is bound by my finite logic. I know that God can do anything He chooses to do. I do, however, believe that God created the logic that we use, and that in this case, it fits the situation.

There are those who argue that in order for Christ to live a sinless life, His mother had to be sinless as well. They believe therefore that Mary was somehow sinless. That will get you quickly to a logical quagmire. Because if Mary had to be sinless in order for Jesus to be sinless, then both of her parents would have had to be sinless in order for Mary to be sinless, and all four of her grandparents would have had to be sinless in order for her parents to be sinless, etc., etc. You see the problem. And if you argue that God somehow worked a miracle and made Mary sinless, then why not start with Jesus instead of Mary? I do believe that Mary deserves our honor and respect, because she was highly favored by God in being chosen to be the mother of the Messiah. However, I do not believe that she was anything more than a godly young woman who was chosen to carry out a difficult yet highly honorable task for the glory of God.

So what does this all mean for us anyway? Why does it matter that Christ was sinless? So what if He did sin? Only that if Christ did sin, then we are no better off than if He had never come to earth at all. Christ died to pay for our sins. He had to be sinless for his death to conform to God's law. We'll talk about that in the next lesson. But let's put that aside for a moment. There is still another reason we needed Him to live a sinless life. Once the debt is wiped clean, paid, what is in its place? If that is it, then it's as though we never existed. No debt, no sin, no life. You see, not only did Christ die for us, He also lived for us. He suffered every temptation that we do[14], and sometimes to a greater degree. Scripture tells us that He spent forty days in the wilderness without food, and then He was tempted by Satan. How many of us have gone forty days without eating?

And although Christ was tempted in every way that we are, He never sinned. Not once. Not even as a child. No wonder He had problems with His brothers.[15] What would it be like growing up with a perfect brother? Some of you may have been compared unfavorably with a sibling and felt that they were treated as though they were perfect. But what if they really were perfect? And what about Mary and Joseph? What would it be like to raise a truly perfect child—a child whom you knew was really God? Can you imagine what you would do if anyone complained to you about Him?

Neighbor: Something is missing from my shop, and I saw your

---

14   Hebrews 2:17-18

15   John 7:5

son Jesus around there right before I noticed it was gone.

Joseph: Well I know he couldn't have taken it because…[he's God!—they'll think I'm crazy!] …well, I just know it wasn't him.

Neighbor: Well, you just keep an eye on him. He's too good. That kind of kid is always up to something.

Notice in Scripture how slow those closest to Him were in believing in Him.[16] They had seen His perfection, and maybe it was just too much for them.

But it's not too much for us; in fact, it makes all the difference for us for all eternity because Jesus' perfect life is credited to us. We have to have lived a life. We have to have a record. So when we accept Christ, God counts His record as our record. Our own record no longer exists; our sins are all forgiven, and it is as though we ourselves have lived Jesus' sinless life. This is the only way we can enter into God's kingdom. We cannot earn our own way in. We can't get rid of our own "sin dirt." We can't make ourselves clean enough or righteous enough to present ourselves to God. But Christ can, and He did. Thanks be to God for His indescribable gift!

---

16   Matthew 13:53-58

LESSON NINE

What does Christ do?

Question 23: What offices does Christ execute as our Redeemer?

Answer: Christ, as our Redeemer, executes the offices of a prophet, of a priest, and of a king, both in His estate of humiliation and exaltation.

Question 24: How does Christ execute the office of a prophet?

Answer: Christ executes the office of a prophet in revealing to us, by His Word and Spirit, the will of God for our salvation.

1. What is the job of a prophet?

   Read Deuteronomy 18:18

2. What does Christ reveal to us by His Word?

   Read Psalm 119:11, 42, 49, 68 104

3. How does Christ reveal things to us by His Spirit?

   Read John 14:26; Luke 12:12

Question 25: How does Christ execute the office of a priest?

Answer: Christ executes the office of a priest in his once offering up of Himself a sacrifice to satisfy divine justice, and reconcile us to God, and in making continual intercession for us.

4. What is the job of a priest?

Read Leviticus 1:5, I Samuel 12:19

5. What was the purpose of the Old Testament sacrificial system?

Read Leviticus 6:7; 16:30

6. What was the requirement for an animal used as an atonement sacrifice?

Read Leviticus 9:3

7. How did Christ serve as a sacrifice for us?

Read I Peter 1:18-19

8. How does Christ make intercession for us?

Read Hebrews 7:24-25; John 17:20-26

Question 26: How does Christ execute the office of a king?

Answer: Christ executes the office of a king in subduing us to Himself, in ruling and defending us, and in restraining and conquering all His and our enemies.

9. What is the job of a king?

Read I Samuel 8:20; Proverbs 8:15, 20:26

10. How does Christ subdue and rule over us?

Read Romans 8:9

11. How does He defend us?

Read Psalm 10:17-18; Romans 5:9

12. How does He restrain and conquer His and our enemies?

Read Romans 12:19-20; Proverbs 14:14; Matthew 25:31-33, 41

Commentary
Lesson 9

What does Christ do?
Questions 23, 24, 25, and 26

If there is one thing that I am not, it is a prophet, at least in the sense of telling the future. I have absolutely no sense of what is likely to happen. In fact, the more sure I am that something is going to happen, the more likely it seems to be that it will not happen. So if there is a gift of prophecy, I definitely haven't got it. The word prophet, or prophecy, has another meaning in the Bible, though; it can also mean a teacher, or one who speaks the Word of God to others. It is in this sense that we will consider Jesus as a prophet, although I'm pretty sure He can predict the future, too.

What better teacher can we have than Jesus? Who better to explain God to us than God Himself? Who better to show us what God is like? Although that was not Jesus' primary purpose for coming to earth, it was certainly a wonderful benefit. The slogan "What Would Jesus Do" has taken a bad rap, because it's a really good question. When we are faced with a dilemma, what better example could we follow? Of course, the only way to know what Jesus would really do is to be thoroughly familiar with what Jesus actually did.

It is a serious mistake to be vaguely aware of the kind of person Jesus was and then imagine what we think He might have done in a given situation. For example, if we are only aware of Jesus as a God of love, we can assume that He would tolerate any and all types of misbehavior. But when we know about His anger at the money-lenders in the Temple, we know that His compassion did not extend to everyone and everything. Jesus did not tolerate those who were defiling the holiness of the Temple. His anger at the Pharisees, the teachers of the law, shows us that he expected those who knew better to do better. He did expect people to behave according to His standards. We need to study the Scriptures to know who Jesus was before we can be confident in knowing what He would do.

We also need to study the Scriptures to read what others have said about Him and what they have to teach us. The entire Bible is the Word of God, and it is the primary way that Jesus teaches us today. The more familiar we are with the teachings of the Bible, the less susceptible we will be to false teachings when we are confronted with them.

I have been told that the way government agencies train people to detect counterfeit money is simply to have them handle real money over and over and over. Then when they come into contact with the counterfeit stuff, it just doesn't feel right. Because they know the real thing so well, they are immediately alert to the fake. I don't know if this is true or not, but it makes my point. That is how it should be with the truths of the Bible. We should be so familiar with the real thing that we are automatically on alert when something doesn't sound right.

And fortunately, we don't have to depend on our own weak memories. (Mine is going by the second.) The Holy Spirit is here to guide us and to help us understand what we learn and to remember it in the future. Without the Holy Spirit, none of the truths of God's Word would make any sense to us anyway, because they are spiritually discerned. To those without the Spirit, as I have said before, these truths can seem as nonsense, or they can seem offensive. We need to remember this for ourselves and for our friends and family who need to believe. First, they need Christ and His Spirit. Otherwise, they cannot understand anything else.

Not only is Jesus our prophet, but He is our priest—and also our sacrifice. In Old Testament times, people sinned just as we do now. They needed a way to atone for their sins, a visible, tangible way that they could see, hear, smell, and feel. So God instituted the sacrificial system. When they sinned, either knowingly or unknowingly (after they figured it out), they were to bring a certain type of sacrifice, and the priest was to burn some or all of it on the altar to atone for the person's sins. The reason I am so vague about the instructions, is that there are so many of them for so many different types of sacrifices. Anyway, if the sacrifice was to be an animal, it was to be an animal without a blemish or imperfection of any kind.

Once a year, the high priest would offer a sacrifice of atonement for his sins and the sins of the nation. At that time, and only at that time, he could enter the section of the Temple behind the veil called the Holy of Holies, where the Ark of the Covenant was kept. He would sprinkle some of the blood of the sacrifice on the Ark as atonement for the sins of the people. This was a major day in the life of the nation of Israel, and it had to occur every year. The blood of an animal is not sufficient to pay for the sins of the people once and for all time.

But the blood of Christ is sufficient. The sacrificial system of the Old Testament merely pointed the way to the sacrifice of Christ. In the previous lesson, we talked about the necessity of Christ's living a sinless life. He had to be sinless to be a sacrifice without blemish, which was required by the law of God. He had to be God for His sacrifice to be big enough to pay for all of our sins. But thanks be to God, it was enough. Since Christ paid for our sins, once and for all time, we no longer need to offer a yearly animal sacrifice. It is finished.

So Christ is the priest and also the sacrifice. As the sacrifice, He has completed the job. Our sins are paid for. As the priest, He continues His work. But Christ is no ordinary priest. First of all, He did not fit the earthly requirements for a Hebrew priest because He was not a descendant of Levi. He is specially ordained for this task.[17] On earth, He acted as a priest by teaching the people the truths of God's Word, and by interceding for them in prayer. He also performed the final sacrifice. Earthly priests could enter the Holy of Holies only once a year, and they brought the blood of an animal to pay for their own sins as well as the sins of the people. Christ is forever in the Holy place, of which the Holy of Holies was just a shadow,[18] and He has brought His own perfect blood. He had no sins of His own, so His blood is the complete and perfect sacrifice for everyone who will believe in Him. And in that Holy place, He still intercedes for us today. He applies His sacrifice to each of us as payment for our sins. He prays for us with God the Father. He will continue as our priest forever.

---

17   Hebrews 5:5-6
18   Hebrews 8:5, 9:24

And speaking of the kingdom, who do you suppose is the king? Silly question. Jesus, of course. We have all heard, and perhaps sung, the famous "Hallelujah Chorus" in the *Messiah*, by Handel. There is something beyond awe-inspiring about singing the words "King of kings and Lord of lords."

This past December, I was privileged to be a part of a church choir that performed a segment of that chorus during our annual Christmas concert. The following Sunday, we decided that rather than concluding the service with the traditional "Amen," we would end with the "King of kings" part of the *Messiah*. The pastor did not know this. However, his sermon was about the Kingship of Christ. He talked about references to the Kingship of Christ in the Scripture passages that deal with Christ's birth. He spoke of the numerous Christmas hymns that mention the Kingship of Christ. He then concluded with a call to make Christ the King of your own life. Those of us in the choir were on the edge of our seats. We couldn't wait to sing that chorus! Those words have never been more meaningful to me. I'm sure the congregation thought that we had put that all together on purpose, but we knew who had really put it together—it was all God.

When we went back to the choir room, we were all talking about the amazing thing that had just happened, until one of the choir members asked, "Why are we always so surprised when God does something wonderful?"

I don't know. Why were we so surprised? We had such joy that morning. Don't you think God enjoyed it too? He is the King, after all. He controls everything, even our morning worship service. He promises to be there even when two or three are gathered in His name, so why are we shocked when He shows up in a really tangible way?

We should want to know He's there. We call on Him in time of need, so shouldn't we be glad He's there in other times as well? As our King, Christ is our defender, and as such, He watches over us and is intimately involved in our lives. He promises to protect us, and in particular, to protect us from the wrath of God. We are not promised freedom from trouble; in fact, we are promised that as believers, we will have trouble. But we are promised that we will not have to go through that trouble alone. Even our greatest enemy Satan cannot stand against the name of Jesus Christ.

For a moment, I want to address the issue of those who do not acknowledge Christ. How does He deal with them? First, He tells us that He will deal with them, and that we are not to seek our own vengeance. In fact, we are to repay evil with good. That is very difficult to do; actually, without Christ, it is probably impossible. It can seem pretty close to impossible sometimes even with Christ. Second, we know that in eternity, they will receive their punishment. Jesus painted a very bleak picture for those who deny Him, or for those who act in His name without serving the God He really is.

For me, another sad part of the picture is painted in Matthew 6:2. Basically, Jesus is warning here not to behave like the Pharisees, who did things for the praise of men, because they have received their reward in full. So what I understand from this passage is that if your goal in this life is praise from men, or lots of money, or something else in this world, you may get it; but that will be all you get. There will be nothing else. It is sort of like the person whose best years were in high school and everything else is downhill from there. I feel sorry for those folks. Only this is much worse. Jesus will give these people what they want. For a few years, a very short time considering the length of eternity, they will have fame, or money, or whatever. Then it will be over. But instead of nothing, they will have punishment and an eternity of regret. They will have received their reward in full.

But for those who trust in Christ, our reward is still to come. We live in expectation of reigning with Christ in glory. In the meantime, while we wait here on earth, Christ is always with us. As our prophet, He continues to teach us the truths about Himself. As our priest, He intercedes for us in the Holiest of holy places, heaven itself. And as our king, He rules over us and defends us against all of our enemies, even Satan himself.

LESSON TEN
The worst thing, or the best thing?

Question 27:

What was Christ's humiliation?

Answer: Christ's humiliation consisted in His being born, and that in a low condition, made under the law, undergoing the miseries of this life, the wrath of God, and the cursed death of the cross, in being buried, and continuing under the power of death for a time.

1. In what ways was Christ's birth a humiliation for Him?

   Read Philippians 2:6-7; Luke 2:7

2. How did Christ undergo the miseries of this life?

   Read Hebrews 2:18; Matthew 8:20; Philippians 2:8

3. How did Christ undergo the wrath of God?

   Read Matthew 27:45-50

4. In what way was Christ's burial a humiliation?

   Read Matthew 27:57-61

Question 28:

What is Christ's exaltation?

Answer: Christ's exaltation consists in His rising again from the dead on the third day, in ascending into heaven, in sitting at the right hand of God the Father, and in coming to judge the world at the last day.

5. What is remarkable about Christ's resurrection?

   Read 2 Timothy 1:10; Hebrews 2:14; I Corinthians 6:14

6. Describe Christ's ascension into Heaven.

   Read Acts 1:9

7. What is significant about Christ's being seated at the right hand of God the Father?

   Read I Peter 3:22

8. What will be the signs of Christ's return?

   Read Matthew 24:29-31; I Thessalonians 4:16-17

Question 29:

How do we take part in the redemption purchased by Christ?

Answer: We take part in the redemption purchased by Christ by the effectual application of it to us by His Holy Spirit.

9. Why can we not achieve redemption, or salvation, on our own?

   Read Romans 3:10-11, 23

10. How do we receive salvation?

   Read Romans 10:9

Question 30:

How does the Spirit apply to us the redemption purchased by Christ?

Answer: The Spirit applies to us the redemption purchased by Christ by working faith in us, and thereby uniting us to Christ in our effectual calling.

11. Where does the faith to believe in Christ come from?

   Read Ephesians 2:8

Commentary
Lesson 10

The worst thing, or the best thing?
Catechism Questions 27 and 28

A few years ago Lael was asked to take part in a friend's wedding as an honorary bridesmaid. The bride already had quite a few bridesmaids, so three girls were asked to participate but not to stand in the front with the rest of the party. Lael was flattered to be asked because she had only known the bride a relatively short amount of time. In fact, she met the bride's parents only a few days before the wedding. When the big day came, everything was absolutely perfect. The couple was gorgeous, the day was beautiful, and everyone was thrilled! The father of the bride announced each member of the wedding party as they walked into the reception hall. When Lael's turn came, he called out the wrong name. She was really, really embarrassed! She just wanted to be known for who she was. I suppose she thought that by being called the wrong name, others would assume that the father didn't know her, and it felt embarrassing not to be known. I think we have all been in situations where we are mistaken for another person or where someone does not recognize us, even when we know who she is.

Now take that embarrassment and multiply it by a million. That was the humiliation Christ suffered for us. Here He is, the King of the Universe, the Creator of every being that He meets, and they have no idea who He is. Not only that, but He is now subject to the laws He set and the people He put in place to govern! His strength is weakened; He has gone from being an all-powerful God to having human strength. He was born in a stable among the animals, the lowliest place He could have been born. He is also subject to temptation and is tested in extreme circumstances, such as fasting in the desert for 40 days and then being tempted with food. He knew where He came from and He knew what He had given up. But for His own purposes, He suffered all this humiliation and in the end died a cruel death because it was the only way we could be saved. I have read a little about death on a cross, and I know that it is one of the most painful and slow ways to die.

But Christ suffered something even more painful than death; He suffered the wrath of God. The Bible tells us that God forsook Jesus while He took on our sins on the cross. In that sense, it was like Jesus was torn from Himself. The triune God—Father, Son, and Holy Spirit—have always had perfect unity and perfect communication. God has always existed and will always exist in those three persons. The Trinity has never been broken, except for that one time.

This is monumental. Forever, for the entire span of eternity, God has existed and will continue to exist in perfect harmony, in perfect communion, in perfect communication—except for that one small period of about three hours. Christ took on the sins of all those He came to save, and God the Father turned away. The Trinity was broken. There was no more communication between the Father and the Son. There was no more harmony. I can't even find the words to stress the significance of this moment in history. It is as if God Himself were torn apart.

No wonder there were signs of this on earth. The moment this happened, light became darkness. We know what was happening because Jesus cried out, "My God, my God, why have you forsaken me!" He did not call out "My Father." The relationship was broken. He called Him "God." And then Jesus suffered alone. Totally alone. He had been forsaken by His friends and finally by His Father. And He did this for us.

And when He had suffered enough, when the penalty was paid, He gave up His spirit. Again, notice what Scripture tells us. Jesus' life was not taken from Him; He gave it up.[19] He chose when to die— when He had accomplished what He had come to earth to do. And what He had done was to open the doors of heaven to all who would believe in Him. Once again, the earth responded: an earthquake shook the ground and rocks broke in two. More importantly, the curtain of the temple covering the Holy of Holies, where the high priest met with God, was torn in two. The curtain that separated the mercy seat of

19   John 10:17-18

God from the people was ripped apart, giving access to the throne of God to anyone who believes. That veil was removed by Jesus; through Him we can now approach the throne of grace with confidence that our sins are forgiven.

But even after Jesus' death, He suffered one last humiliation. He did not receive a funeral or even a proper burial. He was taken away and buried in secret. No one mourned publicly; no one gave a eulogy on his behalf.

But three days later...oh the glory! I have often wondered what happened when Jesus conquered death and came back to life. I wonder what we would have seen in that grave before the angels or Mary saw Him. How awesome that would have been! But even though we did not see it, we receive the benefits from His resurrection, because as Christ rose, so will we. It is because of his death on the cross and resurrection that we can be accepted into heaven; there was no other way for us to be saved.

Jesus stayed on earth for only a short time before He ascended into heaven. I also like to picture this: the disciples watch as Jesus ascends into the sky like a rocket until they can't see anything but a dot. I wonder what they were thinking... Finally, Jesus receives the glory that was all His to begin with! He receives the highest honor from God the Father and is placed at His right hand. Not only that, but He is returned to His position as Ruler of all creation. Praise God!

We can also look forward to Christ's coming again. The Bible tells us that Christ's return will be nothing like His first coming. This time it will be like one of those dramatic scenes from a sci-fi or epic movie. The whole sky will grow dark and Christ will ride in with His power and glory. A trumpet will sound and those who are dead in Christ will be raised, and the living also will be taken up with Him. He will never again suffer the humiliation He suffered the first time. He will finally be recognized; the Scripture says that every knee will bow and every tongue will confess that He is Lord.[20]

My friend Jeff had a professor in college who was extremely antagonistic towards the Christian faith. Day after day Jeff had to listen to this professor criticize Christians or the church or the

---

20   Romans 14:10-12

Bible. One day he had had enough. The professor said something like, "When I die, I'm going to get in God's face and ask him why he didn't do something about some of the problems we have down here." Jeff spoke up boldly and said, "No, you won't. You will get down on your knees and worship your Creator." You see, in the end, everyone will realize who Christ is—who God is. But for many, it will be too late. Even though they will finally acknowledge God, they will not be allowed to spend eternity with Him. There won't be any second chances.

Lael says that she sometimes dreams about the day when Christ is finally known to the world for who He truly is. She has talked to so many people who don't care or don't want to have anything to do with Jesus. Even saying that name causes them embarrassment or anger. Just the name! Our hearts long that they know the truth, and we pray they do before it is too late.

LESSON ELEVEN

Hide and seek, or hide and find?

Question 31:

What is effectual calling?

Answer: Effectual calling is the work of God's Spirit, by which, convincing us of our sin and misery, enlightening our minds in the knowledge of Christ, and renewing our wills, he persuades and enables us to embrace Jesus Christ, freely offered to us in the Gospel.

1. How does the Holy Spirit convince us of our sin?

    Read John 16:7-8; Romans 3:20

2. How does the Holy Spirit enable us to embrace Jesus Christ?

    Read 2 Corinthians 5:17; I Peter 1:23

3. Can we understand the knowledge of Christ without the renewing of our minds by the Holy Spirit?

    Read I Corinthians 2:14

4. Are only those people saved who are effectually called?

    Read John 6:44

5. Is it possible for a person to want to be saved, but not be effectually called?

Read Jeremiah 29:13; John 6:37

6. What is the last point in a person's life that he or she may receive Christ?

Read Luke 23:39-43

7. Is salvation the work of an individual, or the work of God?

Read Ephesians 2:1, 4-5, 8-9

8. When did God decide who would be effectually called?

Read 2 Thessalonians 2:13-14; 2 Timothy 1:9

9. Why did God effectually call us?

Read 2 Timothy 1:9; Ephesians 1:4

10. Why is it not unfair of God to punish those who reject Him?

Read Romans 1:19-21

11. If salvation is the work of God, why do we need evangelism?

Read Romans 10:14; Matthew 28:19

Commetary
Lesson 11

Hide and seek, or hide and find?
Catechism Questions 29, 30, and 31

Have you ever played hide-and-seek? When my siblings and I were younger, we used to love to play Sardines with our cousins. Sardines is a version of hide-and-seek where one person hides and everyone else is "It." Except when you find the person who is hiding, you hide with him. The last person to find the rest of the group "loses" and hides first next time. But we added a little twist to the game, and we played it in the dark. Somehow we managed to convince our parents to stay confined to the kitchen while the seven to ten of us cousins had free rein in a dark house, hiding in all kinds of strange and unusual places. I cannot imagine what my mother was thinking to allow us to do that!

Those are good memories. Sardines, hide-and-seek—those childish games were fun. But in a way, everyone on earth is playing a game of cosmic hide-and-seek, and the "It" they are trying to hide from is God. And while in the child's game, we want to be found, in this cosmic game, we desperately do not. Throughout Scripture, we are told that no one seeks God; no one does good. We run from God and we reject His salvation.

The plan of salvation is very simple. All we have to do is believe in the Lord Jesus Christ and we will be saved. But to do that would mean to submit to Him, to acknowledge and repent of our sins, and to be willing to live for Him. And no one wants to do that. Have you ever talked to someone before she was ready to give her life to Christ? She will offer up every excuse in the world as to why she cannot possibly commit herself to Christ. A former pastor called this hiding behind bushes. If a person is "hiding behind bushes," and you manage to defeat one of her arguments, and thus pull up her bush, she will just run around till she finds another one to hide behind. You cannot argue someone into the kingdom of God if she is not ready to hear the Gospel.

If God left it up to us to choose Him, His heaven would be empty. People basically do not want to choose God. So God chooses us. The Holy Spirit comes to us and convicts us of our sin and our need for a Savior, while at the same time giving us the faith that we need to believe in Christ. We are made into a new creation, one that can now understand the things of God. This is all totally a work of God, something we cannot possibly understand. It is, in every sense of the word, a mystery. How God does this is more than our finite minds can comprehend. Nor can we comprehend why He does this; it is simply for His own purposes. Those who have been called by God need to thank Him continually for this incomprehensible gift. We do not know why we have been called; we only know that we have been changed and that our lives are now His. We should also realize that there is nothing that we have contributed to our salvation. Our salvation is, from beginning to end, the work of God.

And we can't resist it. God makes us into a new creation. He changes us from someone who doesn't want God into someone who does. He changes our minds, so that we can understand the Bible and the truths it teaches. He makes us into someone different. Instead of a person who is unable to believe in Christ, we become a person who is unable not to believe.

For some reason, many people have a problem with this. They want to be responsible for their own salvation, at least a little bit. They want to feel that they were free to either accept God or reject Him. Really? Do they really want that burden? For if my salvation is mine to gain, it is also mine to lose; and I cannot be certain that I am strong enough to hold on to it. I am a very weak person and can be enticed by the sinful desires of this world. Perhaps some of those desires could pull me completely away from Christ. But thankfully, it's not up to me or you. God has called us to Himself, and it is up to Him to keep us in His hand, which He has promised to do. Even if we fail Him, He will never fail us.

Perhaps this is a new doctrine for you, and that's okay. This is honestly one of the most challenging doctrines of our faith. We pride ourselves on our independent spirit. We like to think we can take care of ourselves, that anyone can be anything he wants to be. We don't like the idea of losing control. So we have a problem in allowing even God to have total control over our lives; or to put it more accurately, we have a problem in acknowledging the control that God has over our lives.

But let's look at this from another angle. Have you ever prayed for someone else's salvation? If you ask God to save someone, what are you asking Him to do?

Now, if you believe that salvation is entirely the work of God, the answer is simple. You are asking God to perform that work in the life of that person. But if you believe that salvation is up to the person, then what are you asking of God?

If you believe that the person must somehow recognize, on his own, the necessity for salvation and then come to God in faith, then why are you bothering God with it?

If you believe that a person can be called by God, but choose to reject His message, then what use is God? If man's will is stronger than God's, then what is the point of asking God to save anyone?

Does that make you feel a bit hopeless? If salvation is up to man, it is hopeless. But fortunately, it isn't up to man. It is up to God. All of it. God can do it, and we must trust Him in this. The fact that a person's salvation is entirely up to God is one of the most comforting doctrines in the whole of Scripture, especially to those of us who have lost a loved one. When we are certain that our loved one knew Christ, then we can rest assured that Christ will keep his promises and that our loved one is with Him.

But what if we are not sure that our loved one knew Christ? If you have had a loved one who passed on without knowing Christ, there is amazing comfort in knowing that it is God who is in control of these things and not us. We could not bear that responsibility. My husband and I have experienced several such losses, and it is this basic teaching that kept us going, even when the grief was almost too much to bear. Certainly, we should have talked to these dear ones more about Christ. Surely, we should have prayed for them more often. But no matter how much we failed in our duties, the responsibility for their salvation rests ultimately with God and not with us. We can always know that even at the very end of life it is possible for a person to be called by God, and we can hope to that end for those loved ones. God's timing is perfect, and I believe that sometimes He waits until the last moment to call a person to Himself. We have the example of the dying thief to attest to this. Finally, we must rest in the fact that God is God; He knows what He is doing; and He cares about us.

If you are still uncertain about this doctrine, then there are several passages of Scripture that I would point you to. First, look at Ephesians 1:3-6. Paul tells us here that we were chosen before the foundation of the world and predestined for adoption through Jesus Christ, according to God's purpose. Ephesians 2:4-9 adds that God made us alive with Christ while we were still dead in our sins [*my note*--<u>not</u> after we had received Christ], and saved us through faith, which itself is the gift of God.

Okay, that's Paul. What about the other New Testament writers? In I Peter 1:3, Peter tells us that Jesus Christ in His mercy has caused us to be born again. In his first letter, John tells us, "In this is love, not that we have loved God, but that He loved us and sent His Son to be the propitiation for our sins...We love because He first loved us."

And of course, I've saved the best for last. What did Jesus say about this? Quite a lot, actually, both directly and indirectly.

Matthew 16:17—Blessed are you, Simon Bar-Jonah! For flesh and blood has not revealed this to you, but my Father who is in heaven.

Mark 10:22— All things have been handed over to me by my Father, and no one knows who the Son is except the Father, or who the Father is except the Son and anyone to whom the Son chooses to reveal Him.

John 6:44—No one can come to me unless the Father who sent me draws him.

John 6:65—This is why I told you that no one can come to me unless it is granted him by the Father.

John 10:24-26—So the Jews gathered around Him and said to Him, "How long will you keep us in suspense? If you are the Christ, tell us plainly." Jesus answered them, "I told you, and you do not believe. The works that I do in my Father's name bear witness about me, but you do not believe because you are not part of my flock."

Notice in this last passage, that Jesus could have said, "You are not part of my flock because you do not believe." But that is not what He said. They did not believe because they weren't part of the flock. They couldn't believe. Their minds and hearts had not been changed, and they could not understand the things of God. There are many other passages in the Old and New Testament that speak to this doctrine. The more you read the Bible, the more you will find.

So what about the passages like, "Whoever hears my word and believes Him who sent me has eternal life"? (John 5:24) Isn't this an invitation for anyone to come to Christ? Doesn't this mean that anyone can believe? Many years ago, I was in a Bible study with a young woman who was wrestling with that question, when she suddenly, in the middle of a study, realized the answer. Those verses are statements of fact. Of course, anyone who believes will have eternal life. And yes, in a sense, these invitations are for anyone. However, they are not statements of our ability to believe.

For example, I could tell you that anyone who can fly across the Pacific Ocean, on his own strength, without the aid of any other device, can have my entire bank account. And I could mean it. It would be a statement of fact. But that doesn't mean that you could do it. (And in case you're considering trying, my bank account is not worth the risk.) Anyone who believes will have eternal life. That is a promise of God, and He does not lie. However, the only way we can believe is for Him to change our hearts and make us able to do so.

Let me address another question that has come up from time to time. What if someone feels drawn to God but is afraid he or she is not chosen by God? My answer would be—it can't happen. Those who are not called by God don't want God. They want nothing to do with God. They are certainly not worried about whether He has called them. If a person feels drawn to God, it is probably because he or she is being drawn by God. I would pray with and for that person and encourage him to accept the faith to which God is calling him.

Does this mean that man has no responsibility, or that we are somehow excused if we do not accept Christ? Not at all. Scripture tells us that God has provided enough evidence of His own existence for anyone to believe in Him. No one is off the hook. As I have said in previous lessons, the reason people don't believe in God is simply because they don't want to. They want to have control over their own lives. They enjoy their sins, and they don't want to give them up. We are responsible for our own choices, regardless of the fact that we are unable to choose any differently. I know this doesn't make complete sense to us. But I also know that my mind does not work like God's mind.[21] We cannot understand God's thoughts in this, so we must accept what He tells us in His word. God has given everyone sufficient evidence to believe in Him; however, only those who are changed by the Holy Spirit will want to believe or be able to believe.

So if God has to change hearts, and it's all up to Him anyway, why do we need evangelists and preachers and missionaries? Because that's the way God wants it done. He wants us to share our faith. He wants some to do that in a particular, vocational way. Their life's calling will be to preach the Gospel or to minister to people in a special way. I urge you to support those who are undertaking that work. It is a unique calling, and worthy of our respect, but even more worthy of our gifts and our prayers.

But God calls all of us to tell others about Him, first through our lives, and then through our words. Our lives must come first, though.

21   Isaiah 55:8-9

People must see Christ in our lives before they will believe Christ in our words. They must see the difference He has made in our lives and want that difference for themselves. We must meet people where they are, and accept them as they are, in order to gain a hearing for the Gospel. As Paul said, we may have to become all things to all people that we might win some to Christ.[22]

But even in our evangelism, isn't it wonderful to know that it's still all up to God? We can't argue people into the kingdom; we just need to let those around us know what Christ has done for us. And since that is pretty much everything, it shouldn't be too hard, should it?

---

22   I Corinthians 9:19-22

LESSON TWELVE
What's in it for me?

Question 32:

What benefits are there in this life for those who are effectually called?

Answer: Those who are effectually called partake in justification, adoption, sanctification, and the other benefits that, in this life, do either accompany them or flow from them.

Question 33:

What is justification?

Answer: Justification is an act of God's free grace, in which He pardons all our sins, and accepts us as righteous in His sight, only for the righteousness of Christ imputed to us, and received by faith alone.

1. What did Christ do that made our justification possible?

   Read Romans 5:29; 3:24-25

Question 34:

What is adoption?

Answer: Adoption is an act of God's free grace, by which we are received as sons of God, and have a right to all the privileges of that standing.

2. Why did God choose to adopt us as His children?

Read Ephesians 1:5

3. Why should we not boast in our adoption as children of God?

Read I Corinthians 1:26-30

Question 35:

What is sanctification?

Answer: Sanctification is the work of God's free grace, by which we are renewed in the whole man after the image of God, and are enabled more and more to die to sin and live to righteousness.

4. Which person of the Trinity is primarily involved in working out our sanctification?

Read 2 Thessalonians 2:13

5. How does God use our suffering to aid in our sanctification?

Read Romans 5:1-5

Question 36:

What are the benefits that in this life accompany or flow from justification, adoption, and sanctification?

Answer: The benefits that in this life do accompany or flow from justification, adoption, and sanctification are: assurance of God's love, peace of conscience, joy in the Holy Spirit, increase of grace, and perseverance to the end.

6. How do we know that we are assured of God's love?

Read I John 4:9; Ephesians 2:4-5; I John 3:1

7. How do we know that we will not lose our salvation (that we will persevere to the end)?

Read 2 Corinthians 5:1-5; John 10:29

Question 37:

What benefits do believers receive from Christ at death?

Answer: The souls of believers are at their deaths made perfect in holiness, and do immediately pass into glory, and their bodies, being still united to Christ, do rest in their graves till the resurrection.

8. When do the souls of believers go to heaven?

Read Luke 23:43; Philippians 1:23

Question 38:

What benefits do believers receive from Christ at the resurrection?

Answer: At the resurrection, believers, being raised up in glory, shall be openly acknowledged and acquitted in the day of judgment, and made perfectly blessed in the full enjoying of God to all eternity.

9. What will happen to believers when Christ returns?

Read I Thessalonians 4:16-17

10. What will happen to believers at the judgment?

Read Matthew 10:32; 25:32-34

Commentary

Lesson 12

What's in it for me?

Catechism Questions 32, 33, 34, 35, 36, 37, and 38

My friend Randy had a wreck the other day. He was driving out of a parking lot when a teenage boy, going about 60 miles per hour in a 35 mile per hour zone and talking on his cell phone, came over a hill and ran into the side of Randy's car. Randy had stopped and looked both ways before driving out of the lot, and his daughter Susan, who was a passenger in the car, had also looked. So who do you suppose was blamed for the accident? Randy was, because he had pulled out into oncoming traffic.

That doesn't seem fair, does it? He was pretty upset about it, too. He wanted to be vindicated. He wanted justification. He wanted to be declared not guilty. In his mind, and in mine as well, he was not guilty. But according to the laws of the state, he was at fault.

We can all imagine ourselves in Randy's situation. We don't like to take the blame for something that is clearly not our fault. That is understandable. But we also don't like to take the blame for things that are our fault, like our sins. We want to rationalize those away. We want to be declared not guilty for those also. But we are guilty. The Bible tells us that we have all sinned; that none of us is good; none of us is righteous. We can't explain our sins away, or minimize the seriousness of what we have done. We can't justify ourselves in the eyes of God.

We can't do it, but Christ can. He doesn't rationalize or minimize or sins, however; He paid the penalty for them. When He said on the cross, "It is finished," He was saying that it is all paid for. Every sin that you and I will ever commit has been paid for. We no longer owe that debt. We are free.

Now imagine that you have applied for a very important position. You send in your resume or CV, and on it you have neatly printed your name and address. That's it. No experience, no education, no references. Nothing. Just your name and address. I wouldn't imagine that you would even merit consideration, but let's assume that for some inexplicable reason, the Human Resources manager decides to check you out. He "googles" you, but finds nothing. He checks your social security number. There is nothing—there is nothing negative, but there is nothing positive either. You have no record of any kind. How likely is that you will get that job? Not very.

As Christians, without Christ's sinless life, we would be in a similar state. We would have no record of sin, because Christ paid for our sins by his death on the cross. But we would have no positive record either. The Bible tells us that our righteousness is as filthy rags. Our good deeds, done in our own strength and for our own purposes, count for nothing. So how can we earn a positive record? We can't, so Christ gives us one. His record of perfection is credited to us. That is justification. Not only do we carry no blame, we are seen in God's eyes as righteous, but only because of Christ. By receiving Christ as our Savior and Lord, we are justified.

We are also adopted. Perhaps you were adopted as a child, or maybe you have adopted a child of your own. I have friends who have both biological and adopted children and I honestly can't tell which are which. I know, but it doesn't matter. No one who just met the family would have any idea that one of the children was not a biological child. I have friends who have adopted children only, and I remember the joy in their voices when they called to tell me that a child was waiting for them, that they were finally parents! When faced with an unplanned pregnancy, the gift of arranging an adoptive home is the most precious thing a woman can give her unborn child. I have known women who have made that choice and I honor them for it.

So some of us have been adopted by earthly parents, but if we are believers in Christ, then all of us have been adopted by God. There is an old hymn titled "I'm a Child of the King" and a contemporary Christian song called "My Father's House" which both express that idea. Our Father is God Almighty. He has adopted us. We belong to

Him.

In the movie <u>Anna and the King</u> there are two scenes which I think illustrate this concept beautifully. In the first scene, Anna is introduced to the King of Siam. She is told that her head must never be higher than his head. As the King sits down, everyone in the room bows lower and lower. The king is in total control; no one may enter his throne room or speak to him without his permission, on pain of death.

In a later scene, the king's oldest son gets into a scuffle with Anna's son. One of the king's daughters runs headlong into the throne room and into her father's presence, demanding that he come and do something about the fight. He picks her up and carries her back to the scene of the trouble and solves the problem. She is not punished. She is not even reprimanded. Why? Because she is his daughter. He loves her, and she is allowed to come into his presence whenever she desires.

That is the way God treats us. He is the majestic King of the Universe, Ruler of all of Creation, King of kings and Lord of lords, yet we can run headlong into His throne room and beg for His help in whatever situation we may find ourselves. He will pick us up, carry us if necessary, and stay with us while the situation is being resolved. We are His children.

As His children, we are becoming more and more like Him. That is a long process called sanctification. We are gradually being made more like we should be, and less like we have been. When we accept Christ, we are changed; we are new creations. But we are not sinless. God the Holy Spirit works in us to show us our sins and to help us to live a life that is pleasing to Him. There was a bumper sticker that I used to see that said "Please be patient. God isn't finished with me yet." We need to remember that, not only for ourselves, but especially for others. God is not finished with them yet, either.

Because God has done these things for us—He has justified and adopted us and is sanctifying us daily—we can rest assured that He will continue to bless us. We are His children, and He will never leave us. Nothing can separate us from His love. He will pour out His grace as He shows us what He wants us to learn, and leads us in the ways we should go. We can have peace and because we know that He is not only in control of everything that happens in this world, He cares about what happens to us as individuals.

We can know that when this life is over, we will go immediately to be with Him. Our bodies may remain here, if we die before He returns, but our spirits will be instantly in His presence. My great-grandmother died of tuberculosis at a fairly young age, when my grandmother was only twelve years old. My grandmother told me that as she died, she raised her hands and whispered, "Hallelujah." I know that she is with Jesus now. Her body is buried in Texas, but her spirit is alive with Christ. I am looking forward to meeting her.

If we remain here until Christ returns, we know that He will come for us. The bodies of believers who have already died (like my great-grandmother) will rise first, then those who are still alive will be raised up, body and spirit. Our mortal bodies will be changed to immortal ones, and we will be with the Lord forever. The writer of Hebrews tells us that this world is merely a shadow of the one to come, the one where we will live for eternity. Think of a dark house, with only a night light glowing. You can see things, but not distinctly. You can't really make out colors very well. Then when you turn on all the lights, how different things look. Colors are vivid and everything is clearly distinguishable. Right now, we are living in the dark. The night light is on, but we really can't see very well. In Heaven, all the light (the light of God Himself) will be on. We have no way of even imagining how wonderful that will be!

SECTION TWO

Living Right/Living Well

LESSON THIRTEEN
The Moral Law

Question 39:

What is the duty that God requires of man?

Answer: The duty that God requires of man is obedience to His revealed will.

1. What blessings did God promise the Israelites for obeying His commandments?

   Read Deuteronomy 11:8-15

2. I Samuel 15:22 compares obedience to sacrifice. Which pleases God more? Why do you think this is true?

   Read I Samuel 15:3, 20-22

3. What does obedience to God involve?

   Read Micah 6:8, James 1:27

Question 40:

What did God at first reveal to man for the rule of his obedience?

Answer: The rule that God at first revealed to man for his obedience was the moral law.

4. How does everyone know what God requires?

Read Romans 2:14-15

5. What is meant by the term "moral law"?

Read Exodus 15:26; Deuteronomy 13:18

Question 41:

Where is the moral law found to be summarized?

Answer: The moral law is found summarized in the Ten Command-ments.

6. Where and how were the Ten Commandments given to the people?

Read Exodus 19:20-20:1

7. How did Moses receive the first tablets on which the Ten Commandments were written?

Read Exodus 24:12, 32:16

8. What happened to the first tablets?

Read Exodus 24:18; 32:1-19

9. How were the tablets replaced?

   Read Exodus 34: 1, 2, 28

Question 42:

What is the sum of the Ten Commandments?

Answer: The sum of the Ten Commandments is: to love the Lord our God with all our heart, with all our soul, with all our strength, and with all our mind; and our neighbor as ourselves.

10. Where do we get the summary of the Ten Commandments?

    Read Matthew 22:37-40, Deuteronomy 6:5

11. Name two or three things that you consider to always be wrong.

12. Name two or three things that you have done that you would consider to be wrong.

Commentary

Lesson 13

The Moral Law

Catechism Questions 39, 40, 41, and 42

Is there such a thing as right and wrong? That may seem to you to be a ridiculous question. Of course there is. Some things are right and some things are wrong. Everyone knows that. The problem is that everyone doesn't know it. In today's world, even the very idea of right and wrong is being questioned. More and more people live by the philosophy, "What is wrong for you may not be wrong for me."

But as Tim Keller points out in his book *The Reason for God*, that philosophy really doesn't hold up. There are things that we object to other people doing, even if those things do not seem wrong to them. The terrorists who steered those planes into the World Trade Center towers thought they were doing the right thing, but I doubt that many of us would agree with them, or even support their right to have done what they did. And whether the perpetrators accept the fact or not, child abuse and child pornography are wrong.

But how do we know what is right and what is wrong? To determine right and wrong, there must be a standard. One standard is the law of the land. If something is against the law, it is wrong. That works some of the time. But does that therefore mean that if something is not against the law it is right? There are things that although legal, most of us would consider unethical. For example, corporate executives may lay off hundreds of workers while giving themselves million-dollar bonuses. That is completely legal. In my opinion, it is also completely wrong.

Behavior like that is not against the law of the land, but it is against God's law. It is a basic failure to treat others as you would want to be treated. God demands obedience from all of us, whether we accept His rule or fight against it. He promises blessings to those who obey Him. In the Old Testament passages, those were physical blessings, and He still gives those today. But He does not promise freedom from trouble. He does not promise prosperity for obeying His commands. He does promise to care for us and to see us through all of the difficult circumstances of life.

When my husband was in seminary, there was a period where we had ten dollars to last us through the next two weeks. We had absolutely no idea how we would make it. Then, for the first time, one of our church deacons asked how we were doing financially. We told him, and he promised to see what the church could do to help. Problem solved, right? We thought so too, but that is not how God worked it out. In fact, I don't even remember how it worked out. I only know that we survived that two weeks before we received any help from the church. Our church family did care, and they did help, but that's not what got us through those fourteen days. It was God alone. We did not go into debt and we did not go without meals.

Later in our seminary days, we received a very large gift and had the opportunity to share with others who were in need. We literally went from want to plenty, back and forth, during those years. But we saw how God provided through it all. Did the periods of want mean that we were less obedient? I don't think so. I think God was using those opportunities to show us that He can provide for us no matter what the outward circumstances may be, and that is a far greater blessing than a few dollars in the bank.

Obedience to God must come from the heart and not from outward appearance only. God is not impressed with how many times a week we go to church, read our Bible, pray, witness to others, or any other thing we may do in His name if it is not done for the right reason. Any of it that is done for our own glory is meaningless. Do you worry about whether people know if you have been to church? Then you are going for the wrong reason. Do you pride yourself on the number of people you have led to the Lord? Then you are witnessing for the wrong reason. God can still use you, but He may not be pleased with your attitude. Does it upset you if someone else gets credit for something you have done in the church? Why are you doing it—for your glory or for God's? If it is for God's glory, what does it matter who gets the credit?

Micah tells us that God requires three basic things of us—to act justly, to love mercy, and to walk humbly with our God. Justice means that we want everyone to get what he or she deserves. We do not want to see the innocent hurt or mistreated or put down in any way. We want to see the guilty punished and the innocent spared and we want the punishment to fit the crime. We become angry when we see the powerful in life taking advantage of the less fortunate, and when we have power, we try to make certain that we treat everyone fairly.

Mercy dictates that everyone does <u>not</u> get what he or she deserves. We certainly don't want what we deserve, which is an eternity in hell for the sins we have committed. We want mercy from God. Mercy allows us to forgive others for the wrongs they have committed against us and to treat them with compassion. Mercy calls us to care for those less fortunate than ourselves and to be kind to those around us. Mercy cares for the sick, the prisoners, the elderly, the homeless, the young, and the disabled. As James tells us, mercy cares for the widows and orphans—those with no one else to care for them. Without mercy, our world would be a cold, dark, unloving place to live.

I think it is interesting that we are told in the same verse to act justly and to love mercy. Justice must be tempered by mercy, but mercy must also be guided by justice. The two must work together. There are those who must pay for their crimes or misdeeds, and there are those who should be forgiven in mercy. How do we know which is which? By walking humbly with our God. Through the guidance of the Holy Spirit, we can know how to treat each of our fellow human beings. If we in our own arrogance think we have things figured out and under control, we will quickly find out that things are not quite as simple as we thought. If we humble ourselves and depend on God for guidance, we can make wise decisions which are pleasing to Him.

It is also important to realize that whether they believe in God or not, everyone has a basic concept of what God considers right and wrong. Paul tells us in Romans that everyone has a conscience that can guide him or her in that knowledge. Many people try to ignore their conscience in their desire to please themselves, but that does not mean that it is not there. As a student of communication, I have learned that the more stridently a person argues for a particular position, the more he or she is concerned about the opposing viewpoint. Think about that the next time you hear someone loudly proclaiming his or her right to live in a way that you know is not pleasing to God. The more arduously the person defends his or her position, the more he or she is afraid of the truth of the other side, the truth of God.

God tells us what is right and wrong in His eyes throughout the Bible, but His law is summed up in the Ten Commandments. These ten regulations cover the basic principles by which God wants us to live. They were given to us by God Himself, written by His own hand. They are rules to make our lives easier and more pleasant; they are not meant to be burdensome. If all of mankind were to follow these ten rules, there would be no need for police or military forces, or even a judicial system. We could truly have peace on earth.

God engraved these rules on stone tablets, so they could not fade or decay. They were meant to be permanent. He had to do it twice, though, because Moses broke the first set. Can you picture the scene? Moses has had an amazing, intense forty-day experience with God, and he comes down from the mountain to find that the Israelites have gotten tired of waiting for him. They didn't know what had happened to him, or why he was taking sooooo long on the mountain, so they took matters into their own hands. They decided they needed a god they could see, and they made a golden calf. But God cannot be represented by anything we can see or touch. In fact, His second commandment was that they should not make such an image.

So Moses was angry—really, really angry. And in his rage, he threw down the tablets that God Himself had carved out and engraved. He destroyed the golden calf, ground it up, scattered in on the water, and made the people drink the water. (Maybe that made them sick?) Anyway, he was furious. He wanted to make them pay. God was angry too, and He was ready to destroy the entire nation. What they had done was a terrible thing. But Moses interceded with God for them, and God spared most of them, although some were put to death.

But the tablets were gone. So this time God had Moses carve out new ones, and again God Himself engraved the words on the stones. These laws are permanent and are not to be changed or put away. We are still bound to obey these rules. They are not man's rules, but God's. Christ summarized these laws for us very simply. "You shall love the Lord your God with all your heart and with all your soul and with all your mind," and "You shall love your neighbor as yourself." We are to love God with the totality of our being, with everything that is in us. And we are to love others and treat others as we would love and treat ourselves. In the next few studies, we will look at the introduction to the Ten Commandments, and then at each commandment individually to see exactly how God wants us to do this.

LESSON FOURTEEN
The Introduction:
The Preface to the Ten Commandments

Question 43:

What is the preface to the Ten Commandments?

Answer: The preface to the Ten Commandments is in these words, "I am the LORD your God, who brought you out of the land of Egypt, out of the house of slavery,"

1. What was life like for the Israelites while in slavery in Egypt?

   Read Exodus 1:11-14

2. How did God bless the Israelites in spite of their slavery?

   Read Exodus 1:15-20

3. What kind of slavery are we all born under today?

   Read John 8:34; Romans 8:15

4. What is life like for us under this slavery?

   Read Romans 1:29-32; James 1:14-15; Hebrews 2:15

5. How does God bring us out of this slavery?

Read John 8:36; Hebrews 9:15; I John 4:18; Philippians 4:6-7

Question 44:

What does the preface to the Ten Commandments teach us?

Answer: The preface to the Ten Commandments teaches us that because God is the Lord, and our God and Redeemer, therefore we are bound to keep all His commandments.

6. Why does God have the right to give us commandments about how we are to live?

Read Psalm 146:6, 10; Deuteronomy 32:6; Galatians 4:4-6

7. Does obedience to the commandments earn a person a place in heaven?

Read Romans 3:20; Ephesians 2:8-9

8. What is the purpose of the law?

Read Romans 3:20

9. What sins have you been convicted of through reading or hearing God's Word?

10. Why are we to obey God's commandments?

Read I Peter 1:15-16; I John 5:3; Isaiah 48:17

11. How do we know that God knows what is best for us?

Read Isaiah 40:28

12. What is the result of obeying God's commandments?

Read Isaiah 48:17-18

Commentary
Lesson 14

The Introduction: The Preface to the Ten Commandments
Catechism Questions 43 and 44

The memory of slavery is a big issue in the United States. For too many years, a significant segment of the population was held in bondage by another group. But slavery did not begin in America. Ever since one group of people was strong enough to conquer another group, there have been slaves. And much of the time, slaves were mistreated. In the days of Joseph, the Israelites were an admired and respected people in Egypt. They were given good land and were allowed to live their lives in peace. As the years went by, though, the Egyptians became frightened at their numbers, and they were enslaved. Then they were treated cruelly; they were made to work at strenuous labor for long hours, but they still grew in numbers.

The Pharaoh finally ordered that all the baby boys be killed as soon as they were born, but the midwives did not obey this order. Amazingly, they were not punished by Pharaoh; they were rewarded by God for their righteousness. As the Hebrews increased even more, Pharaoh ordered that all baby boys be thrown into the Nile River. I have often heard that Moses' mother disobeyed this command, but that is not really the case. She did obey it; she threw Moses into the river. She just put him in a basket first. What a clever woman! She found a way to obey the law and still save her son's life. For this she was blessed by being allowed to nurse her son for the next few years. But the Israelites were still slaves and were still mistreated.

We can be thankful that in the United States we have ended this practice, even though it is still in existence in other parts of the world. It is illegal in our country for one person to own another person. But that does not mean that we have no slavery, because everyone in our country is born as a slave. We are not slaves to other people; we are slaves to sin. As slaves to sin, we are bound to do whatever our master wants us to do. We will lie, cheat, steal, dishonor others, refuse to honor God, hate, murder, etc. And the irony is, we think that we are free. We refuse to acknowledge our slavery. We think that we are doing what we want to do, that we are making our own decisions, that we are in control of our own lives. But in reality, all the time we are doing the work of the one who owns us.

There is in each of us a conscience that will let us know that we are doing wrong, but we will ignore it. We are bound to ignore it by virtue of our slavery to sin. We must obey our master. Even if we hear our conscience, we can easily rationalize our actions and ease what little guilt we may feel. We are doomed to live in this slavery until we die, and then we are doomed to face the punishment for our choices.

Even if we wanted to, we couldn't free ourselves. There is no way we can break the chains that hold us in captivity. In ancient times, it was possible for a slave to earn enough money to buy his or her freedom, but that is rarely true in cases of slavery today. A slave is not a paid employee; any money he or she earns goes to the master. Neither can we earn our freedom from slavery to sin. We certainly can't buy our way out. Nor can we do enough good deeds to earn our freedom. God tells us that all of our good deeds are worth nothing. Slaves cannot free themselves.

However, a slave can be set free by someone else. I have heard of several cases of people buying slaves in order to set them free. Someone would have to care a great deal about a slave to pay a large sum of money to buy his or her freedom. Imagine you are a slave. Your life is under the total control of someone else. For years you have to get up very early in the morning and work until late at night doing whatever you are told to do. You don't get days off. You can't leave the house without permission. You and your entire family are subject to the whims of your master. Even if you have a decent master, this is not a pleasant life. Now imagine that a man comes along, buys you and your family, and sets you free. You can now do what you want. What would you say to this man? After "Thank you!" wouldn't your next question be, "Isn't there anything I can do for you?"

Wouldn't you be willing to meet his requests? Not out of fear, but out of gratitude. You would be free not to, but you would probably do whatever he asked. Suppose he asked you to honor him and be kind to his children. Would you be willing to do that? Are you willing to do that for the one who has set you free?

We were all born as slaves, but if we have trusted Christ, then he has bought us and set us free. His death on the cross paid for our freedom. We no longer have to obey our sinful master. We can reject sin and its entanglements and we are free to live a better life. And to help us live that life to the fullest, God has given us rules, which Christ summed up into two: "Love the Lord your God with all your heart and with all your soul and with all your mind." And "Love your neighbor as yourself." In other words, honor and revere God and be kind to His children. We can never obey God's rules perfectly; the purpose of His laws is to show us what we are doing wrong and how we should be living.

So how do we know that these rules are in our best interest? How can we be sure that obeying these rules will bring us the best life possible? There are several reasons we can know this. First, we can know because the One who made the rules is the One who made us. He knows how we operate and what is likely to cause us problems. He knows how we interact together and how to make that work in the best way possible. He not only created our bodies, but also our minds, our emotions, and our personalities. He knows everything there is to know about us, so He knows how to make it work.

If a car manufacturer were to tell you that you must change the oil in your car every 3000 miles for that car to run at its peak efficiency, you would trust him. Why? Because he made the car and he knows how it works, or more importantly, what is likely to make it stop working. You have probably heard the saying, "Children don't come with instructions." But they do. We all have instructions. In the same way the car manufacturer gives us instructions for the upkeep of our car, the God who made us gives us instructions for the upkeep of our lives, and he knows what is likely to make our lives stop working pleasantly. If we would obey a lowly car manufacturer, we should certainly obey the God of the universe!

The second reason we can know that obeying these rules will

work for our best is that God knows far more than we can ever know. He can see consequences to our actions that we can never see. We may not be able to see the harm that may come from our actions, but God can. How much more pleasant are our lives when we live according to our manufacturer's instructions! If we follow His plan, we will have peace in our hearts and righteousness in His sight. That is not to say that it will be easy, but He promises to be with us each step of the way.

LESSON FIFTEEN
The First Commandment:
No Other Gods

Question 45:

What is the First Commandment?

Answer: The First Commandments is, "You shall have no other gods before me."

Question 46:

What is required in the First Commandment?

Answer: The First Commandment requires us to know and acknowledge God to be the only true God, and our God, and to worship and glorify Him accordingly.

1. When we accept that God is the only true God, what else are we obligated to do?

Read Deuteronomy 26:17

2. How does God know if we are acknowledging Him as the only true God?

Read I Chronicles 28:9; Psalm 139:2

3. How are we to worship the Lord?

Read Psalm 29:2; 100:2; John 4:24; Romans 12:1; Hebrews 12:28

4. How are we to glorify the Lord?

Read 1 Thessalonians 5:16-18; Acts 17:11; 2 John 6; 1 John 4:21

Question 47:

What is forbidden in the First Commandment?

Answer: The First Commandment forbids the denying or not worshipping and glorifying, the true God as God, and our God, and the giving to any other of that worship and glory due to Him alone.

5. How does Scripture describe a person who denies God?

Read Psalm 14:1

6. What happens to those who refuse to acknowledge and worship God?

Read Romans 1:18-31

7. How can even Christians give worship and glory to something other than God alone?

Read Colossians 3:5

8. What things are you worshiping other than God alone?

Question 48:

What are we especially taught by the words, "before me," in the First Commandment?

Answer: These words, "before me," in the First Commandment teach us that God, who sees all things, takes notice of, and is much displeased with, the sin of having any other god.

9. How does God describe the worship of other gods?

Read Deuteronomy 27:15; Jeremiah 32:34; I Kings 14:9

10. What is God's response to the worship of other gods?

Read 2 Kings 22:17; Psalm 78:58

11. What does it mean that God is jealous?

2 Corinthians 11:2-3; Deuteronomy 32:16

Commentary
Lesson 15

The First Commandment: No Other Gods

Catechism Questions 45, 46, 47, and 48

"You shall have no other gods before me." What does that mean? I will get to the "no other gods" part in a while, but what does "before me" refer to? Merriam Webster's Online Dictionary gives three definitions for the word "before":

(1) in a higher or more important position than <put quantity before quality>

(2) preceding in time <,just before noon>

(3) in front of or in the presence of <speaking *before* the conference>.

Let's consider each of these definitions to see how well they fit the commandment.

First, the commandment could mean, "You shall have no other gods in a higher position than me." This would allow for the possibility of other gods, but only in a subordinate position to the God of the Bible. Is this what God meant? I don't think so. In Exodus 23:13, God instructs Israel, "Do not invoke the names of other gods; do not let them be heard on your lips." In Deuteronomy 17:2-5, we are told that if a man or woman worshiped another god, he or she was to be stoned to death. Finally, in 2 Kings 17:38, we read, "Do not forget the covenant I have made with you, and do not worship other gods." I think It is pretty clear that God does not allow the worship of any god other than Himself, whether that god is primary or secondary in our worship. So we can rule out definition number one.

Second, we could interpret the commandment as "You shall have no other gods earlier than me." In other words, until you worship me, you should worship no god at all. What this interpretation says is that the worship of any other god is wrong. If we do not know that we are to worship the true God, the worship of any other god is sinful. Actually, this is not exactly wrong, but it does not encompass the full meaning of the commandment. And until we begin to worship the one true God, we are all guilty of breaking the commandment in this way.

Third, we could read the commandment as "You shall have no other gods in my presence." At first, this interpretation might seem to limit the commandment. Have any of you had a son who wanted a pet snake or a pet tarantula? Did any of you give in, with the stipulation, "Just don't bring it in where I can see it"? As long as it wasn't in your presence, you could ignore the fact that it was in your house. So as long as we don't bring other gods into God's presence, then we are okay, right? That is an unanswerable question, since everything in the entire universe is always in the presence of God. Wherever we go, whatever we do, we are always doing it before God. So it is impossible to worship other gods without worshiping them in His presence. I think this is the meaning of the commandment.

You may be thinking by now that this commandment is not relevant to you. People don't pray to idols anymore. We are more sophisticated than that now. But there are certainly religions that worship a different god than the God of the Bible. The true God exists as one God in three persons, which we call a Trinity—Father, Son, and Holy Spirit.[23] Any religion which fails to acknowledge any one of the persons of the Godhead is not worshiping the true God.

There are also still many religions that do incorporate idols into their worship. Many well-meaning folks have fallen for New Age mysticism and the belief in the power of crystals, pyramids, and other talismans. While not exactly idols, these forms of occult power are contrary to the worship of God. In Leviticus and Deuteronomy[24] we are told that divination, sorcery, witchcraft, and spiritism are detestable to the Lord.

But let's assume that you have not engaged in any of these practices. How might you have broken this commandment? My

23   Matthew 28:19
24   Leviticus 20:27; Deuteronomy 18:10-12

sister and I just had a conversation about an event that happened years ago, when I was sixteen and she was eleven. I had just bought a new peppermint-flavored lipstick. I thought it was really cool and asked her if she wanted to taste it. She bit off about half of it! She claims that I was being way too sensitive about that lipstick. I say that "taste" is very different from "eat." I was very upset about that lipstick! Now what does that have to do with the First Commandment? It says nothing about eating lipstick. It does, however, have a lot to say about my attitude toward that lipstick. How upset should I have been? How important was that lipstick? Depending on the degree of my distress, could my attitude have been bordering on worship?

Okay, worship of a lipstick is pretty silly, and I am fairly sure I was not worshiping the lipstick. But what about more important things? What about your home? Your job? Your spouse? Your children? George Robertson, in his study *More Grace, More Love*, says that we worship what we fear losing. In other words, whatever we fear losing the most is the thing we worship the most. Is your biggest fear that you might displease God or act unfaithfully toward Him? If not, then you are probably worshiping something else more than you are worshiping God. Is your biggest fear that you will lose your job, your spouse, or your children? Is your biggest fear that your looks will fade, that you will grow old? We can worship people, jobs, and even youth. Any of this would be a violation of this commandment.

In Colossians 3:5, we are told that greed is the same as idolatry. Why is that true? Because in our greed, our focus shifts from serving God to getting more of the thing or things we want. Those things become the objects of our worship. We may not pray to them or bow down to them, but we orient our lives around them. We give them the place in our lives that God should have and that He rightly deserves.

Our God, the only true God, is a jealous God. He wants the relationship with us that He deserves. He wants the worship that He is due. He wants first place in our lives. You may have been told that jealousy is a harmful emotion; and that is true if you are talking about jealousy in the sense of envy. But there are times when jealousy is healthy. A husband and wife should be jealous of their marriage. They should be angry if someone tries to interfere with that relationship. Marriage is meant to be "till death do us part." If anyone attempts to win the attention and affection of either the husband or the wife, the other spouse has the right, and perhaps even the obligation, to be jealous. This is the kind of jealousy that God has. His relationship with His people is precious. If someone or something else seeks to steal our affection away from Him, He is jealous for that relationship. I'm sure you can think of times in your own life when your first affection was for something or someone other than God.

So, you see, you probably have been worshiping something other than God. We all have; we have all broken Commandment One. Now what can we do about it? First, we can be grateful that God has provided salvation and forgiveness for us through Christ. In Ezekiel 37:23, God makes it clear that He forgives this sin specifically. No matter what you may have been worshiping in the past, God will help you to turn away from that and to worship Him and Him alone. So our second step is to begin to try to worship Him properly and to give Him the place in our lives that He deserves.

To do that requires that God take first priority in our lives. We must obey His Word and seek to live in a way that is pleasing to Him. We must worship Him in spirit and in truth, which means that we must study the Scriptures to understand what pleases Him in worship. We must live our lives in a way that is glorifying to God. Basically, that means that we must first and foremost be obedient to God and to His commands. Paul tells us in I Corinthians that we are to glorify God in our bodies and in our spirits.[25] According to Christ, this means that we should let men see our good works and glorify our Father in heaven.[26] We must look out for the "gods" that might lure us away from giving God the worship that He is rightfully due. In Colossians 3, Paul admonishes us to put to death such things as sexual immorality, impurity, lust, evil desires and greed; and to rid ourselves of all such things as anger, rage, malice, slander, filthy language, and lies. At the same time, he tells us to clothe ourselves with compassion, kindness, humility, gentleness and patience, and to bear with each other and

25   I Corinthians 6:20
26   Matthew 5:16

forgive whatever grievances we may have against one another.

This is a tall order, and we can't do it all at once. This is the process of sanctification. Slowly, little by little, the Holy Spirit will enable us to accomplish more and more of this, although we will never perfect it in this lifetime. However, the more we accomplish, the more our lives will glorify God and the more others will see Him reflected in us.

The worship of God is serious business. It is more than attending church on Sunday. It is the total giving of our lives to His glory. It is giving Him first priority in every part of our lives. The wonderful fact for us is that the more we give our lives to Him, the more peace and joy we can experience.

LESSON SISTEEN
The Second Commandment:
You Shall Not Make a Carved Image

Question 49:

Which is the Second Commandment?

Answer: The Second Commandment is, "You shall not make for yourself a carved image, or any likeness of anything that is in heaven above, or that is in the earth beneath, or that is in the water under the earth. You shall not bow down to them or serve them, for I the LORD your God am a jealous God, visiting the iniquity of the fathers on the children to the third and the fourth generation of those who hate me, but showing steadfast love to thousands of those who love me and keep my commandments."

1. Why is it impossible to represent God by an image?

   Read John 4:24

2. When Moses came down from the mountain with the Ten Commandments, what had the Israelites done that angered him so much?

   Read Exodus 32:7

3. What did Aaron tell the people they were doing when they sacrificed to the calf?

   Read Exodus 32:5-6

Question 50:

What is required in the Second Commandment?

Answer: The Second Commandment requires the receiving, observing, and keeping pure and entire all such religious worship and ordinances as God has appointed in His Word.

4. How are we to worship God?

Read John 4:24

5. What specifically should we do in worship?

Read Acts 2:42; Ephesians 5:19; Malachi 3:10

6. For whom should we pray in our worship?

Read 1 Timothy 2:1-2

Question 51:

What is forbidden in the Second Commandment?

Answer: The Second Commandment forbids the worshiping of God by images, or any other way not appointed in His Word.

7. What does the worship of God by images involve?

Read Isaiah 46:5-7

8. How can we create God in our own image without creating statues or pictures?

Read Isaiah 29:13; Matthew 15:8-10

Question 52: What are the reasons attached to the Second Commandment?

Answer: The reasons attached to the Second Commandment are: God's sovereignty over us, His ownership in us, and the zeal He has for His own Worship.

9. Why does God have the right to tell us how to worship Him?

Read Revelation 4:11

10. What should be our response to God in worship?

Read Romans 12:1

Commentary
Lesson 16

The Second Commandment: You Shall Not Make a Carved Image

Catechism Questions 49, 50, 51, and 52

Have you ever seen that print of the painting of Jesus praying in the Garden of Gethsemane? That print is everywhere. My grandmother had one in her sewing room. And in the little church where my husband preaches, a dear lady donated one for the front of the sanctuary. It was hanging there when he first came to the church. Oh, boy. What do you do? Confront the elders and tell them to take that picture down immediately? Give a series of sermons on idol worship and graven images? Or leave well enough alone?

He decided to leave it, at least for a while. After a time, he mentioned it in a session meeting. The decision was made to leave it there until the lady, who was by then quite elderly, passed on. It has now been replaced by a cross. But does it really even matter? What is the big deal about a picture of Jesus?

Well, first of all, that picture of Jesus probably doesn't look anything like Jesus really looked. If you go to a great art museum, you will see an astounding number of paintings of Jesus or of Mary and the infant Jesus. The interesting thing is that they all look like the people in the place and time that the artist lived. Modern artists are a little bit more in tune with the fact that styles of dress have changed, so they portray Jesus and Mary in more accurate clothing, but they still look like the people the artist lives around. Caucasian painters and sculptors make Him white; African painters and sculptors make Him black; Asians make Him Asian, etc. So in that picture, if I remember correctly, He has brown hair, white skin, and blue eyes.

Jesus lived in the Middle East. He would have fit in with the people He lived with; He would have looked Middle Eastern. I don't think I have ever seen a painting or sculpture with a Middle Eastern Jesus. So, the first thing wrong with most of our paintings and sculptures is that they are just wrong.

That may be the only thing wrong. It depends on our attitude toward the picture. If we are prone to worship or honor the picture in some special way, then we have a problem. Then we are using the picture as a worship image, and that is clearly forbidden in the Second Commandment. (For that matter, if we are using the cross that replaced it as an image to be worshiped, that is also forbidden.)

If you have taught young children, you know how valuable pictures can be to help them understand a story. When you are reading them a book, they always want to see the pictures. According to Dr. D. James Kennedy, in his book *Why the Ten Commandments Matter,* using pictures of Jesus for illustrative purposes is not what is forbidden in this commandment. God is not telling us not to create art depicting Biblical stories, not even stories about Jesus. Jesus did take on a human body. That body lived and walked on earth and then was pierced and killed in payment for our sins. Dr. Kennedy says that we can use our art to depict those events.

What is forbidden is the worship of that art, or the worship of God through that art. There are still many forms of Christianity that use art forms as aids in worship. They may tell you that they are just using the statues or icons as symbols to point the worshipers to God, but isn't that exactly what Aaron did? He told the Israelites that they were to celebrate a festival to the Lord. The golden calf, at least in some ways, was a representation of God. But that was a lame excuse. God does not want to be represented by anything in our worship, because He cannot be represented by anything. He is Spirit, and He is far greater and more magnificent that any of His creation.

Dr. Kennedy likens this to having a really bad picture taken of yourself. Have you ever had that happen? When one of our daughters was in high school, she did not take good pictures. Her school pictures were pretty bad. And the worst part was that everyone kept trying to make her feel better by saying, "They're great. They look just like you." But she didn't want to look like that! Those people were not at all helpful. And the pictures did not look like her. Oh, sure, they looked like she looked for the split second when the picture was being taken, but they did not capture her vibrant personality or sense of humor. They were expressionless and empty. Just like those pictures did not accurately reflect my daughter, nothing that we could draw or paint or sculpt could come remotely close to reflecting the splendor and majesty of God Almighty. So we shouldn't even try.

It's not just through the use of physical objects that we can fail to worship God properly. In both the Old and the New Testaments, God confronts the religious teachers of the day for failing to worship Him properly. He says that they say the right words, but their hearts are far from Him. Instead of worshiping Him in the way He desires, they have made up their own rules for men to follow. How might that be visible in the Church today?

Well, what about the Shorter Catechism that we are studying right now? Or the *Westminster Confession of Faith*? How do you regard that document? If you consider it to be equal to the Bible, then you are guilty of breaking this commandment. These statements were written by godly men, and I truly believe that they are accurate and correct, but they are not, and do not claim to be, divinely inspired. They are not the Word of God.

I grew up in a church where I seldom, if ever, heard the Gospel preached. We were taught how to live nicely and to be kind to others, but I don't remember ever hearing about my need for a Savior. Of course, it could be that I just wasn't ready to hear that message, but I don't think that is the only reason I never heard about my need for Christ. After I became a Christian, I still attended that church for a while and I still did not hear the Gospel. I taught Vacation Church School (that's what they called it) during the summer, and our curriculum included only one Bible story for the entire week. The other stories were just made up by men.

I soon left that church for one that was much better. Several years later, while attending a Christian seminar, I ran into a couple who had both attended that same church. They were now also Christians, and the husband was attending a seminary in Dallas. When I returned home, I was talking with a friend and sharing my excitement that this couple had come to know the Lord, but my friend said, "But that seminary isn't Reformed." He couldn't share in the joy that they now loved the Lord because they didn't share his exact theology!

Folks, Reformed theology is not the Gospel. I believe it, but I can love those who don't. I can rejoice in those who come to know the Lord even if their theology is different from mine. Let's don't let our knowledge of doctrine put a stumbling block between ourselves and other Christians. Let's don't let rules or doctrine, even if they are the right rules and doctrine, separate us from loving our brothers and sisters in Christ.

If we are truly concerned about worshiping God in the proper manner, we will be serving Him with all our heart, with all our soul, with all our mind, and with all our strength. We will offer our bodies as living sacrifices to Him. If God is our focus, other things will fade in comparison. If there are things in your life that you are using as idols, get rid of them and ask for His forgiveness. Focus on God as He truly is. Give Him the glory and honor and worship He is due, in the way He commands it. He will gladly receive your worship, and you will be blessed in giving it.

LESSON SEVENTEEN

The Third Commandment:
The Name of the Lord

Question 53:

Which is the Third Commandment?

Answer: The Third Commandment is, "You shall not take the name of the LORD your God in vain, for the LORD will not hold him guiltless who takes His name in vain."

Question 54:

What is required in the Third Commandment?

Answer: The Third Commandment requires the holy and reverent use of God's names, titles, attributes, ordinances, Word, and works.

1. What is God's name?

   Read Exodus 3:13-15

2. By what other names is God known?

   Read Exodus 15:3; 34:14; Psalm 92:1; Ezekiel 39:25; Amos 5:27; Matthew 1:21, 16:16; John 14:26

3. By what attributes or characteristics is God known?

I Chronicles 16:35; Jeremiah 10:16; 23:6; 50:34; John 14:26:
Romans 8:15

4. What name or names do you usually use for God?

5. What does it mean to "call on the name of the Lord"?

Read Romans 10:9, 13; I Corinthians 1:2; Zechariah 13:9

6. When did people first begin to call on the name of the Lord?

Read Genesis 4:26

Question 55:

What is forbidden in the Third Commandment?

Answer: The Third Commandment forbids all profaning or abusing of anything by which God makes Himself known.

7. How are we to treat the name of the Lord?

Read Deuteronomy 28:58-59; Psalm 68:4, 138:2; Malachi 1:11-14, 2:2

8. How can we profane or abuse God's name?

Read Leviticus 24:11; Deuteronomy 5:11, 28:58; Malachi 1:14, 2:2

Question 56:

What is the reason attached to the Third Commandment?

Answer: The reason attached to the Third Commandment is that, however those who break this commandment may escape punishment from men, yet the Lord our God will not allow them to escape His righteous judgment.

9. How much does God punish those who take His name in vain?

   Read Exodus 34:5-7

10. How have you misused the name of God?

Commentary
Lesson 17

The Third Commandment: The Name of the Lord

Catechism Questions 53, 54, 55, and 56

The story I am about to tell you is true. I hesitated to share it, but I have decided that I need to. My husband was the pastor of a small church in a small town. The longer we served in that church, the more we became concerned about the spiritual well-being of some of the members, and even some of the church officers. Many of the church members seemed to be overly concerned about really trivial details of the church and not at all concerned about spiritual things. One Sunday evening a group of us were decorating the church for an upcoming event, and someone asked if we should move the large Bible from the communion table to make room for a floral arrangement. The basic décor of the church was in the hands of a few of the elderly women, and we were not sure they would approve of our moving the Bible. As we discussed the pros and cons, one woman in the group walked away and said, "Well, you can do what you want to, but I'm not touching that d___ Bible."

Are you shocked? I was speechless. This woman called herself a Christian; her husband was an elder in the church. I'm sure none of you would use such a term in connection with the Holy Bible. Or maybe some of you are not so shocked. Maybe you are thinking, "What's the big deal? It's just a book."

But it's not just a book; it is the living Word of God. Now I don't think the Bible is so "holy" that it should be kept in a special place, that only certain people should be allowed to read it, or that no one should desecrate its pages by writing in them. I have carried Bibles around and written in the pages until they were quite ragged-looking. That is using the Bible for the purpose that God intended—for study and for training in righteousness. But it is a special book because it was written by God Himself through the hands of specially chosen men.

So what does this have to do with taking the Lord's Name in vain? Only that everything about the Lord should be treated with reverence. According to the catechism, this includes His Name, His titles, His attributes, His ordinances, His Word, and His works.

God gave Himself many names and titles in the Bible. He is called I Am; The God of Abraham, Isaac, and Jacob; The Lord; The Lord Almighty; God Almighty; The Sovereign Lord; The Most High; Jesus Christ; The Holy Spirit, and the most unusual, Jealous. His attributes are many, but they include Savior, Redeemer, Our Righteousness, Portion of Jacob, Maker of all things, and Counselor. All of these names, and others you may find in Scripture, are to be used with utmost respect.

Does that mean you should never use phrases such as "Thank God!" Well, that depends on if you really mean it. If you are truly thanking God, then that phrase is appropriate and necessary. But if you are just using it as an expression of happiness, then no, it is inappropriate and actually sinful. Some folks throw around the Name of God so lightly, it is obvious that they are not thinking about God at all. We need to make sure we are never in that position.

I heard of a young man who, whenever he heard someone say "Jesus Christ!" in a profane way, would say "He's here. What did you need Him for?" I'm sure he upset a lot of people, but he got their attention! So many people just don't think about what they are saying.

In an interesting contrast, I was in a philosophy class with a young man who was a self-proclaimed atheist. As we were discussing arguments for or against the existence of God, this man would not even say the word "God." He always spelled it out: G-O-D. It is as if he were afraid that if he said the name, he would bring God into existence. Of course, I think he knew that there really is a God and it scared him to death. But he was very much aware of what he was saying. As an atheist, he showed more respect for the Name of God than many professing Christians do.

Many people, in an effort not to misuse the Name of God, use His attributes instead. For example, rather than say "Oh my God" they will say "Oh my goodness." But is this really any better? According to the Catechism, it is not. Goodness is an attribute of God; only He is totally good. To use His attributes in a profane way is also disrespectful and irreverent. So we all probably need to improve our vocabularies.

So is that it? As long as we don't say anything wrong, we are clear of breaking Commandment Three? Not so fast. Scripture gives us several other ways that we can be guilty of abusing the Name of God. In addition to what we say, we can abuse His Name by what we do or fail to do.

In Deuteronomy, Moses tells us that failure to obey God's laws is dishonoring to His Name. I could discuss this at length, but I won't. Let's just say that God makes it very clear throughout Scripture what He wants us to do and how He wants us to live. Every time we fall short of that, and we all fall short, we are sinning against Him and abusing His Name. We are failing to give Him the glory He deserves. By calling ourselves Christians, using His Name, and failing to live before others as He directs us to live, we are causing others to fail to glorify Him as well.

The prophet Malachi instructs us that by failing to give God His proper offering, we are dishonoring His Name. Whatever you believe the proper offering to be (many people believe that to be ten percent of your income), have you ever failed to give that amount to God? If so, you have profaned His Name. You have told Him that you were more important than He is, and that you could not trust Him to provide for you. Malachi also says that serving God for our own selfish purposes is an abuse of the Name of God. How many times do we do things for God or for the church hoping to receive recognition or reward?

So once again, we are guilty, guilty, guilty. This is getting old, isn't it? Let's face it. We are going to see that we have broken every one of the Ten Commandments. But we should have known that. John tells us in his first letter that if we say we have no sin, we are deceiving ourselves; but if we confess our sins, He is faithful to forgive our sins and to cleanse us from all unrighteousness. So what should we do about this sin? First, let's confess that we have misused God's Name and ask for His forgiveness. Then second, let's get things right. Let's treat God's Name, and everything associated with God, with respect and honor. Let's praise His Name, sing to His Name, rejoice in His Name, and fear His Name. But let's also call on His Name. As His children, we have that privilege. In one sense, to call on the Name of the Lord means to trust in Him for our salvation. This began in the earliest time of human existence, in the days of Adam and Eve and Seth. In another sense, to call on the Name of the Lord can mean to call on Him in times of trouble. As those who believe in Him, we can come to Him with every care and concern, because He is interested and involved in even the smallest aspect of our lives. This is our blessing as His chosen people.

LESSON EIGHTEEN
The Fourth Commandment:
The Sabbath

Question 57:

Which is the Fourth Commandment?

Answer: The Fourth Commandment is, "Remember the Sabbath day, to keep it holy. Six days you shall labor, and do all your work, but the seventh day is a Sabbath to the LORD your God. On it you shall not do any work, you or your son, or your daughter, your male servant, or your female servant, or your livestock, or the sojourner who is within your gates. For in six days the LORD made heaven and earth, the sea, and all that is in them, and rested the seventh day. Therefore the LORD blessed the Sabbath day and made it holy."

1. What is to be done on the six days that are not the Sabbath?

   Read Exodus 20:9

2. What is the purpose of work?

   Read Proverbs 14:23; Ecclesiastes 3:22; Ephesians 4:28; I Thessalonians 4:11-12; 2Thessalonians 3:7-9

3. What is God's attitude toward those who refuse to work?

   Read 2 Thessalonians 3:10

4. Who are we working for?

Read Colossians 3:23

Question 58:

What is required in the Fourth Commandment?

Answer: The Fourth Commandment requires the keeping holy to God such set times as He has appointed in His Word, expressly one whole day in seven, to be a holy Sabbath to Himself.

5. What was the Sabbath Day created for?

Read Leviticus 23:3; Mark 2:27

Question 59:

Which day of the seven has God appointed to be the weekly Sabbath?

Answer: From the beginning of the world to the resurrection of Christ, God appointed the seventh day of the week to be the weekly Sabbath; and the first day of the week ever since, to continue to the end of the world, which is the Christian Sabbath.

6. Why do we celebrate the Sabbath on the first day of the week? (What is the significance of the first day of the week?)

Read Mark 16:2-6

Question 60:

How is the Sabbath to be sanctified?

Answer: The Sabbath is to be sanctified by a holy resting all that day, even from such worldly employments and recreations as are lawful on other days; and spending the whole time in the public and private exercises of God's worship, except so much as is to be taken up in the works of necessity and mercy.

7. What kinds of things should be done on the Sabbath?

   Read Mark 3:1-5; Luke 23:55-56; Acts 17:2-3

Question 61: What is forbidden in the Fourth Commandment?

Answer: The Fourth Commandment forbids the omission, or careless performance, of the duties required, and the profaning the day by idleness, or doing that which is in itself sinful, or by unnecessary thoughts, words, or works, about our worldly employments or recreations.

8. What should we not do on the Sabbath?

   Read Hebrews 10:25; Leviticus 23:3

Question 62:

What are the reasons attached to the Fourth Commandment?

Answer: The reasons attached to the Fourth Commandment are: God's allowing us six days of the week for our own employments, His establishment of a special ownership in the seventh, His own example, and His blessing the Sabbath day.

9. Who was the first person to observe a Sabbath day?

   Read Genesis 2:3

10. What do you usually do on the Sabbath?

11. Is there anything you feel you should change about your activities on the Sabbath?

Commentary
Lesson 18

The Fourth Commandment: The Sabbath

Catechism Questions 57, 58, 59, 60, 61, and 62

I love Sundays. I like going to church, worshipping the Lord, and seeing my friends. I also love the fact that I am commanded not to work. No matter what I see around the house that needs my attention, I am commanded by God to leave it until tomorrow. This is wonderful. I am by nature a Scarlet O'Hara kind of girl—"I'll think about it tomorrow; tomorrow is another day." This doesn't get me very far on most days, but it is exactly the right attitude for Sundays. On Sundays, God commands us to rest. He knows we need it, so He commands us to do it. Why are we so reluctant to take the gift He offers us?

Before we consider that question, though, I want to look at the first half of this commandment: six days you shall labor and do all your work. This is really a two-part commandment. We focus on the second half, but we can't ignore the first. God commands us to work. Work is the way we provide for ourselves and our families; God does not want us to be dependent on others. We should also work so that we have something to give to others. There are times when other people can't work, so we should try to have enough to share. In addition, honest work provides us with a good reputation in the community. It doesn't matter what your work is; if you do it diligently and honestly, others will recognize that and respect you for it.

We are also to enjoy our work. I have been especially blessed to have "stumbled" into a career that is extremely challenging and satisfying. Of course, I don't really think I stumbled into it at all; even though I had no idea what I was doing, God was directing me all along. My personality is split pretty evenly between extroversion and introversion; I love being with people, but I also need a significant amount of time to work alone. In my job as a college professor, I have a good balance of both. I get to work with students and other faculty, but then I get to work alone in my office as well. God has truly blessed me in this, and I am very grateful. If you have not been so fortunate, I would encourage you to think about what you really enjoy doing and see if you can make that an income-producing occupation. It might take some time or some additional education, but God intends that we find fulfillment and enjoyment in what we do. We have to do it for a lot of years, so it helps if we like it!

Whatever we are doing, though, we should be doing it for the Lord. Sometimes we may be tempted to do less than our best, but if we see ourselves as serving Christ, rather than our earthly employers, we will be less likely to act on that temptation. This is one thing I want to impress on my Christian students (especially the ones who make a show of their Christianity). As students, their job is to study. They should do this as though Christ were their instructor. Most of them are content just to get by. I don't think that's what Christ expects from them, or from us either.

So for six days, we are to work diligently. Then we get a day of rest. That is a tremendous gift. God actually tells us to stop. Stop striving, stop stressing, stop running around in circles. Just stop. Rest. Let it go for a while. Come to worship Him. Be inspired and invigorated in your faith. Remind yourself of what is really important and that God is there with you in whatever is going on in your life. Take time to read the Bible. Read an inspiring Christian book. Take a walk and be awed by God's creation. But rest from the labors of the other six days.

Some of you who have small children may find it difficult to rest. Children make the same demands on us on Sunday as they do on every other day of the week. Perhaps you could tuck away some special toys or videos, especially those related to your Christian faith, and let the children use those only on Sunday. While they play or watch the video, you can take a few minutes to rest. Or perhaps you can find an activity, such as taking a walk, which you find restful, but that can be done with the entire family. Read a good book to your children. The important thing is that this day be different, for your children as well as yourself.

Since my husband is a pastor, I want to say a word about pastors and other church workers. Of necessity, they have to work on the Sabbath. They must be there to preach and teach and to keep things going for the rest of us. But they need a day of rest as well. And it's not Saturday. Saturday is the day the entire family can be together and work as a family around the house. This is not a Sabbath for the pastor or church worker. He or she needs another day to truly rest. This is not just my opinion—it's God's opinion. We are all to have a Sabbath rest. God did it and so should we. If you are a church leader or have influence over one, make sure those who work for your church have their Sabbath as well.

So what are we allowed to do on the Sabbath, and what are we not allowed to do? Well, three things are clear: we are allowed to worship God on the Sabbath, we are allowed to do works of mercy on the Sabbath, and we are not allowed to do the work that we would do on the other six days of the week. That leaves a lot of gray area. Should we go out to a restaurant to eat? Should we watch movies? Should we travel? I have friends who believe that we should not do these things, and I have other friends who find no problem with them. How do we know who is right?

I wish I had a clear answer, a list of definite do's and don'ts, but Scripture doesn't give us one, so I certainly won't either. Here is what I do know. In Isaiah 58:13, we are told that we are not to do whatever we please or go our own way on the Sabbath. In 1 Corinthians 10, Paul tells us that all things are lawful for us, but not all things are profitable; and he says that we must do everything for the glory of God. In Romans 14, he explains that believers have different opinions about what is lawful and what is not, such as eating meat or treating one day differently from another. In such regards, if a person thinks something is sinful, but does it anyway, then he has sinned, because he did what he believed to be sinful. If another person does not think it is sinful, then he may do it and it is not sinful. It is the attitude of the heart that is important. If we do what we consider to be sinful, then we are telling the Lord that we are willing to break His law. But if we do not believe it to be sinful, then we believe that we are abiding by His law. However, Paul admonishes us neither to judge one another nor to put a stumbling block in one another's way.

So my interpretation of these passages would be that in those areas where Scripture is silent, each person or family must prayerfully decide what they should and should not do on the Sabbath. Then they should abide by that decision. If they have decided that a certain behavior is sinful, they should not do it. But they must not extend those rules to everyone. If Scripture is silent on an issue, we should not jump in and try to replace it with our own opinion. If a person or family has decided that a certain activity is not sinful, then they can feel free to do it. However, if they will be spending time with others who do consider it sinful, then they should refrain from doing it out of respect for their brothers and sisters in Christ. Remember that this only applies to those gray areas where Scripture does not give us clear direction.

Above all, the Sabbath is a gift from God. It was made for us to give us rest from our labors. It gives us time to focus on the truly important things in life: our relationship with God and with others. We so often want to ruin it by maintaining business as usual. We continue with our stress and worry and busyness, and then we wonder why we feel "burned out." There is seldom anything so important that it can't wait another day. The laundry and the dirty floors will still be there tomorrow. (Unfortunately.) Anything that has to be done can be done early with foresight and advance planning.

We are all guilty of using the Sabbath as just another day. We may go to church, but after that, we get back on the same merry-go-round of work and stress. God is ready and willing to forgive us for this. In Micah chapter 7, He says that He will pass over our rebellious acts and that rather than holding on to His anger, He will cast our sins into the depths of the sea. So again, let's confess that we have been guilty of misusing the Sabbath that God has provided for us. Then let's take His gift and use it as He intended. Enjoy the Sabbath. Worship. Rest. You know you need it and so does God; that's why He gave you a whole day to do it.

LESSON NINETEEN
The Fifth Commandment:
Honor your father and your mother.

Question 63:

Which is the Fifth Commandment?

Answer: The Fifth Commandment is, "Honor your father and your mother, that your days may be long in the land that the LORD your God is giving you."

Question 64:

What is required in the Fifth Commandment?

Answer: The Fifth Commandment requires the preserving of the honor, and performing the duties, belonging to everyone in their various situations and relationships, as superiors, inferiors, or equals.

1. As children, what does honoring your father and mother involve?

   Read Ephesians 6:1

2. As adults, what does honoring our father and mother involve?

   Read Leviticus 19:3; Proverbs 1:8-9; Mark 7:8-13

Question 65:

What is forbidden in the Fifth Commandment?

Answer: The Fifth Commandment forbids the neglecting of, or doing anything against, the honor and duty that belong to everyone in their various situations and relationships.

3. What types of things are we not to do regarding our father and mother?

Read Exodus 21:15, 17; Proverbs 15:20,19:26

Question 66:

What is the reason attached to the Fifth Commandment?

Answer: The reason attached to the Fifth Commandment is a promise of long life and prosperity (as far as it shall serve for God's glory, and their own good) to all who keep this commandment.

4. What is unusual about the Fifth Commandment?

Read Ephesians 6:2-3

5. How does our relationship with our parents change with marriage?

Read Genesis 2:24 or Matthew 19:5

6. Are there other times when we should leave our parents, physically or spiritually?

Read Matthew 19:29

7. What place should our parents take on our priority list?

   Read Matthew 10:37

8. How are we to deal with elderly parents?

   Read Proverbs 23:22; 1 Timothy 5:1-2

9. Does this apply to our own parents only or to all of our elders?

   Read 1 Timothy 5:1-2 again

10. What things do you need to change regarding your treatment of or attitude toward your father and mother?

Commentary
Lesson 19

The Fifth Commandment: Honor your father and your mother.
Catechism Questions 63, 64, 65, and 66

Missionaries and parents have a similar career goal—to work themselves out of a job. Missionaries are trying to establish churches that national Christians can then take over and support on their own. Parents are seeking to raise children who can be independent and productive adults. Some of you who are reading this are both a parent and a child. Some of you are parents, but have lost your own parents. Some of you are children and have no children of your own. Some have lost your own parents but have no children. There is a place for all of you in this study.

The Fifth Commandment tells us to honor our father and mother. We are going to explore exactly what that does and does not mean. But before proceeding any further, we need to remember that much of this applies on a larger scale than just our immediate family. All of the elderly are to be treated in some respects as our parents. Most of the provisions attached to this commandment apply to everyone with whom you have a relationship, whether they are related to you or not.

First, how do we honor our parents? As children, we honor them by our obedience. Our parents were given to us by God to guide and direct us until we were old enough to navigate this world on our own. However, this stipulation does have an ending point. I do not believe we are called upon to obey our parents for our entire lives. That is fairly obvious for those who get married. Scripture makes it very clear that when a man and woman marry, they become one flesh. They form a new family. They leave their father and mother. This doesn't mean that they never see them again, but it does mean that they are no longer under their authority.

What about adults who have not married? Are they still bound to be obedient to their parents? This is just my opinion, but I think that when a person reaches the age that they begin to seriously contemplate marriage, or the age of financial independence, then they should be independent of their parents. They should become a new family of one.

Many parents have a hard time with this. They still want their son to be "mommy's little boy" or their daughter to be "daddy's little girl." I don't think this is a healthy relationship. Adult children need to be treated as adults and given the respect and independence that we would give our friends. If they ask for advice, give it. Otherwise, stay out of it. A young woman I know said that when she was in the hospital after giving birth to her first child, her mother-in-law came to her house and rearranged and redecorated it completely. This is way out of line! I don't care if this young woman has the worst decorating sense in the world [and she doesn't], it is her house. If you would not do something in a friend's home, don't do it in your children's. And if you would do things like that in your friend's home, then call me. We need to have a long talk.

So we honor our parents by our obedience only up to a certain age. After that, what should we do? We need to continue to respect them, listen to their instruction, and provide for them when they are older. We all know how to treat people with respect, but too often we fail to do that within families. We know each other's quirks and frailties so very well, and it is easy to make jokes of these. Do you laugh at the "stupid" things your mother has done? Do you joke about your father's lack of handyman skills? Is this respect? We can so easily hurt the feelings of others without meaning to and without their letting us know what we have done.

We also need to listen to the advice and instruction of those older and wiser than we are. People learn a lot through experience. Listening to advice can save us a lot of heartaches and headaches. That is not to say that our parents are always right and that we must always do what they advise. But we should at least listen and consider their opinion. They may not know all the facts or have all the knowledge they need, but before we write them off completely, see what they do have to say. They may be wiser and smarter than you think. If not, what did it cost you but a little time?

When our parents are elderly, we need to be sure their needs are taken care of. In today's world, that usually does not mean that we must provide for them monetarily, although sometimes it might. It might mean that we need to become our parents' advisors in making wise financial decisions. As people live longer, more of the elderly become easy prey for those who would take advantage of them. Just recently, I got my first email from Africa. A Mrs. Edith Matthews said that her husband had died, and she had some money that she needed to get transferred into the United States. If I would just send X number of dollars, she could open a U. S. bank account, etc., etc. Have you been on Mrs. Matthews' mailing list? This is a familiar email scam to most of us, but some of our elderly parents are not as Internet savvy and are more trusting of others. As their children, we need to help protect them against those who would harm them for their own financial gain.

Does honoring our parents mean that they must take first place in our lives? Absolutely not. That place is reserved for God. We must never put anyone in the place He deserves. If we are married, our spouse must come before our parents as well. Hopefully, you will never have to choose between God and your parents, but some people do. Some people leave their parents, families, and everything to follow Christ. Those of us in the church must become their family. Others are called to leave their homes to serve God far away. Sometimes parents can try to stand in the way of their going. If you find yourself faced with such a dilemma, consider your parents' reasons for their objection. Seek godly counsel. And pray for clear direction from God. You may find that you are still called to go. Our parents cannot stand between us and doing the will of God.

And I want to add a note to the parents here—don't be those parents. If your child is called to serve God far away, especially overseas, rejoice in that. It will not be the easiest thing you have ever done in your life, but you will be greatly blessed. We've been there and done it—we even have the T-shirts! The first time my two older daughters took a plane to a mission trip destination, I literally panicked. During the time they were at their mission site, a plane crashed nearby. I was a basket case. I am not exaggerating. I had friends coming to my house to counsel with me and pray with me. My friend Judy put a rubber band around her wrist to remind her to pray for me. My girls were gone for a week and I thought I wouldn't make it. When we went to the airport to pick them up, Judy and I stood together waiting for the plane. As we saw the plane approaching, the rubber band on her wrist popped off and flew across the hallway. Judy said, "Well, I guess I don't need to pray for you any more."

As I am writing this, my two younger daughters are both overseas and my oldest daughter is planning to go in a couple of weeks. Before they leave, I pray with them, give them a kiss, tell them I love them, and send them on their way. I sleep soundly that night. Did I do this on my own? Are you kidding! God has done a transforming work in me because He wants my kids overseas, and He doesn't want me to be a hindrance to them.

Yes, we are commanded by God to honor our parents. But as parents, let's be the type of parents that are easy to honor. If you have difficult parents, respect and honor them in spite of that. If you have young children, teach them obedience, and set the example by honoring your own parents. If you have adult children, treat them with the respect that you want from them. God promises blessings if you do.

LESSON TWENTY
The Sixth Commandment:
You shall not murder.

Question 67:

Which is the Sixth Commandment?

Answer: The Sixth Commandment is, "You shall not murder."

1. Summarizing what you read in these verses, what is the definition of "murder"?

Read Numbers 35:16-21

2. Summarizing what you read in these verses, is the accidental killing of another person considered murder?

Read Numbers 35:22-24

3. Is killing other people in a righteous war considered murder?

Read Joshua 8:1, 24

4. Is executing a person who is guilty of a crime considered murder?

Read Exodus 21:14; Leviticus 20:2

5. When does a person become a person?

Read Jeremiah 1:5

Question 68: What is required in the Sixth Commandment?

Answer: The Sixth Commandment requires all lawful endeavors to preserve our own lives, and the lives of others.

6. How should a person treat his or her own body?

Read Ephesians 5:29

7. How should we protect the lives of others?

Read Matthew 25:34-36; Proverbs 31:8; Joshua 2:1-6

Question 69: What is forbidden in the Sixth Commandment?

Answer: The Sixth Commandment forbids the taking away of our own lives or the lives of our neighbors unjustly, or whatever tends to do so.

8. How does the Bible describe our body?

Read I Corinthians 6:19-20

9. Is it possible to commit murder in our thoughts?

Read Matthew 5:21-22

10. How should we treat the elderly among us?

Read Leviticus 19:32; 1 Timothy 5:1-2, 4, 16

11. How should we treat the disabled among us?

Read Job 29:11-15; Luke 14:12-14

12. What instances can you think of where you have committed murder in your words or thoughts?

Commentary
Lesson 20

The Sixth Commandment: You shall not murder.

Catechism Questions 67, 68, and 69

After my grandfather died, my grandmother moved in with my mother. It was not a good match. They had very different ideas about how to do a lot of things. As my grandmother got older and more forgetful, it got worse. Those little things that Mother could have put up with on an occasional visit were hard to deal with on a day to day basis. One weekend they were visiting our house and my mother and I were having a conversation in the kitchen. My grandmother came in and asked us a question that she had already asked several times before, but that was getting fairly normal by this time. After she left the room, my mother turned to me and said, "If I ever get like that, just shoot me."

Have you ever felt like that? Just shoot me. Or just shoot them? We all have; of course, we don't mean it, any more than my mother did. We get exasperated and say things we don't mean. However, Jesus tells us that even saying things in anger is a sin like murder. But some people not only say it, they do it. And most of the time they go to prison. We know that it is very wrong to take a human life, no matter how irritating that life may be. It seems pretty clear, but where do we draw the line? Is killing another person always wrong? If not, when is it not wrong? When does the prohibition against murder begin to apply? What about taking one's own life? What about the terminally ill, the disabled, or the unwanted? Let's look at all of these cases.

First, is it always wrong to take another life? The answer from the Bible is clearly "no." There are times when taking a life is justified and even commanded. In times of war, lives will be lost. War is not a nice thing. It is not glorious. It is horrible in every sense of the word. But sometimes it is necessary. As Edmund Burke said, "All that's necessary for the forces of evil to win in the world is for enough good men to do nothing." Sometimes those good men have to go to war against the forces of evil. And some on each side will die. It isn't pleasant to think about, and no one wants it to happen; but there are times when we have to do it anyway.

There are also certain crimes that are so evil that God commands that those who commit them be put to death. Think of serial murderers such as Jeffrey Dahmer, Ted Bundy, John Wayne Gacy, and Charles Manson. These men showed no respect for human life and by their own actions, they convicted themselves of crimes worthy of death. Some of them were actually sentenced to death and some were not. But according to the Bible, they all deserved the death penalty. For the government to execute a person who has been found guilty of such a crime beyond the shadow of a doubt is not wrong. Personally, I think we need to be very careful before imposing such a punishment so that we don't execute innocent people, but in some cases the evidence is so overwhelming that there is simply no doubt as to who committed the crimes.

So not all killing is murder. But any intentional killing of an innocent human being is murder; so when does the prohibition against murder begin to apply? When does a person become a person? According to God, we become a person before we are born. Most scientists who are Christians believe that occurs at the moment of conception. At the precise instant that two cells unite to become one new cell, a genetically new individual is created. This one cell has its own unique DNA and will soon grow to become a recognizable and distinct individual. In week 5 of its development, its heart will begin to beat. In week 6, the basic facial features will begin to form. In week 8, it will develop fingers and toes, eyelids, ears, the upper lip and the nose. By week 9, hair follicles appear and many internal organs are forming. By week 10, its bones are forming. By week 12, its gender is obvious and it has fingernails and toenails.[27] But if its mother doesn't want it, a doctor can legally go into the womb, rip it apart and throw it away. Is this the deliberate killing of an innocent human being? I don't see how we can call it anything else.

---

27   MayoClinic.com

But what if the baby is not whole, if there is something seriously wrong? What if the child will be mentally retarded or severely disabled? I would challenge you to ask a parent of such a child how they feel about parenting that child. Almost all of those I have talked to speak of the joy they have received from their children. Yes, their life is not the same as they dreamed it would be; but for many, it is actually better. But even if not, let me ask you about another scenario— suppose you have a healthy, perfectly normal child who is seriously disabled as the result of an accident. What would you do? Would you have a doctor come in and kill that child because your life was now going to be different from what you had expected? I hope and expect that your answer would be "Of course not!" You would love that child and do whatever was in your power to make his or her life a good one. So what's the difference? Whether there is a problem before birth or after birth, the child deserves to be loved and nurtured because he or she, just like all the rest of us, is created in the image of God.

What about those who want to die? Why is killing yourself considered wrong? Because, as I just said, God considers each of us to be precious. We are all made in His image, and He has a purpose for each of us. He intends for us to nourish and take care of our bodies. We may fight against that purpose, or life may impose unbelievably difficult circumstances on us, but that does not mean that He wants us to give up. God is always with us, no matter what the circumstances. All we have to do is call on Him; He promises that He will never turn us away.[28] We need to reach out to those who are in distress and who are in severe pain; perhaps our laws need to be changed to offer a greater variety of medical help to those who are suffering from terminal illness. When my sister's mother-in-law was dying of cancer, her doctor acknowledged that many families have resorted to buying heroin illegally to relieve the suffering of their loved ones. Maybe we should reconsider whether drugs such as this should be available for doctors to use for the terminally ill. Our compassion should be as great as it can possibly be, but only God should decide when life is over.

There is always the danger that society can cross over the line between a person's choosing to end his or her own life and society's

---

28   John 6:37

choosing when his or her life should end. When we accept that death is an acceptable solution when our life is painful or unhappy or unproductive, then it is not too far to the next step of society's deciding that the elderly or the disabled are too much of a drain on society and that they should be "allowed" to "end their lives with dignity." What might begin as an attempt to allow the voluntary ending of one's life to relieve pain and suffering may become the expected action to take when we become too old or infirm to "contribute productively to society." I don't know what society views as productive, but as far as I am concerned, there are lots of ways to be of use to others.

My father's mother lived to be 103 years old. At the age of ninety, she started wondering why God was keeping her on earth. She was a strong Christian and she was ready to go home. I told her He was keeping her here for us, her children and grandchildren. She was an amazing inspiration to me, and through me she is an inspiration to my children. She was not earning any money, or able to do much work to help others physically, but she was a great joy and an emotional encouragement to all who knew her. Is that "contributing productively"? I think so, but I don't know how society as a whole would view it. I hope I never have to find out.

So as long as we are not involved in the taking of a life, we can breathe a sigh of relief on the sixth commandment, right? Not so fast. Remember back at the beginning of this lesson when I said that saying things in anger is a sin like murder? Well, have you ever done that? In Ephesians, Paul tells us to get rid of bitterness, rage, anger, brawling, slander, and malice;[29]   in Colossians he adds filthy language to the list.[30] James says that our anger does not bring about the righteous life that God desires us to live.[31] When we harbor bitterness and anger in our hearts, we are also guilty of the sin of murder. We are desiring evil, or even death, for the person against whom we are angry. And we are only hurting ourselves in the process. In teaching us to pray, Jesus used the phrase, "Forgive us our debts as we forgive our debtors." And when Peter asked Him how many times we are to forgive a person for the same offense, Jesus told Him not to add to the number of times

29   Ephesians 4:31
30   Colossians 3:8
31   James 1:20

he guessed we should forgive, but to multiply. We are to continue to forgive others, not so much for their benefit as for our own. To refuse to do that, to store up resentment and anger in our hearts, is to be guilty of breaking this commandment. So once again, we are all guilty.

But once again, praise the Lord, there is forgiveness if we ask for it. Whether we have broken this commandment through our words, or even committed the actual act, God can still forgive. James tells us in chapter 4 that if we draw near to God, He will draw near to us. He says that if we humble ourselves before the Lord, then He will exalt us. Even a heinous sin like murder can be forgiven by God.

All of life is meaningful to God. He created all of it, and expects us to honor and preserve it in thought and in deed. The taking of human life is necessary at times, but only when it is determined by law and cannot be avoided. We should treat every human being with the dignity and respect he or she is due as a person made in the image of God. In doing this, we can live with the peace of knowing that our hearts are right before others and before God.

LESSON TWENTY-ONE
The Seventh Commandment:
You shall not commit adultery.

Question 70:

Which is the Seventh Commandment?

Answer: The Seventh Commandment is, "You shall not commit adultery."

1. What is the meaning of the word "adultery"?

   Read Leviticus 20:10; Hebrews 13:4

Question 71:

What is required in the Seventh Commandment?

Answer: The Seventh Commandment requires the preservation of our own and our neighbor's chastity, in heart, speech, and behavior.

2. Is it possible to commit adultery even if a person never cheats on his or her spouse?

   Read Matthew 19:9; Mark 10:11-12

3. What is God's plan for marriage?

   Read Genesis 2:24; Mark 10:6-8

4. How many wives are church leaders supposed to have?

Read 1Timothy 3:12; Titus 1:6

5. What does Jesus say is an acceptable reason for divorce?

Read Matthew 19:9

6. What reason does Paul add as an acceptable reason for divorce?

Read 1 Corinthians 7:12-15

Question 72:

What is forbidden in the Seventh Commandment?

Answer: The Seventh Commandment forbids all unchaste thoughts, words, and actions.

7. Is it possible to commit adultery in our thoughts?

Read Matthew 5:27-28

8. How can you commit adultery in your speech?

Read Ephesians 5:3-4

9. What does God have to say about sex before marriage?

Read 1 Corinthians 7:1-2, 8-9; Ephesians 5:3

10. What does God have to say about sex within marriage?

Read 1 Corinthians 7:3-5

11. In what ways could you change your behavior or speech to avoid the sin of adultery?

Commentary
Lesson 21

The Seventh Commandment: You shall not commit adultery.
Catechism Questions 70, 71, and 72

I warned you way back in Lesson Five that we would find out that we have broken all of the commandments, but some of you thought you were safe on this one, didn't you? You have never cheated on your spouse, so you were sure you have never committed adultery. I hope you see after answering the questions that it's not so simple.

We would all probably like to work with a really narrow definition of the word "adultery." In fact, Dictionary.com gives as its definition of the word "voluntary sexual intercourse between a married person and someone other than his or her lawful spouse." If that were God's definition, most of us could rest easy here. But that is man's definition, not God's. Included in God's definition are all kinds of sexual immorality, including our thoughts, words, and behavior towards everyone we meet.

Let's start with behavior, since that's the most obvious. Why is God so opposed to adultery? Well, can you think of three good things that come out of an act of adultery? [I will give you two: the two people involved have a few moments of pleasure.] But there is no third good thing. Every other result is negative. Those two "good" things that I gave you aren't even really good because the people involved do not have lasting benefits; they are usually caught up in a tangle of lies and deceit and probably guilt. So those few moments of pleasure end up causing many more moments of discomfort and even pain. And what about the other people involved. The spouses of the people involved feel nothing but pain, as do the children, if there are children and they find out.

I saw a movie once where a husband cheated on his wife. In response, the wife took all of his belongings and put them in his car.

Then she poured gasoline all over the car and set it on fire. This seems to me to be a completely understandable reaction. It is not something you should do, of course, but I can appreciate why you would want to. Adultery takes something precious between a husband and wife and throws it in the garbage. The pain it causes the innocent spouse can be almost unbearable. In fact, Jesus doesn't even ask the spouse who has been sinned against to continue to live with the adulterer; He says that this is a legitimate reason to dissolve the marriage. Anyone, including a pastor, who would advise a person to tolerate this kind of behavior is not giving Biblical advice.

But suppose there are no spouses. Suppose the two people involved are single and simply want to enjoy each other physically. What could be wrong with that? The problem is that God did not wire us that way emotionally. We are made to join together with another person and to become one with that person. The marriage act is the ultimate form of that union. When we give ourselves to a person, we have invested some of our emotional energy into that relationship. Even for a brief time, we have become one with that person. How many times can a person do that without severe emotional impact?

And the consequences are not only emotional, they are also physical. According to the American Social Health Association, over 65 million people in the United States have some form of sexually transmitted disease. Each year, one in four teens contracts an STD. About half of all hepatitis B infections are transmitted sexually. ASHA estimates that one in five Americans has genital herpes, but that 90% of those people are not aware that they have the disease. The Centers for Disease Control revealed in 2008 that 26% of American girls aged 14-19 have at least one of the four most common types of STDs.

How can we avoid these horrible diseases? By remaining abstinent until marriage. We have all heard that the way around these STDs and unwanted pregnancies is "safe sex," but the failure rate for "safe sex" is anywhere from 2% to 20%. I think that even the conservative 2% failure rate is too high. That would mean that the method would fail once in every fifty sexual encounters. If you knew that once in every fifty flights a plane would crash, would you fly? Or if every fiftieth driver were certain to be involved in a serious accident, would you be afraid to drive? In the paragraph above, you can see the results of taking the chance on having even protected sex outside of marriage.

I cannot leave our discussion of sexual behavior without discussing relationships between people of the same gender. Although such behavior has always existed, it seems that it has become more open and more widespread in this generation. What did God have to say about it? In the Old Testament, these acts were considered capital crimes, punishable by death.[32] In the New Testament, Romans 1:26-27 calls these acts unnatural, shameful, indecent, and perversions. There are those who want to excuse this behavior on the basis that it is genetic, that a person is born with a predisposition to homosexuality, and that he or she cannot control the behavior. I am not sure that this is the case, but even if it were, how does society view other genetic conditions?

Let's look at one other type of condition, that of addiction. *The Handbook of Addictive Disorders* lists the following as mental health disorders: chemical dependency, workaholism, compulsive gambling, eating disorders, sex addiction, and compulsive buying. It is commonly accepted that addictive disorders have a strong genetic component; people are born with a tendency to engage in these behaviors. But how does society view this? Do we simply tolerate these behaviors and expect others to view them as acceptable lifestyle choices. Of course not. The subtitle of the above-mentioned book is *A Practical Guide to Diagnosis and Treatment.* We expect people with a predisposition to addictive behavior to get treatment for their behavior so that it does not continue. We do not condone the behavior because it has a genetic component.

We should look at alternative sexual preferences in the same way. No matter what the cause, these are unacceptable in God's eyes. And just like addictive behaviors, they need to be dealt with. If a person is an alcoholic, the best thing for her to do is to avoid alcohol and places where alcohol is served. If a person is a compulsive gambler, the best thing to do is to avoid people and places that promote gambling behavior. Likewise, if a person has a tendency toward homo-

---

32   Leviticus 20:13;

sexual behavior, it would seem to me that the best thing for that person to do would be to avoid people and places that promote that lifestyle. Remaining celibate is an honorable choice for many people; there are lots of single people in the world, some with heterosexual and some with homosexual tendencies. They can avoid much of the emotional and physical pain that comes with extra-marital sex by making that choice.

How do we know that this commandment was not just culturally based? Perhaps our society has evolved to a point where sex outside of marriage is no longer frowned upon as it once was. Maybe this rule was given to or made up by a very restrictive society. Well, if the commandment had been written two hundred years ago, I would see your point. But it was given four thousand years ago. And in many of the cultures of the time, sex outside of marriage was practiced in their religion. Both male and female temple prostitutes are mentioned in the Old Testament. So far from being a restrictive society, the world of the Old Testament was probably more open to extramarital sex even than our society is today. Yet God forbids it.

The obvious conclusion is that God knows what is best for us. He did not give us rules to punish us or to make our lives miserable, but to keep us safe and happy. God is not opposed to sex; He created it. He is very much in favor of it in the proper context of marriage. He even gave consideration to women's enjoyment of the sexual union, which is something not found in most other ancient religious texts. In other ancient religions, women were not given much regard when it came to sexual matters (or any other matters). In the brief reading I have done, it appears that the Buddha gave instructions only to men when it came to sexual matters. The Hindu religion regarded the wife as the property of the husband, to the point of burning her alive on his funeral pyre. Yet the Bible gives as much consideration to the wife as it does to the husband in the sexual relationship. How progressive!

It is pretty clear that the rules for our sexual behavior have been given for our protection, with due concern for our enjoyment of sex within the context of marriage. Let's widen the scope of our attention now to our thoughts and our words.

Jesus makes it crystal clear that even thinking about someone in a lustful way is a form of adultery. It is not the same as committing the behavior, but it is adultery nonetheless. Now think of all the ways that society encourages this type of behavior. How many advertisements have you seen that entice the viewer through sexual images? And it seems that almost every movie made today has one or more sexually charged scenes. The world does its best to draw us all in to its lifestyle. And it works. My husband and I know of several ministers who have been drawn in and who have left their wives and families for another woman. We all need to be very careful; no one is above temptation.

In addition to our thoughts, we need to watch our words. The Bible warns us about obscene talk and coarse joking for a reason. Jesus warns us that the things that come out of the mouth come from the heart, including sexually immoral speech. If we are speaking in such a way, then we are thinking in such a way. And all of it is sinful.

In our day and time, sexual purity is seen as prudery. Both men and women flaunt their bodies to attract the opposite sex. Living together outside of marriage has become the norm; many languages have words to describe unmarried couples. I am not saying that we should sit in judgment of those who behave in such a manner. As Jesus said, "Let he who is without sin cast the first stone." Violating this commandment is no worse than violating any of the other nine.

Everyone has sinned, and as we have seen in this lesson, everyone has broken the seventh commandment. As with all sins, adultery can be forgiven. In Paul's first letter to the Corinthians, he says that no one who indulges in adulterous behavior can inherit the kingdom of God; but he adds that if we are cleansed by the blood of Christ, we can be justified before God. No matter what we have done, God is ready to receive anyone who calls on Him. Those who do not know Christ do not need us to condemn their behavior; they need us to lovingly lead them to the Savior. Accept others where they are and point them to Christ, while making sure that you are living a life that is in all ways glorifying to Him. Watch your thoughts, your words, and your actions to keep yourself pure. You will be blessed if you do.

LESSON TWENTY-TWO
The Eighth Commandment:
You shall not steal.

Question 73:

Which is the Eighth Commandment?

Answer: The Eighth Commandment is, "You shall not steal."

1. How can we steal from our neighbor?

   Read Leviticus 19:13; Job 24:2

2. How can we steal from our employers?

   Read Titus 2: 9-10

3. How can we steal from the less fortunate?

   Read Deuteronomy 24:14-17; Isaiah 10:12

4. How can we steal from God?

   Read Proverbs 3:9; Malachi 3:8, 1:14

Question 74:

What is required in the Eighth Commandment?

Answer: The Eighth Commandment requires that we utilize only lawful means in obtaining and furthering the wealth and outward estate of ourselves and others.

5. How should we acquire whatever wealth we may acquire?

Read Proverbs 10:4; Psalm 112:1-3; Proverbs 3:13-16

6. What is the danger of trusting in wealth?

Read Proverbs 27:24; I Timothy 6:7; Matthew 6:19

7. What should we trust in rather than riches?

Read Philippians 4:19

8. What should be our request of God concerning wealth?

Read Proverbs 30:7-9

Question 75:

What is forbidden in the Eighth Commandment?

Answer: The Eighth Commandment forbids whatever does, or may, unjustly hinder our own, or our neighbor's, wealth or outward estate.

9. How can we correct our actions in regard to this commandment?

Read Ephesians 4:28

10. Where should our treasure be?

Read Matthew 6:20

11. In what ways have you been stealing from God or your fellow man?

Commentary
Lesson 22

The Eighth Commandment: You shall not steal.

Catechism Questions 73, 74, and 75

As I write this lesson, the economy of our country is in a shambles. I don't know if it will get worse or better. There is gloom and doom in every economic report I read or hear. What has gone wrong? Well, part of the problem is that a lot of people have broken the Tenth Commandment, but I'll get to that later. Another part of the problem is that some major players in the financial game have broken this one. People are willing to take other people's money in order to make themselves richer. And eventually it all comes crashing down. When people invest in a house of cards, it will eventually collapse.

Theft is a horrible thing, and there are so many ways to do it. The most obvious is simply to take what belongs to someone else. If you have ever had your house burglarized or your car or even your purse stolen, you know how traumatic it can be. On her first day of a visit overseas, my friend Ann had her purse stolen, including her passport. We had to spend over half of the next day at the embassy getting the passport replaced. The thief stole not only the objects in the purse, but our time as well. Objects can be replaced, but the time cannot.

Sometimes even objects can't be replaced. I have an heirloom ring that was given to me by my father-in-law. This is a very special ring to me because of the history behind it. My father-in-law, whom we called "D," had told my husband that when he wanted to get married, if D approved of his choice of a wife, he could have the ring for an engagement ring. Because they had very different value systems, my husband-to-be was not going to allow his father to have veto power over his choice of a wife, so he did not even ask for the ring. Several years later, D gave it to me anyway. Either he approved of me or realized he wasn't going to get rid of me, but either way, I felt accepted into the family. So I now have the ring. I have had it insured so that if it gets lost or stolen I can replace it. But I can't really replace it; I can buy a new ring, but it won't be the one D gave me.

I'm sure you wouldn't even think of breaking into someone's home or car and stealing things. But there are so many other ways to steal. What about at work? When we are at work, we are supposed to be doing work. How often have you made personal phone calls or sent personal emails on company time? In effect, you are being paid to make those calls or send those emails. Or have you ever "borrowed" office supplies to use at home?

In my line of work, I often have to deal with two other types of theft. In a 1998 poll by *Who's Who Among American High School Students*, 80% of the nation's best high school students admitted to cheating. According to *U. S. News and World Report*, 75% of college students admit to cheating, and 85% of college students think cheating is necessary to get ahead. Cheating on tests is nothing but theft of the work of other students. In other words, I will not try to prepare for the exam; I will let you work and prepare, and then I will steal your answers.

Another rampant type of theft is plagiarism, copying someone else's work and passing it off as your own. There are actually websites that encourage this. [There are also websites that can help instructors catch it!] In my department we teach public speaking and we require the students to turn in outlines of their speeches. Another professor told me about a student in her class who turned in a perfect outline. It was indeed perfect, because it was the exact outline that this professor had handed out as a sample outline in a previous semester! Sometimes plagiarism is pretty easy to catch! Parents and teachers must begin early to teach our children that stealing the work of others is exactly that—stealing.

Many otherwise law-abiding citizens steal from the government every year by cheating on their income tax. According to the Internal Revenue Service, the "tax gap" for tax year 2001, tax that should have been paid but was not, totaled $345 billion. Of that amount the IRS estimates that it will eventually recover only $55 billion. I realize that we do not all approve of the ways that our money is used by the government. But what did Jesus say about taxes? When asked specifically whether we should pay taxes, He told us to give to Caesar what is Caesar's.[33] In other words, yes. Pay your taxes. I'm absolutely certain that Christ did not approve of everything that was done by the Roman government or by the Jewish leaders at the time, but still He paid the taxes He owed. We should do no less. To fail to pay taxes is to steal from those God has put in authority over us.

We can also steal from those who are less fortunate by failing to help them in their need, and by depriving them of their rights. Before we judge others, let's be certain of all of our facts; or better yet, let's not judge others at all. We are often quick to stereotype those on government assistance, but often we don't have the full story, or even half of the story. It actually should be the job of the church to help these people, but we have fallen down on the job, and the government has stepped in to do what we should have been doing. So let's be cautious about criticizing the government for doing what ought to be our job.

And finally, we can steal from God Himself. Whatever you believe the tithe should be, and many people believe that it should be ten percent of your entire salary, you should be giving that to the Lord in some form. Not to do that is to say two things to God: 1) I am not grateful for what You have given me and done for me, and I don't feel that I owe You anything, and 2) I don't trust You to provide for my needs and I feel that I have to do it myself. If you want to provide for yourself, God will let you, but He has more resources at His disposal than you do, so you are missing out on the riches that are available to Him.

So is wealth wrong? Not intrinsically, no. God does provide wealth to some people. Money is not the root of all evil, the love of money is. My husband and I have a friend who is very wealthy but who gives thousands of dollars a year to the work of various missionaries and missions agencies. He has been blessed, and he uses his blessings to bless others. To meet him, you would not know he was wealthy. He is not pretentious in the least. He is a really good

---

33   Matthew 20:21

business man and has a knack for investments, and God has blessed his talent. But he in turn uses his talent for God.

Which do you love more, God or money? Remember the story of the rich young ruler. When he asked Jesus what he needed to do to inherit eternal life, Jesus told him that the one thing he needed to do was to sell all of his possessions and give the proceeds to the poor. He couldn't do it. Jesus had found his weakness, the one thing he loved more than God.

What would you do with wealth if you had it? Buy more stuff for yourself? Give more to others? The prayer of Proverbs is a good one for all of us because the writer is asking for just enough—not so much that he will forget that it all comes from God and not so little that he will be tempted to steal to provide for his family. If we have just enough, then we can be content.

So what if you have realized that you have been stealing? Then stop. Do diligent work. Be honest in all your dealings. Give to those in need. Give to God. In Malachi 3:10, God actually invites us to test Him in the act of giving to see if He will bless us when we give to Him. It may be that God will give you wealth. If He gives it to you and allows you to enjoy it, that is a blessing from Him. Use it wisely. It may be that He will give you just enough. If you have enough, can you be content?

LESSON TWENTY-THREE
The Ninth Commandment:
You shall not bear false witness

Question 76:

Which is the Ninth Commandment?

Answer: The Ninth Commandment is, "You shall not bear false witness against your neighbor."

1. How does God deal with those who testify falsely against others?

Read Proverbs 19: 5, 9

2. Other than giving false testimony, what other types of dishonesty in legal proceedings are we warned against?

Read Exodus 23:1, 7

Question 77:

What is required in the Ninth Commandment?

Answer: The Ninth Commandment requires the maintaining and promoting of truth between man and man, and of our own and our neighbor's good name, especially in testifying as witnesses.

3. How are we to speak to others?

Read Ephesians 4:25; 1 Thessalonians 5:11, 14

Question 78:

What is forbidden in the Ninth Commandment?

Answer: The Ninth Commandment forbids whatever is prejudicial to truth, or injurious to our own or our neighbor's good name.

4. How does God feel about those who tell lies?

Read Psalm 5:6; Proverbs 6:16-19

5. Who is the father of lies?

Read John 8:44

6. In what ways can we lie?

Read Psalm 12:2; Ezekiel 13:8; Micah 6:11

7. What happens if a ruler is influenced by lies?

Read Proverbs 29:12; Psalm 62:4

8. Why are we misled by lies?

Read Jeremiah 5:30-31; Hosea 7:3

9. What does the Bible have to say about those who teach false doctrine?

   Read Psalm 78:35-37; Matthew 7:15; 1 Timothy 6:3-4

10. How did Rahab lie to the authorities over her?

   Read Joshua 2:1-16

11. What was God's response to this lie?

   Read Matthew 1:5; Hebrews 11:31; James 2:25

12. If God detests liars, why do you think He considered Rahab to be righteous because of her lie?

Commentary
Lesson 23

The Ninth Commandment: You shall not bear false witness

Catechism Questions 76, 77, and 78

Do you want to be lied to? Think about your answer. Our first response is, "Of course not," but perhaps there are times when we wouldn't mind a little white lie. What is the correct answer to the question, "Does this make me look fat?" Every husband knows, or ought to know, that the correct answer is always "No." Whether it's the truth or not, that's the answer. When a woman asks that question, she is not asking for the truth; she is asking for reassurance that she is attractive.

So how are we to interpret the Ninth Commandment? There are those who argue that this commandment means that we are to speak the truth in all circumstances and let God handle the consequences. Then there are those who say that although the truth is to be preferred, it is our reason for withholding the truth that is at stake, and that there may be good reasons, even godly reasons, for lying. I will tell you right now that my opinion lies with the second group.

First of all, the commandment is specifically addressed to lying in court, as a witness in a legal proceeding. We are always to tell the truth in that situation. Interestingly, we are not told here not to bear false witness in favor of our neighbor, but I would hesitate to do that for practical reasons. For example, if your neighbor is accused of a crime, and you testify that he was at home when you know he was not, you may be helping a criminal to go free. You may be a part of perpetrating that crime on the next victim.

But the commandment specifically warns us against testifying falsely against our neighbor. God tells us that He will not let those actions go unpunished. Not only are we not to testify falsely against someone, we are not to have anything to do with false charges or putting an innocent person to death. I am not opposed to the death penalty, but if I were to serve on a jury in a capital case, I would have to know beyond a shadow of a doubt that the accused person was guilty before I could sentence him or her to die.

So is that it? As long as we don't lie in court, we haven't broken this commandment? Not so fast. Even though the commandment addresses honesty in the courtroom, God tells us how He feels about honesty in our daily lives. God says that He hates liars; they are detestable to Him. We are to put off falsehood and speak the truth to our neighbor. So we are back to the question that began this lesson. Are we supposed to tell the truth all the time, every time, no matter the consequences? I still don't think so.

Look at the example of Rahab. Rahab was a prostitute—not a very godly occupation—in the city of Jericho. When the two Israelite spies entered the city, she hid them and told their pursuers that yes, the spies had been there, but that they had gone away at dusk. After the gates of the city had been closed, she helped the spies escape and told them how to avoid being captured. There is no way around the fact that Rahab told an outright lie to the soldiers who were pursuing the spies. So what was God's response to this? He blessed her and her family: first, by not killing them when Jericho was destroyed by the Israelites; second, by considering her actions to be righteous; and third, by giving her a place in the ancestry of Jesus Christ and honoring her by listing her name in His genealogy.

Clearly, this was a lie; and clearly, God was not opposed to it. What is the difference? What makes one lie sinful and another lie righteous? I think it has to do with the attitude of the heart. In my field of communication, we study lying. It is after all a form of communication. There are basically seven reasons for lying: to save face, to avoid tension or conflict, to guide social interaction, to expand or reduce relationships, to gain power, to benefit the listener, or to benefit a third party. Let's examine each one of these to see how God might view them.

First, lying to save face, or to save ourselves from embarrassment. "The check is in the mail." Who is benefiting from this lie?

Only the person who is lying. We all want to look good in the eyes of others, so when we are afraid we might look bad, we lie to cover up our shortcomings. Paul warns us in his letter to the Galatians[34] and his first letter to the Thessalonians that we should be trying to please God rather than men. If this is our motive for lying, I think it's safe to say that God would not approve.

Second, lying to avoid tension or conflict. "I'm not upset; I just need to readjust to the change in plans." Again, what is our motive? Why do we not want to admit our true feelings? Couldn't we say, "Sure, I'm a little upset, but I'll readjust and it will be okay"? God does tell us that as much as it is within our power that we should live at peace with others. But I think most of the time we can do that and still tell the truth. When we lie for this reason, we are still more concerned about our image with other people than our obedience to God.

Third, lying to guide social interaction. "I have been meaning to call you." Once again, aren't we concerned about how we appear to others? What could we say instead? How about, "How have you been? It's been such a long time since I've seen you." Why lie?

Fourth, lying to expand or reduce relationships. "You're going downtown? Me too. Can I give you a ride?" or "I'd love to see you, but my schedule is really packed this week." This one gets a little tricky. We often lie at the beginning of a relationship because we aren't sure how the other person feels about us. It's hard to say, "I'm really kind of interested in you and I am willing to go completely out of my way in order to spend time with you. Hop in." I don't think this is a type of lie that we need to be concerned about, especially if the aim is to reduce discomfort for the other person involved. In the second example, though, we need to be careful about giving false impressions. Sometimes the truth, although it may hurt, is the best in the long run.

Fifth, lying to gain power. "If elected, I will _____." Enough said. This is always wrong. Always.

Sixth, lying to benefit the listener. This is the "Does this make

_____
34   Galatians 1:10; 1 Thessalonians 2:4

me look fat?" type of lie. In addition to telling us to speak truthfully, God also tells us to encourage one another, especially those who are weak or timid. Sometimes the truth can hurt or discourage. The best advice here is probably what your mother told you. If you can't say something nice, don't say anything at all. But if you are asked, there is an alternative rather than lying; equivocation. "How do you like my new hairstyle?" "It's really you." Or "It's so unique and different." Equivocal statements can be understood in more than one way. They don't really say anything. And they are perfect for this type of situation. But if equivocation won't work, and the truth will be hurtful and not helpful, then I would opt for encouragement instead.

Seventh, lying to benefit a third party. This is Rahab's type of lie. When she lied, she had nothing to gain. She did gain later, but at the time, she didn't know what would happen. She could have been caught and killed. She was lying to protect the innocent. Corrie ten Boom and her family did the same thing for the Jews during the Holocaust. If you have nothing to gain, and your lie is to protect the innocent from harm, then I think God will honor it.

What about false prophets and teachers? Where do they fall in this scheme of things? Probably in category five, lying to gain power. False teachers can worm their way into any church and any congregation. We are easy prey for them, because we like what they tell us, since they tell us what we want to hear. But as Christ warned us, they appear in sheep's clothing, but inwardly they are ferocious wolves. They do not have our best interests at heart. They are concerned only for themselves. Worst of all, they have no concern for the truth of God. They are following their real father, the devil, who is the father of lies.

So what conclusions can we come to? Any lie told for our own benefit is wrong. We are to seek the approval of God rather than the approval of men. Any lie told in order to harm others is wrong. We are to treat others as we would want to be treated, and we are to be just and fair in our dealings with others. However, if we are faced with the situation of telling the truth and endangering innocent life, or lying and protecting that life, then I think God will honor our decision to withhold the truth. And in those cases where the truth will hurt rather than help, we must use our best judgment as to what we should say or do.

The question to ask ourselves is this: In my everyday life, am I generally truthful? Can my word be trusted? God is opposed to those who have a lifestyle of lying. We must examine our hearts to make sure our motives are pure before God, in our speech, and in all of our actions.

LESSON TWENTY-FOUR
The Tenth Commandment:
You shall not covet.

Question 79:

Which is the Tenth Commandment?

Answer: The Tenth Commandment is, "You shall not covet your neighbor's house; you shall not covet your neighbor's wife, or his male servant, or his female servant, or his ox, or his donkey, or anything that is your neighbor's."

1. What does "covet" mean?

   Read Deuteronomy 7:25; Micah 2:2 (You may also want to consult a good dictionary.)

Question 80:

What is required in the Tenth Commandment?

Answer: The Tenth Commandment requires full contentment with our own condition, with a right and charitable frame of spirit toward our neighbor and all that is his.

2. What does it mean to have full contentment with out condition?

   Read Philippians 4:11-12; 1 Timothy 6:8

3. How can we accomplish that kind of contentment?

   Read Hebrews 13:5

Question 81:

What is forbidden in the Tenth Commandment?

Answer: The Tenth Commandment forbids all discontentment with our own estate, envying or grieving at the good of our neighbor, and all unreasonable motions and affections toward anything that is his.

4. How does the Bible describe people who envy and covet what others have?

Read Micah 2:1-2

5. How are our needs provided for?

Read Matthew 6:8, 31-33

6. Does God only give us the basic necessities of life?

Read Luke 11:13; Ephesians 3:20

7. What is the end result of covetousness and envy?

Read James 4:2-3; Proverbs 14:30; Titus 3:3

8. What is the end result of working hard so we can have what our neighbors have?

Read Ecclesiastes 4:4

9. What should our attitude be towards our neighbors?

Read Philippians 2:3

10. What should we do if we need something that we cannot afford?

Read Luke 11:9; 1 John 5:13-15

11. What things are you coveting that you need to let go?

Commentary
Lesson 24

The Tenth Commandment: You shall not covet.
Catechism Questions 79, 80, and 81

I like jewelry. I really, really like jewelry. I buy sterling silver jewelry because I like the color silver more than the color gold, and also because it is cheaper than gold and I can buy more of it. I have bought several pieces of jewelry from a certain shopping channel on television. My co-worker Alison also really likes jewelry, and she buys from that same shopping channel. At lunch one day, I was talking with Alison about that channel and I mentioned that I had seen a pair of earrings that I really liked, but I told her I had not bought them because I decided I didn't need them. She stopped eating, looked me straight in the eye, and said, "Paula. We don't <u>need</u> any of the jewelry we already have, much less any more jewelry."

No kidding. I could live my entire life without one piece of jewelry. It is certainly not a necessity. So when does my love of jewelry turn into covetousness? What exactly is covetousness? Dictionary.com gives as its first definition of the word covet: to desire wrongfully, inordinately, or without due regard for the rights of others. This would involve wanting what someone else has; not another one like it, but the exact thing they have. As the second definition, we are given: to wish for, esp. eagerly. This can be wrong, but it can be a good thing, depending on what we are coveting. (We'll get to that later.) The third definition is: to have an inordinate or wrongful desire. This desire could be for anything, whether it belongs to your neighbor or not.

Let's take each of these definitions and see how they might affect us. First, to desire wrongfully without regard for the rights of others, to want what others have. What does this lead to? At the very least, it leads to envy; why do they get to have that and I don't? At the very worst, it leads to murder. Look at the example of David and

Bathsheba. What was the first sin David committed? It was actually lust. He saw Bathsheba and lusted after her. This led really quickly to coveting; he wanted her. So he took her, which was adultery. When the affair led to a baby, he called for her husband to come home from war, assuming that he would sleep with his wife and then think the baby was his. The plan was to get out of the mess by lying. But her husband would not indulge in those pleasures when the other soldiers were still at war. In the end, to save his reputation, David had Bathsheba's husband killed by military maneuvering. He resorted to murder. How many of the commandments did he break in this one event?

Does this kind of thing happen today? Of course it does. We hear about people murdering others for insurance money, for property, or even for a pair of expensive tennis shoes. But you are probably thinking, I might want something someone has, but I certainly wouldn't murder them for it. So let's look at definition two: to wish for eagerly.

Wishing for something is not necessarily wrong. In 1 Corinthians 12, in the King James version of the Bible, we are told to covet the greater spiritual gifts. More modern translations use the word desire, rather than covet, but it really means the same thing. If we are eagerly desiring the glory of God, or the prayers of others when we are in a difficult situation, or the wisdom to know how God is leading us, these things are not wrong. We are told to desire and seek these things. But if we are wishing for something to satisfy our own longings, we can be heading down the road to definition three: to have an inordinate or wrongful desire.

Why is it wrong to want something that much? Because it can take God's place in our lives. In Colossians 3:5, Paul tells us that greed, or covetousness, is the same thing as idolatry. We give first priority in our lives to the thing we are coveting; but first priority always belongs to God. By breaking the Tenth Commandment, we have come full circle back to breaking the First one.

So how are we to live? Very simply, we are to be content with what God has given us. When children are little, and even when they are a little older, they ask for things that their parents know they should not have. If a four-year-old wants to play with a butcher knife, will you let him? If a ten-year-old wants to drive to the grocery store, does she get the keys to the car? Of course not. We know that children at those ages are not ready for those responsibilities. In the same way, God knows what gifts and what responsibilities we are ready to handle. He gives us what we need, and He gives us what we can handle. He will not give us gifts that we will only use to further our sins. For example, if we have a tendency to be greedy and selfish, He will probably not give us more money just so we can spend it on ourselves.

Now, if you don't have a lot of money, I am not accusing you of being greedy and selfish. There are other reasons God may not give us certain things. My husband and I have had the "pleasure" of being in need and we know how hard that is. But we learned through those times how faithful God is. We have also had the pleasure of having more than enough to meet our needs, but we know that we cannot depend on our jobs or our bank accounts in the long run. We must always remember that all of our resources come from God alone.

One of the biggest problems in our society today is consumer debt. Where does that debt come from? From all of us wanting more than we can afford. Eventually that debt comes back to bite us. Proverbs 22:7 tells us that the rich rule over the poor, that the borrower is a servant of the lender. These two things are connected. The rich rule over the poor because the poor owe them money. The poor have borrowed from the rich and must now pay them back with interest. If you are in a position of debt, there are some great programs and books that can help you get out of debt. It will take work, but it will be worth it.

But what if our friends and neighbors have more than we have? How should we handle that? We should be humble and realize that God has given those things to them (or that they have accumulated a lot of debt and have more problems than we are even aware of). We should not be envious of their possessions or their lifestyle. We should focus on the things God has given us and not the things He hasn't. If you have a lot of trouble with this, look at some pictures of people in refugee camps, then make a list of everything you have that they don't. You will need more than one sheet of paper.

Finally, those who have been blessed and have plenty need to be careful of their attitude towards possessions. If you have wealth, do you flaunt your possessions? Do you talk about what you have bought, where you have been, or what you have inherited? Don't take pride in your possessions. They can go in an instant. Instead, make sure that your treasure is in heaven because that can never be destroyed. Be considerate of those who don't have what you have.

My church has a women's retreat every year and the cost to attend is minimal. But even that cost is too much for some of the women, so the retreat organizers wisely instituted a scholarship fund. Those who have resources can contribute to the fund, and those who have less can discreetly request a scholarship. No one but the scholarship committee knows who paid and who is on scholarship. In my opinion, there should never be a church function that is financially out of reach for anyone who wants to attend. And we must remember that what is a reasonable cost to some may be an exorbitant amount to others. My husband and I once had only ten dollars to buy food for two weeks. There may be people in your church in a similar situation.

Covetousness is a sin that can lead to many other sins. It is a sneaky thing that can creep up on us until it consumes our lives. We must constantly be on guard to make sure that nothing, absolutely nothing, takes the place in our lives that God should have. We must be content and at peace with the blessings God has given us, and we must not envy the things He gives our neighbors.

SECTION THREE

Communion with Our God

LESSON TWENTY-FIVE
A Sin is Still a Sin

Question 82:

Is any man able to keep perfectly the commandments of God?

Answer: No mere man, since the Fall, is able, in this life, to keep perfectly the commandments of God, but does break them daily, in thought, word, and deed.

1. What does God require us to do?

   Read 1 Kings 8:61; I John 2:3

2. Does anyone do this?

   Read Ecclesiastes 7:20; Romans 3:12

3. If we fail to obey God's commands, what does this mean for us?

   Read Romans 3:10; Psalm 143:2

4. What are we doing to ourselves and to God if we claim that we have not sinned?

   Read 1 John 1:8, 10

Question 83:

Are all transgressions of the law equally wicked?

Answer: Some sins in themselves, and by reason of aggravating circumstances, are more wicked in the sight of God than others.

5. Under Old Testament law, what was the penalty for murder or kidnapping?

   Read Exodus 21:12-16

6. Under Old Testament law, what was the penalty for theft?

   Read Exodus 22:1-3

Question 84:

What does every sin deserve?

Answer: Every sin deserves God's wrath and curse, both in this life and that which is to come.

7. What was the first sin?

   Read Genesis 3:6

8. How was Eve tempted to eat the fruit?

   Read Genesis 3:5

9. What are the reasons for the wrath of God?

Read Micah 7:9; Romans 2:8; Ephesians 2:3

10. What are the reasons for the curse of God?

Read Deuteronomy 11:26-28; Malachi 2:2; Galatians 3:10

11. Why can we not be trusted to know what is right and wrong?

Read Proverbs 12:15, 14:12, 21:2

Commentary
Lesson 25

A Sin is Still a Sin.

Catechism Questions 82, 83, and 84

Can you think of anything you have ever done wrong? I hope you think that is a ridiculous question. My list would take pages and pages. How about yours? Of course, we all do things we shouldn't or don't do things we should. That's just human nature, right? Well, sort of. It's not *human* nature, it's our human *sin* nature. The first humans didn't have that nature. They were able to live totally without sin, at least for a while. But then they chose to do the one thing they were not supposed to do, and from that point on we have all inherited that sinfulness.

The problem is that God's law requires that we keep it perfectly, that we never, ever do anything we are not supposed to do or fail to do anything we are supposed to do. Let's review the Ten Commandments, the summary of the Law of God. I am including my own short explanation of each commandment for clarification.

1. You shall have no other gods before me. [You shall not give anything other than God first priority in your life.]

2. You shall not make for yourselves a carved image. You shall not bow down to them or serve them. [You shall not use a representation of God as an aid to worship or worship anything man-made.]

3. You shall not take the name of the Lord your God in vain. [You shall always speak of God and all His attributes and all His works in an honorable way.]

4. Remember the Sabbath day to keep it holy. [Do all your work in six days, and rest and honor the Lord on the seventh day.]

5. Honor your father and your mother. [Respect your parents,

speak well of them, and provide for them in their need.]

6. You shall not murder. [Do not take the life of an innocent person or wish ill on anyone.]

7. You shall not commit adultery. [Do not have sex outside of marriage or use impure language or have impure thoughts.]

8. You shall not steal. [Do not take anything that does not belong to you, including ideas, and give to the Lord what He is due.]

9. You shall not bear false witness against your neighbor. [Do not lie to one another, especially to cause trouble for an innocent person or to make yourself look better.]

10. You shall not covet. [Do not want anything that someone else has.]

In reviewing that list, can you find one or two of those commandments that you have broken? If you have broken even one of them, one time, you have not kept God's law perfectly. And we know that we have all broken more than one, many more times than once. So we are faced with the wrath of God, which we will get to in a bit.

You have probably heard that all sins are equal in the sight of God, and in one sense that is true. But in another sense it is not. Even when He was giving the specific laws for the punishment of criminals, God did not order the same punishment for every crime. Taking a life is not the same as stealing an object, and God did not treat those crimes the same. We instinctively know that. Even criminals know that. In prison, those who have committed crimes against children are subject to much more cruel treatment from other prisoners than those who have broken other laws.

So why are we told that all sins are the same? Because in another sense, they are the same. The first sin ever recorded doesn't really seem so bad; Adam and Eve ate something they weren't supposed to eat. They didn't kill anyone; they didn't even take something that didn't belong to them. They just ate fruit that they were told not to eat. As a result of that sin, they were thrown out of the Garden of Eden and made to work hard for the rest of their lives. At first glance, it doesn't seem like the punishment fit the crime.

But what really was the crime? It was much more than eating the fruit. It was wanting to be like God. It was actually wanting to be their own god, to make their own rules. When they ate that fruit, they were saying to God, "We don't care what your rules are; we will do what we want to do. We will be our own gods and we will make our own rules." And the punishment fits that crime very well.

Whenever we sin, that is exactly what we are saying to God. We are saying that we are going to be our own god and make our own rules. We are going to feel free to disobey God's rules and obey our own. Have you ever heard a child say to another child, "You're not the boss of me"? Well, that is exactly what we are saying to God every time we fail to do what we know is right.

In that sense, every sin is the same. Every sin is rebellion against God, or wanting to be our own god. Every sin involves our saying to God, "I will take charge of my life now and follow my own rules. I am not interested in following your rules because you are not the boss of me. I am my own god." We create rules which please us, following them when it suits us and forgiving ourselves when we don't. We act in every way as gods. But there are big problems with this scenario.

The first problem is that we can't be trusted to know what is best because we are very foolish people. We make decisions on little knowledge, on what seems good at the moment. But God has all knowledge. He knows all of the potential consequences for all of our actions, and He knows how our actions can affect others.

Have you ever been in the car with someone who is obviously lost but absolutely will not stop to ask for directions? These people will tell you that they know what they're doing, that they will get there pretty soon, that the road signs are all messed up, anything but admit that they are hopelessly lost. Meanwhile, everyone else in the car has to suffer along until they give up or miraculously stumble on the right road. That's a pretty good picture of how we run our own lives. We think we know what we're doing, but we can get everything all turned around and get ourselves hopelessly lost. And everyone else in our lives has to suffer along with us until we get things right. The way that seems right to us can be the road that ends in death. God not only knows the way, He is the way. If we will follow His direction, we will always be on the right road.

The second problem is that we are not gods. We are created beings acting in rebellion against the One True God. And in our rebellion, we deserve God's wrath and curse. We break the first commandment by setting ourselves up as our own gods, and then proceed to keep or discard each of the other nine commandments as we see fit. But God does not give us that privilege. He demands obedience. By breaking His law, we actually put ourselves under His wrath and curse.

Did you ever watch *The Cosby Show*? Bill Cosby played a father of five children, and one of his most famous lines from that program was, "I'm your father. I brought you into this world, and I can take you out." All parents can identify with that line. We wouldn't really take out our children, but we understand the feeling. And fathers don't really bring their children into the world, either. They contribute half of the genetic material, but all human beings are created by God. So it is God who brings us into the world, and it is God who takes us out. If we would be afraid to make our earthly fathers angry, how much more should we fear the God of the Universe?

God created us and sustains us and He deserves to be worshipped and obeyed. We deserve His displeasure, His wrath even, when we don't. But we don't have to continue in His wrath. He loved us enough to provide a way out, if we will only take it.

LESSON TWENTY-SIX
A Perfect Standard and a Perfect Sacrifice

Question 85:

What does God require of us, that we may escape his wrath and curse, due to us for sin?

Answer: To escape the wrath and curse of God, due to us for sin, God requires of us faith in Jesus Christ, repentance to life, with the diligent use of all the outward means by which Christ communicates to us the benefits of redemption.

Question 86:

What is faith in Jesus Christ?

Answer: Faith in Jesus Christ is a saving grace, by which we receive and rest on Him alone for salvation, as He is offered to us in the Gospel.

1. If we receive salvation through Christ, what are we saved from?

   Read 1 Thessalonians 5:9

2. Why do we deserve God's wrath?

   Read Ecclesiastes 7:20; Romans 3:12

3. What does God require as payment for our sins?

   Read Leviticus 5:13-15;5:5-7

4. Why was the death of Christ necessary to satisfy the requirement of a sacrifice for sin?

Read Hebrews 10:4-10

5. What happens to those who do not accept Christ's death as a sacrifice for their sins?

Read Revelation 21:8

6. What is the simplest expression of our faith in Christ?

Read Romans 10:9

7. What else happens when we first believe in Christ?

Read Mark 1:15

8. What is repentance?

Read I Kings 8:47

9. Are we able to turn to Christ on our own, without help?

Read John 6:65

10. How are we made able to come to Christ?

Read 1 Corinthians 12:3

11. How are we to live if we believe in Christ?

Read James 1:22; Philippians 2:5-8

Commentary
Lesson 26

A Perfect Standard and a Perfect Sacrifice
Catechism Questions 85 and 86

You may be getting tired of reading and hearing that you deserve God's wrath, but there is really no other way to say it—we are all miserable failures at living up to God's demands. We mess up at every turn. Even the good things that we manage to do, we usually do for selfish motives. If we are truly honest with ourselves, we will be very disappointed with the way we live.

God made it crystal clear from the beginning of time that He expected perfection from His creation. From our vantage point, it looks like He made it pretty easy for Adam and Eve—just one rule to obey—but they blew it. I'm not going to go through the whole argument here [I've laid it all out in Lesson 6], but suffice it to say, we would have done the same thing. We would all have yielded to the temptation.

So none of us is perfect. Isn't God expecting too much? He has given us a standard that we are incapable of living up to. Isn't that unfair? It depends on how you look at it. I am a teacher. I am actually a pretty demanding teacher. I have fairly strict standards. However, I am also very willing to help any student meet those standards. For example, in my public speaking classes, I require an outline for every speech, and those outlines must adhere to rigid guidelines. However, if a student comes to my office before an outline is due, I will see to it that his or her outline meets every one of the guidelines perfectly. His or her score on the outline will be 100%. If a student writes an outline on his/her own that meets the guidelines, he or she will also score 100%. But if a student decides not to take advantage of my help and the outline does not meet the guidelines, I do not feel guilty for giving that outline the score it deserves. Am I being unfair? Am I overly demanding? Some of those students who get low scores think so. But why were their scores low? First, they did not meet the requirements. But second, they did not ask for help.

Yes, God has impossibly high standards. But He has also promised to give us help in meeting those standards. What did He say about asking for help?

"No temptation has seized you except what is common to man. And God is unpredictable; sometimes, he will not let you be tempted beyond what you can bear. And sometimes, when you are tempted, he will provide a way out." Is that what you believe? Is that what the verse says? Look at 1 Corinthians 10:13. Which words did I change? God is not unpredictable—He is <u>faithful</u>. And there is no "sometimes" about it. He will not let you be tempted beyond what you can bear; He will provide a way out. We may say we believe this verse, but we act like we believe my heretical interpretation. Or maybe we believe it, but we don't want a way out. We actually enjoy the temptation and the accompanying sin very much, thank you, and really don't want to think about giving it up. We would much prefer to rationalize that we are only human and are not perfect, anyway.

So we are sinners, and we deserve God's wrath. What is the ultimate result of that wrath for us? It couldn't be that bad, could it? The ultimate result is Hell itself. In graduate school, it was somehow obvious that I was a Christian, or at least that I was really moral. Even though I had not gone out of my way to publicly announce my faith, my fellow grad students were careful not to use profanity around me and to treat me with the utmost respect. Until the subject of Hell came up. One of them finally asked me one day whether I really believed in a literal Heaven, or more importantly, in a literal Hell. I told him that yes, since Jesus taught that there is a Hell, I had no choice but to believe in it. From that moment on, he decided that I was a "religious nut." He still treated me differently, but for different reasons.

What does Jesus say about Hell? He told his disciples that it is an eternal fire, prepared for the devil and his angels, and that there will be darkness and weeping and gnashing of teeth. He also said that those who have not done His will are to be sent there.

This is not a pretty picture, but it is a picture painted by Christ Himself. He wanted us to know that it is a real place, and He wanted us to not want to go there.

So what is God's standard? How do we avoid Hell? By obeying God perfectly. Some of you may be thinking now, "Well, thank you very much. That is sooo helpful. I am quite sure I can do that. No problem. You might as well have told me to fly to the moon once a month to gather groceries." And I really might as well. We all know we are not going to be able to do that. God would help us do it if we asked, but we know we're not always going to ask. And even if we do ask, we're not always going to follow the instructions we are given.

But fortunately, God knows that too. And for some amazing reason that I absolutely do not understand, God wants us in His Heaven in spite of the way we behave. His love is so great that He provided a way for us to get there when there was no way to do it ourselves. At first, He created a system of sacrificing animals to pay for the sins of the people. These animals had to be perfect specimens of whatever type of animal they were. They had to be sacrificed by a priest, and some of their blood had to be sprinkled on the altar. Once a year, a special day was set aside to pay for the sins of all the people for the whole year—the Day of Atonement. But these sacrifices had to be made over and over. No animal could pay for the sins of a human being forever.

What was required was the sacrifice of a perfect human. It is interesting to me to study different religions. I have found in doing this that every religion has gotten something right; there is an element of truth in every religion. There is much more that is wrong, but there is truth there. Satan has taken the truth and twisted it, but you can find truth in every system of worship. Think about those ancient pagan religions that practiced human sacrifice. How abhorrent! Yet, wasn't this really on the right track? Didn't God require a human sacrifice to pay for our sin? They just weren't relying on the right human.

You see, the only human sacrifice that would do was one that was perfect. Does that mean he or she had to be perfect looking? Not at all. In fact, the Bible tells us that Jesus was not more handsome or majestic than other men [Isaiah 53:2]. God does not judge by outward appearance; He judges the heart. In other words, the perfect human sacrifice had to be perfect in heart, or completely sinless. No such person has ever existed. Every created human being since the first man and woman has sinned. So God Himself came to earth. God the Son took on a human body and was born of a woman. She was a virgin so He would have both a human nature and a divine nature. With His human nature, He could experience all of the temptations that every other person on earth experiences; but with His divine nature, He could resist them. Since He could resist every temptation, He could be the perfect human sacrifice; and He was willing to do that so that our sins could be paid for.

But God even goes further than that. In order for Christ's death to pay for our sins, we have to accept that payment. Suppose one day, your friend receives an inheritance check for several million dollars. She is an instant multi-millionaire, but only if she will take the check to the bank and deposit the money in her account. Now suppose that when you tell her this, she doesn't believe you. She argues that all she has to do is have the check. For them to require her to bring in the check is too demanding. She does not have time to make a special trip downtown just to confirm what she already knows—she has a multi-million dollar check. So she never takes the check to the bank. As a result, although she can tell everyone she has inherited a great deal of money, she will have nothing to show for it but a bunch of numbers on a piece of paper.

Without God's help, we would treat Christ's death just like this. God tells us that we must accept Christ's death as a sacrifice for our own personal sins; the sacrifice is there, and it is perfectly sufficient to pay for our sins. But we must each accept it personally, or it doesn't count. We can complain that God is being too demanding, or we can ignore Him completely, but our excuses will not matter to God. And the thing is, not one single one of us would accept this sacrifice on our own unless God changed our heart and made us want to do it. That is what Jesus meant when He talked about being "born again." When we are born the first time, we come into this world. When we are born the second time, we come into God's world. We become able to see things from God's perspective. We suddenly want to please God. And the first step in this process is that we want to accept Christ's sacrifice as payment for our sins. So Christ pays for our sins and then sends His

Spirit to cause us to want that payment.

We take this for granted, but think for a minute about what this means. The only way for you to escape the fires of Hell was for a perfect human being to be sacrificed to pay for your sins. There are no perfect human beings. So there was no one to sacrifice. But God wanted you in Heaven. In spite of everything you have done to ignore Him, displease Him, frustrate Him, anger Him, etc., He wanted you there. In fact, He wanted you there badly enough to become a man Himself and suffer a cruel, cruel death to make it possible. Then His Spirit works in you to help you to understand just what He has done for you. What kind of love is that?! What kind of response does that kind of love deserve?

LESSON TWENTY-SEVEN
Repentance and Grace

Question 87:

What is repentance to life?

Answer: Repentance to life is a saving grace, by which a sinner, out of a true sense of his sin, and understanding of the mercy of God in Christ, does, with grief and hatred of his sin, turn from it to God, with full intention of, and endeavor after, new obedience.

1. What is the life that true repentance leads us to?

   Read 1 John 5:13; John 10:10

2. The dictionary defines grace as "unmerited favor and love" or "favor rendered by one who need not do so."[1] How are these passages examples of these definitions of grace?

   Read Ephesians 2:1-10; 2 Timothy 1:9

3. What makes a person a sinner?

   Read Isaiah 42:24; Romans 3:23

4. How do we gain a true sense of our own sin?

   Read Romans 3:20; John 16:7-8

5. How do we gain an understanding of the mercy of God in Christ?

Read Romans 5:6-8;

6. How are we able to turn from our sins to God?

Read Romans 8:5-9

7. Can we overcome our sins in our own strength?

Read Galatians 3:3, 10; Romans 8:3, 5

8. What is the new obedience that we should endeavor after?

Read 1 John 2:3; Luke 11:28

9. If we are obedient, does this mean that we will never sin?

Read 1 John 1:8, 10

10. What should we do when we sin?

Read 1 John 1:9

Commentary
Lesson 27
Repentance and Grace
Catechism Question 87

You have probably seen signs along the road, or perhaps even someone holding a sign, which says, "Repent!" The problem is that those signs rarely tell us what we are to repent from or how exactly we are to accomplish that repentance. But since Jesus Himself told us to repent, this is not a concept that we can dismiss out of hand. What exactly is repentance, and how can we achieve it?

While still a very young man, Benjamin Franklin, determined, as he put it, to "arrive at moral perfection." He "wished to live without committing any fault at any time." He identified twelve Virtues by which a moral man should live; and when a Quaker friend commented on his pride, he added a thirteenth Virtue of humility. This is Franklin's list:

1. TEMPERANCE: Eat not to dullness. Drink not to elevation.

2. SILENCE: Speak not but what may benefit others or yourself. Avoid trifling conversation.

3. ORDER: Let all your things have their places. Let each part of your business have its time.

4. RESOLUTION: Resolve to perform what you ought. Perform without fail what you resolve.

5. FRUGALITY: Make no expense but to do good to others or yourself, i.e., waste nothing.

6. INDUSTRY: Lose no time. Be always employed in something useful. Cut off all unnecessary actions.

7. SINCERITY: Use no hurtful deceit. Think innocently and justly; if you speak, speak accordingly.

8. JUSTICE: Wrong none by doing injuries or omitting the benefits that are your duty.

9. MODERATION: Avoid extremes. Forbear resenting injuries so much as you think they deserve.

10. CLEANLINESS: Tolerate no uncleanliness in body, clothes, or habitation.

11. TRANQUILITY: Be not disturbed at trifles or at accidents common or unavoidable.

12. CHASTITY: Rarely use venery [*sexual pleasure*] but for health or offspring-never to dullness, weakness, or the injury of your own or another's peace or reputation.

13. HUMILITY: Imitate Jesus and Socrates.[2]

Franklin chose the order of the Virtues very carefully. He placed Temperance first, reasoning that once he had conquered that virtue, the others would be easier to attain. Each of the succeeding virtues were meant to make the ones after it easier to accomplish. Franklin focused on one virtue per week, and kept a notebook in which he noted his progress and marked his failures for the day.

What Franklin discovered was that he "was surpris'd to find myself so much fuller of Faults than I had imagined." To avoid having to use new notebooks, or scraping off the ink in the old notebook, which would soon leave it full of holes, "I mark'd my Faults with a black Lead Pencil, which Marks I could easily wipe out with a wet Sponge."[3]

You are probably not surprised at Franklin's failure to achieve his goal. No mere human being can achieve moral perfection on his own. In fact, on a website encouraging young people to follow Franklin's example, the author writes, "The thirteen virtues are a good guide for you to follow. In fact, keeping track of how well you do in maintaining the virtues and having positive character traits, as Franklin did, is worth trying. You also need to realize that no one is perfect. The main idea is to follow the advice of Benjamin Franklin and try to be a person of good character."[4]

What Franklin was attempting was a type of repentance, but it was not repentance to life. So where did our beloved founding father go wrong?

First, he was using the wrong list. God had already given us a list of rules that we are to follow perfectly. That list is hard enough; we certainly don't need another one. By creating his own list, Franklin was acting as his own god, and establishing his own "Thirteen Commandments." Some of Franklin's "Commandments" do relate to God's law, but notice how vastly they differ. And ironically, even though Franklin made up his own laws, even he was not able to obey them.

Second, Franklin refused to call a sin a sin. He merely saw his failures as moral shortcomings which could be overcome by his own personal diligence. Franklin had a sense of sin, but he did not acknowledge it as sin. He developed his list of virtues out of his own sense of morality, which in some cases went in direct contradiction to the law of God. Look at Virtue number 12. Do you see the idea of marriage anywhere in that statement? If you read about Franklin's personal life, you will understand why. His first son was born out of wedlock, and there is serious question whether he and his wife were ever really legally married. In my opinion, Franklin did the honorable thing by raising his oldest son in his home and treating him as legitimate, but the point is that he apparently saw nothing wrong with the circumstances surrounding that son's birth.

Third, Franklin tried to accomplish moral perfection on his own power. Although he believed in God, he did not turn to God to help him in his quest. Franklin wrote a letter shortly before his death in which he stated that his view of Jesus Christ was that he believed in His system of morals and His religion, but he also "understood" that it had been corrupted. Franklin said that he had doubts about the divinity of Christ but that he had not studied it and would not do so "when I expect soon an opportunity of knowing the truth with less trouble." He also did not believe that God looked upon unbelievers in the world with any particular displeasure.[5]

A man with such a belief about God and Christ would not be quick to ask for their assistance in becoming a better person. And in light of his thoughts about unbelievers, he would not be likely to think that God would care. How sad for Dr. Franklin! But fortunately, we are not condemned to live as he did. We can have the same goal—to live a morally pure life--but we can have the aid of an all-powerful God as we go through the process of trying to attain it.

Of course, we won't attain it any more than Dr. Franklin did. And that is his fourth mistake. He actually thought he could do it! He did not understand the total sinfulness of man. He really thought that by focusing on one virtue per week, after a few years of practice, he could become perfect. And he was surprised at how often he failed. Our advantage, if you will, is that we know we can't do it. We know that we are supposed to try, but we are not surprised when we don't make it. We are not discouraged or disillusioned because we know that we are sinful people and that we will never attain perfection in this life.

So what's the point of repentance? Well, there are two ways in which you can repent. The first way is one that I don't think Dr. Franklin ever tried, unless it was at the very end of his life; if he had, his whole list of virtues might never have been made. That is the turning away from our sin nature, *in general*, and turning to God. That happens the moment we come to Christ, when we are born again. Scripture teaches us that the only way we are able to do this is because the Holy Spirit changes our nature, making us able to repent and believe in Christ. So the only way we can repent in the first place is because of God and Him alone.

This should not be taken lightly. None of us wants God. We love our sins, and we do not want to give them up. We are unable, on our own, to choose God. That is why Jesus told us, "No one can come to me unless the Father who sent me draws him" [John 6:44]. And "No one can come to me unless the Father has enabled him." [John 6:65] Without the Holy Spirit's first changing our hearts, we would forever reject Christ. But if we believe, then the Holy Spirit has changed us and enabled us to repent and believe. We have turned from love of sin to love of Christ.

Now that is true in a general sense, in the sense that leads to salvation. But does that mean that we no longer sin? Of course not. If we were to keep a notebook like Dr. Franklin's and make a mark every time we fail, we would find, just as he did, that it is soon full of marks. Our sin nature still needs to be conquered. In one sense it has been conquered. But in another sense, it is still there tempting us to go astray.

So that is the other meaning for the idea of repentance—daily, or by the minute, turning from our sins and turning to God. Whenever we are tempted, we are to turn to God, who has promised that He will always provide a way of escape. And if we do sin, we are to confess our sins with the assurance that we will be forgiven. But we don't have to do this alone either. The Holy Spirit is still there, guiding us along the right path, warning us when there is trouble ahead, and admonishing us when we have gotten off the path entirely. Unlike Benjamin Franklin, we have lots of help, and it is help of the most powerful kind. The God who created the universe walks with us each step of the way and will be there every minute to offer help and encouragement. All we have to do is listen and follow.

LESSON TWENTY-EIGHT
The Word of God

Question 88:

What are the outward means by which Christ communicates to us the benefits of redemption?

Answer: The outward and ordinary means by which Christ communicates to us the benefits of redemption are His ordinances, especially the Word, sacraments, and prayer, all of which are made effectual to the elect for salvation.

1. What is meant by the Word?

   Read 2 Peter 1:20-21

2. What are the sacraments?

   Read Matthew 28:19; 1 Corinthians 11:23-26

3. What is the best example of how to pray?

   Read Matthew 6:9-13

4. Who are the elect?

   Read Mark 13:20; I Peter 2:9; 2 Timothy 2:10

Question 89:

How is the Word made effectual to salvation?

Answer: The Spirit of God makes the reading, but especially the preaching, of the Word an effectual means of convincing and converting sinners, and of building them up in holiness and comfort, through faith to salvation.

5. Who is described as preaching in the New Testament?

Read Matthew 4:23; Mark 1:4; Luke 9:1-2; Acts 8:25, 40; Acts 17:13

6. What did Paul tell Timothy to do in his absence?

Read 1 Timothy 4:13

7. Why is preaching necessary?

Read Romans 10:14

Question 90:

How is the Word to be read and heard, that it may become effectual to salvation?

Answer: That the Word may become effectual to salvation we must attend to it with diligence, preparation, and prayer; receive it with faith and love; lay it up in our hearts; and practice it in our lives.

8. How do we attend to the Word with diligence?

Read 2 Peter 1:19; Proverbs 8:34

9. How should we prepare and pray to hear or read the Word?

Psalm 119:18

10. How are we to receive the Word?

Read Luke 8:15; Psalm 119:42

11. Why is it important to lay up the Word in our hearts?

Read Psalm 119:11; Hebrews 12:5

12. Is listening to or reading the Word enough?

Read James 1:22

Commentary
Lesson 28

The Word of God

Catechism Questions 88, 89, and 90

I was recently diagnosed with a medical condition. It isn't life-threatening, but it does require some attention on my part or it will affect my lifestyle. My doctor gave me a booklet to read that tells me what to do to deal with this condition most effectively. Two things concern me: I have to take daily medication and I am supposed to exercise. I am not fond of living on medication and I really do not like to exercise, so how do I know I can trust this booklet? What if the people who wrote it had some ulterior motives? What if they own stock in a pharmaceutical company or a fitness center? I think I'll just ignore the whole thing. Besides, I think I heard somewhere that medical booklets are unreliable anyway.

So what do you think of my decision? If you are a rational, sensible person, you probably think I'm nuts. Exercise is good for me, and taking one little pill is not going to ruin my day. Why would I doubt the accuracy of the booklet? The only reason I can think of is that I don't like some of what's in there. I am trying to rationalize the fact that I am not following the instructions by discrediting the source.

That's what lots of folks do with the Bible. They don't like some of what's in there, so they try to discredit the source. In this lesson, I first want to explore several arguments for the accuracy of the Bible. Then I want to talk about our response to the Bible.

First, let's look at how we can know that the Bible is really the Word of God. I cannot possibly go into these arguments in detail, so I will give you some websites that you can consult on your own if you would like more information. We will look at four arguments: the argument from prophecy, the argument from history, the argument from science, and the argument from eyewitnesses.

The Bible is full of prophecies, predictions of events that would happen in the future. In contrast to every other prophet or prophetic book, every event that the Bible has predicted to happen by now has actually happened. Let me repeat that. Every single one of the prophecies that should have happened has happened. There was not one mistake. This is not true of any other supposed prophet. I see many magazine articles about the prophecies of Nostradamus, but not only are his prophecies vague, they are often completely wrong. For instance, according to many people, he predicted that the world would end in 1999. The prophecies of the Bible have never been wrong. Not once.

The book of Micah was written approximately 700 years before the birth of Jesus, yet he prophesied that the Messiah, the Savior, would be born in Bethlehem. This was remarkable because Bethlehem was not much of a town. It was a historic city, the home of David, but it was not the seat of government or a prominent place in Israel. In fact, Micah calls it "the least" or "little." It would not have been the most likely place for such an important person to be born. But it was true. Jesus, who is called the Messiah, was born in Bethlehem.

Likewise, the book of Isaiah was written almost 700 years before Christ's birth, but he prophesied exactly what would happen to Jesus. He describes Him as a man of sorrows who is led to His death without uttering a word in His defense. He even explains that He took on our sins and paid for our iniquities. All of this was fulfilled in Jesus' trials before Herod and Pontius Pilate and His agonizing death on the cross. Isaiah did not know that His name would be Jesus, but he accurately portrayed what He would do for His people.

These are only two of hundreds of prophecies in the Bible that have already been fulfilled. So one reason we can trust the Bible is its record of 100% accuracy in predicting the future. Mere man has never achieved that result; someone or something else must have been involved. Of course that someone else is God.

A second argument for the truth of the Bible is the argument from history. For many years, historians and archeologists argued that the Bible included people and places that were not mentioned anywhere else, and that it therefore could not be trusted. However, the more we have discovered through archeology, the more the accuracy of the Bible has been proved. For example, the tribe of the Hittites was believed to be a non-existent group until the early twentieth century, when an archeological excavation discovered remains of the culture in Bogazkoy, Turkey. Similarly, the Assyrian king Sargon was thought to be mythological until French archeologists found his royal city in Khorsabad, Iraq, in the nineteenth century. Dr. Nelson Glueck, Biblical Archaeologist and President of the Hebrew Union College-Jewish Institute of Religion, is quoted as saying, "No archeological discovery has ever controverted a Biblical reference. Scores of archeological findings have been made which confirm in clear outline or in exact detail historical statements in the Bible.

So according to archeology and history, the Bible is overwhelmingly accurate. Even people and places that were thought to be non-existent have recently been found. If the Bible mentions people and places that men did not even know about, who do you think did know? Which leads us to argument three: the argument from science. Not only did God know about people and places, He also had scientific knowledge that man did not have at the time the Bible was written.

In about 1600 BC, Job told us that the earth hangs on nothing. This is common knowledge today, but in ancient Mesopotamia, where Job lived, the world was believed to be a flat disk floating in the ocean. At the same time, the Hindus believed that the earth was supported by four elephants, the ancient Greeks believed that the god Atlas carried the earth on his shoulders, and the Egyptians thought the earth rested on crystal spheres. The first people to advance the theory that the earth was a sphere were Pythagorus and Thales of Miletus in the 500's BC. Likewise, the first theory that the earth floated in space was not until the 500's BC, and we didn't really understand how gravity held the earth in place until Sir Isaac Newton published his theories in 1687 AD. This means that hundreds or even thousands of years passed before scientific knowledge caught up with what Job said in the Bible.

The next two verses in Job deal with wind and water. Job also refers to the weight of the wind. According to NASA, the fact that air has weight was not discovered until the year 1640 AD. That is over 2000 years after Job made his statement. How did he know this? It was also in the 1600's that people understood that rain is produced from water that has evaporated from lakes, rivers, and even the oceans. But the book of Job explained this thousands of years earlier. I think it is safe to assume that either the writers of the Bible were incredibly advanced scientifically or that God Himself had a hand in writing the Bible.

Finally, let's look at the Bible from the argument of eyewitness accounts. John says in his gospel account, "We have seen His glory." Paul tells us in his first letter to the Corinthians that after His resurrection, Jesus appeared to more than five hundred people, most of whom were still alive when he wrote the letter. These men appealed to the fact that there were eyewitnesses of what they were writing about who were still alive and who could testify for or against the accuracy of the reports. There is no record that any eyewitness accused either man of speaking falsely or even stretching the truth.

So I have given you four arguments. In light of fulfilled prophecies, historical accuracy, scientific knowledge that pre-dates that of "science" itself, and eyewitness accounts, what conclusion should we come to? The only logical conclusion is that there is more to this book than just a book. It is undoubtedly the work of God Himself.

So what are we to do with this knowledge? If the Bible is the actual Word of God, how should it affect our lives? First of all, it should be taken seriously. When we read or hear the Word of God, we should focus on the Word and the Word alone. We should find a place free of other distractions and concentrate on what we are hearing or reading.

I am a real fan of mystery novels, but I try to stay away from the really creepy ones. Once, by accident, I started one that scared the pants off of me—not because it was particularly violent, but because of the location and circumstances of the crime. A woman was led into a vast underground cavern, and then left there alone to die. I have been on tours of underground caves where the guide turned out all of the lights to show us how dark total darkness truly is. The idea of being left alone in such a situation is completely horrifying to me. Fortunately, in the novel, the woman was rescued. When she saw her rescuers coming, she almost attacked them in her eagerness to get to the light.

This should really be our attitude toward the Word of God. We live in a world of total darkness. Most of those around us have no concept of who God really is and no guidance from His Holy Spirit. As we try to move and live in that world, we should run almost screaming and crying in our eagerness to get the truth and the light that is given to us in Scripture. It is our only lifeline to what is real and true and what will save us from the horrors of the world in which we now live.

Then second, we should believe it and act on it. It is not enough to just read or hear the Word; we must also obey it. We should try to memorize key Scripture passages so that we can recall them at times when our Bible isn't handy and we need to be reminded of what God has told us. If memorizing Scripture is hard for you, then don't try to learn long passages. Focus on short bits that have great meaning for you. "When you walk through the fire, I will be with you," for example. Or "I know the plans I have for you; plans for good and not for evil." Those are not difficult passages, but they can bring great comfort to an anxious soul.

Third, and maybe most important, the Word needs to be preached. This is the means that God has chosen for conveying His Word to those who do not yet know Him. He could have called people to Himself in a number of ways, and He has used other ways on occasion. But the primary means that God uses for spreading His Word is the preaching and teaching of it. And He has promised that His Word will not return to Him without accomplishing its purpose. If we are given the opportunity to teach the Word of God, we should do so humbly, in total dependence on God, and be very careful that what we say and do are in complete agreement with what He says in His Word.

God's Word is exactly what the phrase implies—the actual words of God Himself. He has chosen to speak to us directly through the pages of Scripture and through the mouths of those He has chosen to preach and teach His Word. Let's be careful to focus on what He has to say and to apply it to our lives on a daily basis.

If you would like more information on the arguments for the accuracy of the Bible, I found the following websites to be very useful. I hope they are still active:

http://www.clarifyingchristianity.com/science.shtml

http://www.christiananswers.net/q-eden/edn-t003.html

http://www.faithfacts.org/search-for-truth/questions-of-christians/how-do-you-know-that-the-bible-is-true.

LESSON TWENTY-NINE
The Sacrament of Baptism

Question 91:

How do the sacraments become effectual means of salvation?

Answer: The sacraments become effectual means of salvation, not from any virtue in them, or in him who administers them, but only by the blessing of Christ, and the working of His Spirit in those who by faith receive them.

1. How does the Holy Spirit work in those who receive Christ?

    Read Luke 12:11-12; John 14:26; Acts 1:8; Romans 5:5

Question 92:

What is a sacrament?

Answer: A sacrament is a holy ordinance instituted by Christ, in which, by perceptible signs, Christ and the benefits of the new covenant are represented, sealed, and applied to believers.

Question 93:

What are the sacraments of the New Testament?

Answer: The sacraments of the New Testament are Baptism and the Lord's Supper.

2. How did Christ institute the sacrament of Baptism?

    Read Matthew 28:19

3. How did Christ institute the sacrament of the Lord's Supper?

Read Matthew 26:19-20; 26-28

Question 94:

What is Baptism?

Answer: Baptism is a sacrament, in which the washing with water, in the name of the Father, and of the Son, and of the Holy Spirit, does signify and seal our grafting into Christ and receiving of the benefits of the Covenant of Grace, and our engagement to be the Lord's.

4. Who told us to baptize in the name of the Father and of the Son and of the Holy Spirit?

Read Matthew 28:18-19

5. Is it possible to be saved if you are not baptized?

Read Luke 23:39-43

Question 95:

To whom is Baptism to be administered?

Answer: Baptism is not to be administered to any who are out of the visible church, till they profess their faith in Christ and obedience to Him; but the infants of those who are members of the visible Church are to be baptized.

6. What is required for an adult to be baptized?

Read Acts 8:12, 13

7. What was the sign of the covenant between God and man in the Old Testament?

Read Genesis 17:9-11

8. Who participated in the covenant sign of circumcision?

Read Genesis 17: 12

9. Is the covenant between God and man still represented by the sign of circumcision?

Read Galatians 5:2-6

10. What is now the sign of our covenant with God?

Read Acts 2:41

11. Were children baptized in the New Testament?

Read Acts 16:15, 33

12. When the Ethiopian eunuch was baptized, who "went down into the water"?

Read Acts 8:36-38

13. What happened when the apostles received the baptism of the Holy Spirit?

Read Acts 1:5; 2:1-4

14. Have you been baptized? If not, why not? If so, what does your baptism mean to you?

Commentary
Lesson 29

The Sacrament of Baptism

Catechism Questions 91, 92, 93, 94, and 95

Do you remember your own baptism? If you were baptized as an older child or as an adult, undoubtedly you do. But if you're like me, there is no way you would remember it. I was baptized when I was only a few months old. There are many questions that go along with the subject of baptism, and the purpose of this lesson is to answer those questions the best I can according to the theological perspective of the Westminster Confession of Faith. If you have been taught another view of baptism, I ask that you be open-minded as you consider my arguments and that you try to separate tradition from Scriptural instruction.

First of all, in whose name(s) are we to be baptized? For many of us, this is pretty clear, but there is a school of thought that says that since Peter said that we should be baptized in Jesus' name [Acts 2:38], our baptism should be in Jesus' name only. I have two problems with this. First, I don't think Peter was trying to supplant Christ's instructions about baptism. Notice in Matthew 28:19, Jesus says that we are to baptize in the name [singular] of the Father, Son, and Holy Spirit. There is one name, but three persons. I think that Peter was trying to emphasize that baptism should coincide with our belief in Christ. John the Baptist had been baptizing for forgiveness of sins, and others also had been baptizing. Peter wanted us to identify baptism with becoming part of Christ's kingdom. But even if Peter had been arguing that we should be baptized in Jesus' name only, whom should we follow? Christ or Peter? I'm not even going to answer that question.

Second, is baptism necessary for salvation? There are denominations that say that it is. But through the example of the dying thief on the cross, I think Christ has taught us that baptism is not essential. There was absolutely no way that the thief could have been baptized, and yet Christ told him that he would enter paradise. If a person has no opportunity to be baptized, the lack of baptism will not hinder her salvation. However, if a person has the opportunity to be baptized and chooses not to do so, such a choice would leave serious doubt as to his decision to follow and obey Christ. He made it clear that we are to be baptized when we believe.

Third, should everyone be baptized? Any adult or older child who has not made a sincere profession of faith should not be baptized. Furthermore, there is no age at which a child should suddenly make a profession of faith and be baptized. My three daughters came to know the Lord at the ages of 3, 2 ½ , and 6 years of age. [In case you are wondering about those very young ages, I had a long talk with my pastor at the time about the validity of those professions. He agreed with me that they were genuine.] Many churches have a confirmation class and ceremony, which sometimes includes believers' baptism, at around 8 years of age. I think they would have a hard time defending that practice from Scripture. Nowhere in the Bible can you find that 8 years of age, or any other age, is the age at which children come to know the Lord.

So what about children? Can we baptize them, and when should we baptize them? This is perhaps the most divisive issue in the Christian church regarding baptism, so let's look at the argument in favor of infant baptism. In the Old Testament, God gave Abraham the sign of circumcision to designate that a man was a part of the nation of Israel, the chosen nation of God. These people were to believe, love, and obey God. Male children as young as eight days old were to be given this sign. Did that mean that those infants could understand the commandments of God and agree to obey them? Of course not. It meant that those children were included in the covenant God had made with Abraham, that He would be their God and they would be His people. As they grew older, it would be up to each of them to believe and obey God. The sign of circumcision did not save them, but it did set them apart as God's people.

In the New Testament, the sign of circumcision was abolished. In its place, the sign that a person has believed in Jesus and is willing to obey Him is baptism. We now have a new sign for a new covenant, but this sign still signifies that God will be our God and we will be His people. So should it be a sign given to infants? Since the first Christian converts were Jews, who were accustomed to the sign of circumcision being given to infants, don't you think God would have told them explicitly if the new sign of baptism were not to be applied in the same manner? God very explicitly told them that circumcision was no longer necessary. Would He not also have told them that no longer were infants to be included in the sign of the covenant?

And why would God have stopped including infants in His covenant family? They were included in the Old Testament covenant—why not in the New Covenant as well? Infants who are born into Christian families are still a part of the family of God. The sign has changed, but I doubt seriously that God's relationship with the youngest of His children has changed as well.

Finally, we have examples in Scripture where entire households and families were baptized. Surely there were some young children or infants in those families. Since the practice in the Old Testament was to apply the sign of the covenant to very young children, and since God has never told us not to baptize our children, then I think it is very safe to assume that He means for us to continue to do so.

This leads to the fourth question: How are people to be baptized? There are many Christians who believe that baptism must be done by immersion. This leads them to think that obviously this would preclude baptizing young children, since they cannot be immersed. [Actually, some churches do immerse babies, so that argument doesn't hold up even on a practical level.] But does baptism mean that one must be immersed? The Greek word baptism can mean "to immerse," but it can also mean "to pour" or "to sprinkle." In many instances, the word for "sprinkle" or "anoint" in the Old Testament is the same as the word for baptism. Also, as you have seen in Acts chapter 2, the apostles were baptized by the Holy Spirit through tongues of fire. They were not immersed in fire; fire appeared above their heads and settled on them. The word baptism in this instance clearly does not mean "to immerse." Also, when Phillip baptized the Ethiopian, Scripture tells us that they both "went down into the water." If this phrase means that the Ethiopian was immersed, then Phillip was immersed as well. If this is our understanding of this passage, then every pastor who baptizes by immersion should go under the water with every person he baptizes.

The writers of the Westminster Confession of Faith understood the importance of baptism, and they also understood how it should be applied. All adult believers should be baptized to show that they have believed in Christ and that they are now part of the Covenant with God. When we baptize our children, we are showing that they are also a part of the family of God; but just as circumcised children in the Old Testament, they must grow up and establish their own personal relationship with God. Baptism of a child does not save that child; every person must acknowledge for himself that Jesus is Lord and agree to follow and obey Him. The manner of baptism is not significant; we can be immersed or we can be sprinkled. The sign of baptism is what is important because it sets us apart from the world as children of God.

LESSON THIRTY
The Sacrament of the Lord's Supper

Question 96:

What is the Lord's Supper?

Answer: The Lord's Supper is a sacrament, in which by giving and receiving bread and wine, according to Christ's direction, His death is shown forth; and the worthy receivers are, not after a corporal and carnal manner, but by faith, made partakers of His body and blood, with all His benefits, to their spiritual nourishment and growth in grace.

1. When was the Lord's Supper instituted?

   Matthew 26:18-30

2. What does the bread of the Lord's Supper represent?

   Read Matthew 26:26

3. What does the wine of the Lord's Supper represent?

   Read Matthew 26:27-28

Question 97:

What is required to be worthy of receiving the Lord's Supper?

Answer: It is required of those who would receive the Lord's Supper worthily that they examine themselves, as to their knowledge to discern the Lord's body, as to their faith to feed on

Him, and as to their repentance, love, and new obedience; lest,
coming unworthily, they eat and drink judgment on themselves.

4. How were the Corinthians observing the Lord's Supper?

Read I Corinthians 11:21

5. What did this show about their attitudes toward God and others?

Read I Corinthians 11: 22

6. What are we to do before eating the bread and drinking the wine?

Read I Corinthians 11:28

7. How does Paul tell the Corinthians to behave when observing the Lord's Supper?

Read I Corinthians 11: 33-34

8. What happens when we eat the bread and drink the wine?

Read I Corinthians 11: 26

9. Did Jesus tell us how often we are to observe the Lord's Supper?

Read I Corinthians 11:25-26

10. Where did Paul receive the instructions he gives us concerning the Lord's Supper?

Read I Corinthians 11: 23

11. With what attitude do you come to the Lord's Supper?

Commentary
Lesson 30

The Sacrament of the Lord's Supper

Catechism Questions 96 and 97

"The Lord's Supper." What do those words bring to mind? In many churches, this sacrament is celebrated with tiny pieces of bread or wafers and tiny little cups full of grape juice or wine. In others, a full loaf of bread is used with a large cup of wine or juice which is shared by everyone. In this lesson we will explore the meaning of this sacrament and the proper attitude toward its celebration.

When Christ instituted what we call the "Lord's Supper," it may have been during a Passover meal. This is a full meal, not the traditional bit of bread and taste of wine or juice that we commonly use in our communion services today. This will be important to remember later. Each element in the meal has special significance. The order of the meal would be as follows:

1. Light the Passover candles and recite two blessings over the candles as you light them.

2. Bless the wine, and then pour a cup for each guest and a cup for the prophet Elijah. Everyone drinks the first cup, which symbolizes God's promise to take His people out of Egypt. Then pour the second cup. Elijah's cup will remain untouched.

3. Wash your hands, then eat parsley or some other green vegetable dipped in salt water. The vegetable symbolizes rebirth and the salt water is symbolic of the tears shed by the Jews held in slavery in Egypt.

4. There will be a pile of three matzohs (pieces of unleavened bread) on the table. Break the middle one and return half of it to the pile. Hide the other half. Later, the children will hunt for it and eat it.

5. Tell the story of the exodus from Egypt and the first Pass over. At the end of the story, recite a blessing over the second cup of wine and drink it. This cup represents God's promise to deliver the Hebrews from slavery.

6. Wash your hands and say a blessing, then recite two blessings over the matzoh. Eat a piece of matzoh after saying the blessings.

7. Recite a blessing over a bitter vegetable (usually raw horse-radish), symbolizing the bitterness of slavery. Dip the bitter vegetable into a paste called charoset (made of chopped nuts, cinnamon, and apples) and eat it. Then make a sandwich using another piece of bitter vegetable and charoset between two small pieces of matzoh.

8. Eat a festive meal. During this time, the children hunt for the hidden piece of matzoh.

9. Pour the third cup of wine, recite a grace after the meal, then bless and drink the wine. This is the cup of redemption, and it God's promise to redeem His people. Then pour a fourth cup of wine for everyone. Have a child open a door for the prophet Elijah, who is supposed to arrive on Passover to announce the coming of the Messiah.

10. Recite a series of psalms and a blessing over the last cup of wine, representing God's promise to acquire Israel as a nation, and drink the fourth cup of wine.

11. Announce that the Passover celebration has been completed and that you wish to celebrate it next year in Jerusalem, which is a wish that for the Messiah to come.

Again, notice that this is a meal. Whether it was a Passover meal or not, Jesus and His disciples ate a full meal in the upper room on the last night before His crucifixion. Since it was Passover week, when He referred to the bread, He was probably referring to matzoh, or unleavened bread. When He spoke of the wine, most scholars agree that He was talking about the third cup of wine in the Seder meal, the symbol of God's promise to redeem His people. He was saying that from that time forward, whenever anyone partook of this meal, they should remember that the promise to redeem was fulfilled in Him. They should also remember that the middle piece of matzoh, the piece that was broken and hidden (ie, buried) was also a representation of Himself.

When Paul wrote his instructions about the observation of the Lord's Supper, this was apparently still the practice; the Christians were still eating the full meal of the Passover. However, they were doing so to satisfy their own appetites and not to glorify God. Apparently, when they gathered to observe this meal, these Christians were not following the patterns set out for them, but they were each eating and drinking as they pleased. Some were taking more than they should and leaving nothing for others.

After admonishing them for their behavior, Paul reminds them of what had happened when Jesus instituted the Lord's Supper and that this observance is meant as a proclamation of the death of the Lord Jesus Christ. He then cautions them again not to eat the bread or drink the wine in an unworthy manner, but to examine themselves to be certain that their motives are pure in taking part.

It is important for us to understand the historical significance of the Passover, the basis of the Lord's Supper, to fully understand the admonition Paul is giving us. What are we to examine ourselves about?

First, we are to be sure that we have received a new birth through the Holy Spirit and that we understand what we are doing. We must understand that Christ died as a substitute for our sins and that only through Him can we receive eternal life.

Second, we must be sure that we have repented of a life of sin and are endeavoring to the best of our abilities to live as Christ would have us live. We must desire to follow Christ. We must trust in Him to guide and direct our lives.

Third, we must be sure that we have no unconfessed sin. Maybe. It depends on what you mean by "unconfessed sin." If you mean that a person must have confessed and repented of every sin he has committed, then no, that is not a requirement for participating in the Lord's Supper.

There is no one alive who is even aware of all of his sins, let alone has confessed all of them. "Eating the bread or drinking the cup in an unworthy manner" does not mean that we are sinless, or even aware of all of our sins. However, if you mean that a person has a sin or sins that he is very much aware of, but is not ready to repent of, to give up, then I would say that he should not participate. Such a person is not really trying to follow Christ to the best of his abilities. But remember that this admonition was given by Paul primarily so that we would not behave as he has described in verse 21 of I Corinthians 11.

So what happens when we receive the Lord's Supper in an appropriate manner? First of all, Scripture tells us that by doing so, we are proclaiming to everyone around us the death of Jesus Christ for our sins. This observance is a visible reminder of what Christ did on the cross. As His body was beaten and broken and His blood was shed for our sins, the bread and wine are visible representations of His love for us.

Second, we are connected spiritually in a special way with Christ. We do not believe that the bread and wine actually become the physical body and blood of Christ; but we do believe that He is spiritually present in these elements, and that when we eat and drink them, we have a special communion (intimate communication) with Christ.

So how often should we do this? There is a great deal of debate over this question, and different churches have answered it in different ways. Some churches observe the Lord's Supper every Sunday; others once a month; others a few times a year. Since Scripture does not specify how often a group is to observe this Supper, I would not presume to dictate a specific time frame. The important thing is that it should be done, and it should be done with reverence and with full attention to the significance of the event.

Scripture does not tell us to examine our denomination, our church, or even our family. We are told to examine ourselves. Next time you have a chance to participate in the Lord's Supper, examine your motives for doing so. If your desire is to live in a way that is pleasing to Christ, and if you are participating to strengthen your relationship with Him, that is all He asks.

LESSON THIRTY-ONE
Prayer

Question 98:

What is prayer?

Answer: Prayer is an offering up of our desires to God, for things agreeable to His will, in the name of Christ, with confession of our sins, and thankful acknowledgment of His mercies.

1. What does prayer involve?

   Read 2 Chronicles 6:21; 30:27; Nehemiah 1:6; 11:17

2. What kinds of things can we ask God for in prayer?

   Read Psalm 5:2; 6:9; Jeremiah 42:3; 2 Chronicles 6:29; James 5:16; Matthew 26:41; I

   Timothy 5:5

3. What kinds of things did Paul pray for?

   Read Romans 1:10; 15:31; 2 Corinthians 13:9; Ephesians 3:16-18; 6:19

4. What promises do we have that God will hear our prayers?

Read Deuteronomy 4:7; 2 Chronicles 7:14

5. What if our prayers are not answered immediately?

Read Luke 18:1

6. How should we pray?

Read Matthew 6:6-7

7. What if we don't know what to pray for?

Read Romans 8:26

8. What result can we expect from prayer?

Read Philippians 4:6-7

9. How can we know our prayers will work?

Read James 5:16

Commentary

Lesson 31

Prayer

Catechism Question 98

Have you ever heard a young child pray? "God bless mommy and daddy and grandmommy and granddaddy and all my friends and keep me safe all through the night. Amen." Isn't that beautiful?

How about an adult? "God bless all my family and friends and help me to earn more money and get that promotion I have been wanting. Heal all my aches and pains and please keep my car from breaking down. Please don't let the bad economy ruin my 401K, and provide a way for me to go on vacation this year. In Jesus name, Amen."

What happened? When do we become so selfish? Is that how you pray? (Be honest.)

In this lesson, we will look at prayer in general, then in the next few lessons we will look more specifically at the Lord's Prayer. So first of all, what is prayer? Richard Pratt, in his book *Pray With Your Eyes Open*,[6] defines prayer as "a believer's communication with God." Since I teach communication, I particularly like this definition. In communication studies, it is generally understood that in order for communication to take place, there must be three elements present: a source of the communication, a receiver of the communication, and a message that is being communicated. There are more elements, but these are the essential three. So let's look at each of the elements as they apply to a believer's prayer.

First is the source of the communication—the person who is praying. I would venture to say that most of us could do with a more vibrant and active prayer life, so let's first look at reasons we may have for failing to pray as we should. In the book *Plain Talk on Prayer*, Manford Gutzke[7] gives us five reasons:

•Ignorance—We don't realize we can or need to pray. We become so accustomed to trying to do things on our own that we don't even think about praying.

•Indifference—We don't expect God to act. We forget that He is the God of the Universe who loves us. He can do whatever He desires, and He desires the best for us.

•Indolence—We are too lazy to pray. We will not make the time or use the mental energy to pray as we ought.

•Irresponsibility—We decide that "it's not my problem." We live in our own little world; if it doesn't affect us directly, we aren't concerned

•Indwelling sin—We don't want to come face to face with God. We are unwilling to confront our sin and ask for God's forgiveness; we are unwilling to repent.

Do any of these apply to you? That could be your first matter of prayer—talk to God about letting go of that particular sinful attitude.

We must also think about how often we pray. Scripture tells us to pray without ceasing. What does that mean for us? In my opinion, it means that God and His concerns must be first in our minds and hearts; we must continually see the world and those in it through His eyes. We can keep up a running conversation with God about the things we see, hear, and experience to know how to deal with those things. However, it can also help to set aside specific times during the day to pray.

So we ourselves are the source of the communication of prayer, and a lot of us are not doing a very good job of it. But when we do pray, who is the receiver of the communication? The Lord Almighty, the Creator of the Universe, who is also the Father of all who believe. If you are a believer in Christ, then think about what God has done for you. Through His death and resurrection, Jesus has opened the way for us to have direct access to God. He is also our High Priest and represents us before the heavenly altar, praying for us. Search the Scripture to learn all you can about who God is. Pratt cautions us that if we have a limited concept of God, our prayers can become repetitious and boring. The better you know God, the more you will pray to Him and the more intimate your prayers will be.

The third element of communication is the message itself—the prayer. In order to understand what prayer is, I think it might be helpful if we first understand what it is not. In this, I can definitely not set myself up as an example. I have prayed for a better understanding of prayer so that I could write this study, and I think God has answered that prayer. In fact, I am now convinced that my prayer life falls so short of what it should be that I hesitate to even write this at all. So this is without a doubt a "do what I say, not what I do" type of lesson.

First of all, prayer is not a type of wish list. As a child, you may have made up a list for Santa Claus. I found with my own children that if I allowed them to look at Christmas catalogs or newspaper ads, their lists for Santa got longer and longer—even when they knew that it was Mom and Dad who were providing the goodies. Our prayers are not meant to be wish lists for God to fill. Yes, we may ask for things we need, and even for things we want, but I feel that there should be a higher purpose for our asking than just "gimme, gimme, gimme." I have looked at examples of prayer in Scripture, and I did not find one example where a person prayed for a new tent, a new robe, or a new camel. I have concluded therefore that these things are not supposed to be all that important. In fact, Jesus even tells us specifically not to worry about these things. (Matthew 6:25).

Second, true prayer is not a repetition of memorized phrases. (Matthew 6:7). We are to enter into prayer with our minds as well as our words (1 Corinthians 14:1). Prayer is personal; you are talking and someone else is listening. That someone else just happens to be God.

Third, to pray "in Jesus name" does not mean that we should tack that phrase onto the end of our prayers as a kind of magic spell. In the tale of Aladdin, one had to say the phrase "Open Sesame" to unlock the door to the treasure cave. "In Jesus name" is not the spell to unlock the treasures of heaven. God is not bound to give us everything we ask for. He is not a cosmic Santa Claus or a genie in a bottle; there are no magic words to make Him respond. God will give us some of the things we ask for because He wants to bless us. He will give us some things we haven't even thought to ask for. He will also not give us some of the things we want.

Does that mean He doesn't care about us, or that He is too busy to be bothered with us? Of course not. Would you give a child everything he asked for? Some parents do, and they end up with spoiled, selfish children. Sometimes they end up with extremely dysfunctional families as well. God knows what we can handle and what will be the best for us. If He does not give us a specific blessing, there is a very good reason.

So if prayer is not a wish list, a magic spell, or repetition of well-worn phrases, then what is it? If I am not supposed to ask for all the things I want, what am I supposed to pray for? How am I supposed to talk to God? Let's back up a minute to that phrase "in Jesus name." I have said that these are not "magic words." I have not said what I believe the phrase really means. As I have been praying about this lesson, I have come to believe that this phrase directs us to think of all of life from Jesus' point of view. If we look at our lives from His perspective, we will see our blessings and our needs more clearly. We will be able to distinguish easily between needs and wants. We will be more thankful for the things we have and less envious of the things that others have. If we look at our lives through the eyes of Christ, we will be more sensitive to the needs of others. We will truly care about others, just as He does. We will want what is really best for them and for us, and we will trust Him to decide what that will be. We will be willing to relinquish control to Christ.

Actually, I think this is what the term *sanctification* means. I have been told that it means becoming more and more like Christ. Would it not also follow that as we become more like Christ, we would see things as He sees them? Those things that seem so important to us would become less important and the things we desire would correspond more and more to what He desires for us. As we see the world through the eyes of Christ, we won't want to make a wish list. We won't want most of that stuff anyway; we will see how foolish it all is.

So how do we pray? Ordinarily, our prayers should begin

with praise. Think about who God is and what He has done. What specifically can you praise Him for? Let this be different each time you pray—today, at this very moment, what stands out to you that you want to praise God for? Think of all the attributes of God. Which are particularly relevant to you today?

Second, we should thank God for what He has done specifically for us. If you were to make a list of everything you could think of for which you could thank God, you should have a really long list. It isn't necessary to go through the whole list in every prayer. Focus on the things that you are really thankful for today.

Then third, we should confess our sins. God has said that He will forgive us for our sins and cast them as far away as the east is from the west. If we confess, we can have the blessing of knowing that our sins are forgiven. And once a sin has been confessed and forgiven, let it go.

Finally, we can pray for ourselves and others. In this, we should try to see our lives and the lives of those around us as Christ sees us. We should not ask for things that we know are against His will, or things that we know will tempt us to sin or cause us to struggle in our Christian lives.

We can be honest with God about our disappointments, our frustrations, and our unmet longings. The Psalms give us examples of all kinds of things said to God in prayer. In Psalm 18:46, the psalmist is praising God; in Psalm 22:2, he is crying out to God because of unanswered prayer; in Psalm 38:18, he is confessing his sins; in Psalm 71:20, he is making a statement; in Psalm 13:1, he is asking a question. We should talk to God in an immediate and personal way; you may speak to God as you would a friend, or your language may be more formal. It doesn't matter, as long as you give God the respect and worship He is due. Nothing is hidden from God anyway, so we might as well talk to Him about it all.

But let's keep it fresh. Beware of repeating the same thing over and over. Imagine you have a friend who calls you at 7:30 and says, "Hello _____. I am so glad you are my friend. You are a wonderful, caring, and loving person. You have helped me so many times in the past. I am grateful that you are my friend. I would like to ask you to continue to help me in my need, and I will be truly grateful." Then she hangs up. You are a little shocked, but the call has made you feel good. The next day, at 7:30, she calls again, and says, "Hello _____. I am so glad you are my friend. You are a wonderful, caring, and loving person. You have helped me so many times in the past. I am grateful that you are my friend. I would like to ask you to continue to help me in my need, and I will be truly grateful." This time you are not as shocked, but you don't feel as good about it as you did yesterday. The third day, you are kind of expecting the call, and sure enough, at 7:30 the phone rings. The voice at the other end says, "Hello _____. I am so glad you are my friend. You are a wonderful, caring, and loving person. You have helped me so many times in the past. I am grateful that you are my friend. I would like to ask you to continue to help me in my need, and I will be truly grateful."

Aren't you ready to ask this caller, who really means well, "Can't you think of anything else to say?! I appreciate what you are trying to do, but can't we have a conversation? Can't you be more specific about what is going on in your life? Can't I talk to you?"

Which brings up an element of communication that I didn't mention earlier—the feedback. The receiver of the communication can send a message back to the source. Take time to be quiet and listen to what God may be telling you. Read His Word. Hear what God has to say to you.

One of the best promises that God gives us is that if we don't know how to pray in a certain situation or if we pray for the wrong thing, the Holy Spirit will take our prayers and present them to God the Father as they should be. He will pray for us in a way that goes beyond our words. Not only can we pray to God, but we can give our problems to Him and ask Him to pray for us! We don't have to know what to ask for.

God also promises that He will hear and answer our prayers. He tells us in His Word that the prayer of a righteous person is powerful and effective. So who are the righteous? According to God, that would be everyone who has been saved by Christ. When we receive Christ as our Savior, not only are our sins forgiven, but the righteous life that

Jesus lived is credited to us. It is as though we ourselves lived a perfectly righteous life. So all who trust in Christ are the righteous ones, the ones whose prayers are powerful and effective.

Do you believe that? When you pray, do you believe that there is power in your prayers? Do you expect God to act? If not, are you praying selfishly, looking at the world through your own eyes and not through the eyes of Christ? Let that be the thing you pray for—to see with the eyes of Christ.

LESSON THIRTY-TWO
"Our Father who is in Heaven"

Question 99:

What rule has God given for our direction in prayer?

Answer: The whole Word of God is of use to direct us in prayer, but the special rule of direction is the form of prayer that Christ taught His disciples, commonly called "the Lord's Prayer.

1. Where was Jesus when he taught the disciples "the Lord's Prayer"?

    Read Matthew 4:23-25

2. When was this instruction repeated?

    Read Luke 11:1-4

3. Do you think that repeating the Lord's Prayer over and over mindlessly is an acceptable form of prayer?

    Read Matthew 6:7

4. How are we to pray the Lord's Prayer (or any other prayer)?

    Read I Corinthians 14:15

Question 100:

What does the preface of the Lord's Prayer teach us?

Answer: The preface of the Lord's Prayer, which is, "Our Father in heaven," teaches us to draw near to God with all holy reverence and confidence, as children to a father, able and ready to help us; and that we should pray with and for others.

5. How does a person become a child of God?

Read John 1:12

6. Why were the Pharisees so angry with Jesus?

Mark 14:60-64

7. According to the Bible, who are Jesus' brothers and sisters?

Read Matthew 12:50

8. According to Scripture, who is our brother?

Read Philemon 1:8-16; I Corinthians 7:12; I Corinthians 5:11

9. How are we to treat those who are not our brothers?

Read Matthew 5:44; Romans 12:20

Commentary
Lesson 32

"Our Father who is in Heaven"

Catechism Questions 99 and 100

How often do you pray the Lord's Prayer? Or, more importantly, how do you pray the Lord's Prayer? Jesus gave us this prayer in answer to his disciples' request to teach them to pray. According to most Bible scholars, it is meant as a guide for prayer, not as a prayer to be repeated over and over without thinking about its meaning. We know that Jesus did not intend this as merely a rote or repetitive prayer because he tells us in the book of Matthew not to keep babbling like pagans, who think their prayers will be heard because of their many words. Paul tells us in I Corinthians that we should pray with our minds.

Does this mean that we should not repeat the Lord's Prayer as part of a church worship service? I don't think so, but it does mean that we should focus our minds on what we are praying. Whether we are praying the Lord's Prayer or any other prayer, our minds should be totally engaged.

It stands to reason, then, that we need to know what the words of the Lord's Prayer really mean. Whether we use this prayer as a prayer by itself or as a guide to how we should form other prayers, Jesus gave us this example in answer to the disciples' question about how we should pray. If we are going to understand it as we pray it, or understand how it should guide our prayers, we need to be clear about what it is really saying.

So let's start with the first phrase, "Our Father in Heaven" (or "Our Father who is in Heaven"). Did you know that in the entire Old Testament, not once does anyone call God his father? God is called *the* Father, but not *my* Father. To have called God your Father would have meant that you considered yourself equal with God. Think about earthly fathers. Have you ever heard of anyone who escaped trouble with authorities because of who his or her father was? Of course you have. Even in society today, we are sometimes identified by who our father is or was. To call someone like Donald Trump or Ronald Reagan your father implies a relationship that most people do not have with these men and would almost automatically cause a person to be treated differently.

This is the kind of relationship that Jesus claimed to have with His Father and that He in turn gave to us with our Father.

This is why the Pharisees were so angry with Jesus' teaching. Of course they were offended when he called them a brood of vipers and a whited sephulchre. But the worst offense was that He claimed to be equal with God; He called God His Father and said that He was one with the Father. According to Jewish law, this was a crime worthy of death—unless, of course, it was the truth.

Christians today are so accustomed to using the term "Father" to refer to God that we don't give it a second thought. Most of our prayers begin with the term. We may add descriptors such as "Our heavenly Father" or "Almighty Father," but the concept is almost always there. We have numerous hymns which also reinforce the idea that we are God's children. So we lose sight of how awesome that really is.

Before I accepted the Lord Jesus as my Savior and turned my life over to Him, I had a strong sense of obligation to God. I knew there was a God. I knew Jesus was His Son. And I was determined to do what I could to please Him (at least some of the time). I read my Bible every night, went to church every Sunday, and tried not to cuss. I was almost superstitious about doing these things; I did not want to offend God.

When I began attending a college Sunday School class, I realized that the other students in the class had a different relationship with God than I had, and I wanted it, too. I scheduled an appointment with the pastor and asked him, "How do I get the kind of relationship with God that those other students have?" (Wouldn't you love to be asked that kind of question?!) He explained God's plan of salvation, and I immediately prayed to receive Christ.

I remember walking to class the next day with a feeling of complete awe. As I looked at the world around me, I knew that the God who had created it all loved me personally. He had chosen me to be His child. I was a child of the King of the Universe! To this day I continue to be awed by that knowledge. If you have been a Christian for a while, reflect on who you are before God. He loves you, each of you, individually and personally. You are not just part of a vast population of humans—you are unique and special to God. And this relationship does not apply to everyone.

In the nineteenth century, according to R.C. Sproul,[8] a philosopher named Adolf von Harnack developed a view of religion that had two concepts at its core: the universal fatherhood of God and the universal brotherhood of man. You have probably heard those concepts expressed in one form or another. But are they true? And how do they affect the way we see ourselves before God?

If God is a universal Father, then He is the father of everyone in the same manner. Think of an earthly father. He may have several children with different mothers, but he is equally the father of all of them. If he were to single out one or two of his children for special favors, we would condemn him for his unequal treatment of his children. We would feel that all of his children belong to him and deserve an equal share of his love and attention.

Now think of a potter with a vast collection of pottery that he has created. Suppose he decides to put one of his pots on the coffee table in his living room and he uses another pot outside to hold the potting soil for his garden. He is treating those pots very differently, but would we condemn him for that? Would we insist that he must treat all of his creations equally? Of course not. He made the pots and he can decide how they are to be used.

So which one of the examples above is a better picture of God? Although many of us would prefer it to be the example of the father, that is not the picture that the Bible gives us. According to Romans 9, God has created us just as a potter creates a clay pot. He owns us because He has created us. And since we belong to Him, it is His decision how we are to be treated.

Now suppose that the potter is miraculously able to breathe life into his pots, and he chooses to do so. He selects certain pots, gives them life, and adopts them as his children. Think of the story of Pinocchio. He was a puppet, not a pot, but the idea is pretty much the same. Is the potter obligated to breathe life into all the pots? Not at all. He created them, they belong to him, and he can use them however he wants.

That is the picture of God. He has created us, He owns us, and He gives eternal life to whomever He chooses. Those are the people who are His children. We are given life and adopted by Him. He is the only one who can give us the right, or even the power, to become His children.

Now, back to the pots. How should those pots who have been brought to life behave? Should they look down on the other pots and misuse or abuse them? No, because all of the pots are the work of the potter. They should all be treated with dignity because they are all his creations. If the living pots love the potter, then they will take care of what he has made. Should the living pots feel pride that they have been given life? I wouldn't think so. Instead they should feel supremely grateful that they are alive.

So what about the "universal brotherhood of man"? Is everyone your brother or sister? Contrary to what you may have been taught, the answer is no. Although every human being is a creation of God, all human beings are not children of God. In both the Old and New Testaments, the term "brother" has one of two meanings. First, the word can refer to a sibling, the son of your father, mother, or both. Second, the word can refer to someone who shares your belief in God. Those who are outside the family of faith are referred to as friends, neighbors, or even enemies, but never as brothers. God also gives us instructions about how we are to treat people who are outside the faith, and we are always told to be kind to them. But there are special instructions about how we are to treat our "brothers."

If we have been adopted by God, we should not be proud of that fact, but humbly grateful for the incredible gift of life and sonship. We should give others who are also His children special consideration. And because everyone is a creation of God, and thus our neighbor, we should treat everyone we know with dignity and respect.

LESSON THIRTY-THREE
Praying to Honor God

Question 101: For what do we pray in the first petition?

Answer: In the first petition, which is, "Hallowed be your name," we pray that God would enable us, and others, to glorify Him in all the means by which he makes Himself known, and that he would arrange all things to His own glory.

1. What does the word "hallowed" mean?

Read Exodus 20:11 in the King James Version, then in a more modern translation.

2. What does the word "holy" mean?

Read Isaiah 5:16; Ephesians 5:27

3. God is holy. What other things does He call holy?

Read Genesis 2:3; Leviticus 27:21, 30; Numbers 18:19; Isaiah 56:7

4. How does God describe His people in Rome and Corinth?

Read Romans 1:7; 1 Corinthians 1:2

5. Were the Christians in Rome and Corinth completely righteous and blameless?

Read Romans 14:10; 1 Corinthians 3:3

6. Why were these people considered to be holy?

Read Leviticus 20:26; Deuteronomy 7:6; 1 Peter 2:9

7. How do we keep the name of God holy?

Read Isaiah 29:23; Ezekiel 20:39; Exodus 20:7

Question 102:

For what do we pray in the second petition?

Answer: In the second petition, which is, "Your kingdom come," we pray that Satan's kingdom may be destroyed, and that the kingdom of grace may be advanced, ourselves and others brought into it, and kept in it, and that the kingdom of glory may be hastened.

8. Where is the kingdom of God?

Read John 18:36

9. What are characteristics of those who are living in the kingdom of God?

Read Romans 14:17

10. How do we enter the kingdom of God?

Read John 3:3

Commentary
Lesson 33

Praying to Honor God
Catechism Questions 101 and 102

My grandfather was adamant about protecting the name of God. Nothing made him more angry than for someone to misuse God's name. On one occasion, my mother was driving him somewhere, and when they got out of the car, she accidentally slammed the car door on his hand. In her moment of distress, she said, "Oh my God!" With his hand still stuck in the door, my grandfather berated her for misusing God's name. He was more concerned with honoring God than with the pain he was obviously in.

And he was right. We must be careful not to use God's name when we are not specifically referring to Him. But there is much more involved in hallowing God's name; we must revere and honor all things having to do with God. And we must center our lives around giving Him all the glory.

I am in the middle of reading the book *Radical* by David Platt. Because I do not believe that anything happens by chance, I do not believe that it is by coincidence that the chapter I read last night concerned our duty to extend the glory of God. God knew I would be writing this today, and He wanted me to expand my understanding of what it means to glorify Him. Please indulge me as I tell you a couple of things Platt says in his book.

First, Platt says[9] that we were all created for two purposes: to enjoy God's grace and to extend His glory. (Sound familiar? If not, look at Catechism question 1, in the book *Created by God/Purchased by Christ*.) If we bother to think about God's grace at all, we are usually pretty good at enjoying it. It is not hard to be thankful for God's saving us and His providing for all of our needs. So that is not where Platt places his emphasis.

What does it mean to extend the glory of God and how do we do it? Platt refers to several Old Testament stories (Abraham; the Israelites crossing the Red Sea; Shadrach, Meshach, and Abednego; and Daniel. As he reminds us, the end result in each of these stories was that others besides the main characters began to glorify God. God blessed the men in these stories, but in doing so, He extended His glory to come from others.

Second, Platt begins to hit where it hurts. He asks what the gospel is all about. What is your answer? In your answer, is the word "me" or "I" in there somewhere? Is the gospel that Christ died for me? Or that God gave His Son so I could have eternal life? That is only a small part of the correct answer. The gospel is that the triune God determined that God the Son would come to earth, live a sinless life, die a cruel death, and be raised from the dead to save those whom the Father had given Him and who would believe in Him so that He might be glorified.

Do you see the difference? In the first two answers, the focus of the gospel is on me; in the last, the focus is on God. Where should the focus be? Does God bless me so that I can have a comfortable life? Does God design churches so I can be at ease as I attempt to worship Him? What does God want for my life—for me to be happy or for me to glorify Him? Or perhaps, does He want me to glorify Him so I can be truly and deeply joyful in His kingdom?

God's Kingdom is not of this world. When we pray for His kingdom to come, we are praying for one of two things. First, we could be praying for Christ to return and take us to His heavenly kingdom. Or second, we could be praying for Christ to enlarge His kingdom here on earth. I have decided to focus on the second option. How does Christ enlarge His kingdom here on earth? He could do it any way He wanted to, but in His infinite wisdom, He has decided to use people.

Look at Matthew 28:19 – "Go therefore and make disciples of all nations, baptizing them in the name of the Father and of the Son and of the Holy Spirit, [20]teaching them to observe all that I have commanded you." Is this a request, an invitation, or a command? Does Jesus tell us, "It would be really great if you would go into all the world and teach others about me"? Does He say, "Everyone is invited to participate in the sharing of the good news of the gospel with the rest of the world"? Does He say, "If you are called to do so, go into all the world and share the gospel"? Or does He simply tell us, "Go"?

What if we don't feel "called" to go? Then we should get over it, because we are all called. When we become part of the kingdom of God, we are called to go and tell others. If you have confessed your sins and yielded control of your life to Jesus (and that's what being born again means), then your primary purpose in God's kingdom is to spread the news—wherever God puts you. "Going" does not necessarily involve leaving your home town; there are plenty of people who need the gospel who live all around you. But "going" might involve a move. Would you be willing to do that?

I was at a church missions conference many years ago, and at the end of one sermon, the preacher asked us to stand if we were willing to serve God wherever He would lead us to go. Only a handful of people stood up. I was horrified. The preacher was not asking us to volunteer to go to Outer Mongolia or the inner city, he was just asking if we were willing to do what God wanted us to do! At least two hundred people in that congregation smugly sat there telling God, "Not me, buster. I'm staying right here."

So let me ask you. Are you willing? Will you do whatever God asks of you? Will you go wherever He sends you? He may want to keep you right where you are and have you extend His glory to those around you; but He might want to uproot you from where you have grown comfortable and complacent and plant you in a place where you can be of more service to Him. It's really not about us; it's all about Him.

Please don't say that missions is not your gift. It's not on the gift list. Everyone is commanded to serve God using the particular gifts God has given them. That's what missions is. My definition of missions is to extend the good news of Christ and the love of Christ to those who do not believe. It doesn't matter if they are on the other side of the world or live next door. There are so many types of missions. If our gift is mercy, we can serve the poor; if our gift is hospitality, we can house the homeless; if our gift is teaching, we can teach the prisoners, the children, and all those who need the gospel; if our gift is encouraging, we can lift up those who are troubled and discouraged.

Many people use the excuse that they don't want to go over-seas because they are concerned about the needs here at home. But are they truly serving God to help meet those needs? Do they volunteer at homeless shelters? Do they visit prisons? Do they help women with unplanned pregnancies? Do they assist victims of domestic abuse? Do they build homes for those who need them? Do they visit the sick (those they don't know)? There are lots of ways to glorify God. What are you doing?

Maybe you are thinking that you are doing some of those things, but you are using your gifts to serve the church. Of course we can use our gifts within the church; God wants us to do that. Churches are made up of people with needs and problems, and they need our help. But nowhere in Scripture does God tell us to limit the use of our gifts to the church. Certainly, we should glorify God by serving Him in the church, but let's not stop there. The Great Commission calls us to spread the Gospel, not just maintain it.

And while we're on the subject, are you concerned about getting credit for what you do in the church? If someone in your church made a list of people who have served in your church, would you be upset if your name wasn't on it? I think all of us are still sinful enough that we would resent that. But who is supposed to get the glory for the things done in God's name? Us or God? If our service is done to glorify ourselves, then maybe that's not the kind of service God wants.

God moves some people to places other than where they were born. He wants those people to serve him there. We call those people missionaries. Why? They are doing the same thing we are all supposed to be doing, they are just doing it in a new and different place. That doesn't excuse the rest of us for not doing anything. We each have gifts; if God has left us where we are, then He expects us to use those gifts where we are. What are you doing with your gift to help those both inside and outside the church body? Where do you think God wants to use you?

LESSON THIRTY-FOUR
Praying for God's Will and Our Own Needs

Question 103:

For what do we pray in the third petition?

Answer: In the third petition, which is, "Your will be done, on earth as it is in heaven," we pray that God, by His grace, would make us able and willing to know, obey, and submit to His will in all things, as the angels do in heaven.

1. What is God's will for us?

   Read 1 Thessalonians 4:3-6; 5:16-18

2. What else is God's will for us?

   Read 1 Peter 2:13-15; 3:17

3. What were we created for?

   Read Ephesians 2:10

4. What have we been predestined for?

   Read Romans 8:28-29

Question 104:

For what do we pray in the fourth petition?

Answer: In the fourth petition, which is, "Give us this day our daily bread," we pray that, of God's free gift, we may receive a sufficient portion of good things of this life, and enjoy His blessing with them.

5. What things do we need physically?

Read Matthew 6:31-32; Matthew 9:12; Psalm 142:6

6. How much do we need?

Read Exodus 16:18; Proverbs 30:8-9

7. What things do we need spiritually?

Read Luke 10:38-42; Acts 3:19; I Corinthians 12:21

Commentary
Lesson 34

Praying for God's Will and Our Own Needs

Catechism Questions 103 and 104

One thing I have noticed as I have been writing these Bible studies is that the more I deal with the doctrines of our faith, the more I realize how far I fall short of what God expects of me. This lesson has affected me greatly in this way. So as you read this study, please be aware that this one was written to me, and I pray that you will be convicted as I have been.

To begin, in the third petition of the Lord's Prayer, we pray for God's will to be done on earth. What exactly does that mean? And do we really, honestly, want that?

Let's look at what the Bible tells us about God's will for us. First, God's will is that we should be sanctified and conformed to the image of His Son, Jesus Christ. This requires that we live in a certain way. We should avoid sexual immorality and control our own bodies, and we should not wrong or take advantage of our brothers. We should be joyful always, pray continually, and give thanks in all circumstances. (All circumstances, not just the ones we like.) We are to submit to all earthy authorities and do good works to silence our critics. And finally, sometimes it is God's will for us to suffer for the sake of Christ.

Is this what you think about when you pray for God's will to be done? Are you really asking for God's will to prevail, or are you asking that God put His rubber stamp on your will? Are you thinking only of the "positive" aspects of God's will—that all men serve and love Him? Have you ever considered that God's will might mean your suffering for Him? That God might want you to change some of your behavior, or even your thoughts? Are there times when you have been opposed to your earthly authorities and said something like, "He's not my President!" But he is (or she is), no matter who holds that office.

He is your President because he has been elected by the people of the country; but more importantly, he is your President because God has put him in that position. Are you fighting God's will in this regard?

Are you joyful always? Of course we are all joyful at times, but I'm afraid that in my case that usually occurs when I get something I want or when everything's going my way. I am not usually joyful when I am suffering or especially when my children are suffering. I am not joyful when I hear dire predictions about the future of my country or its economy. I am not joyful when I have to do things I really don't want to do.

But I should be. God's will for me is to be joyful at all times, and He also wants me to be thankful in all circumstances. I must be thankful when God showers His blessings on me, and I must be thankful when He teaches me the lessons I need to learn. Those lessons are often not a lot of fun. They can be painful and require a lot of hard work and soul-searching. But I must be thankful. I must be thankful when I have plenty; and I must be thankful when I don't. I must be thankful when my friends support and encourage me; and I must be thankful when they criticize or neglect me. God tells us to be thankful in everything.

In the Lord's Prayer, we pray that God's will be done on earth as it is in Heaven; that is, that God's will be done perfectly. In Heaven, there is no sin; all of the angels and the saints who have been taken to be with the Lord are in perfect obedience to Him. Is that what you want for your life? To be in perfect obedience? What would you have to give up or change in order to accomplish that goal? Is that what you are praying for?

Not only do we pray for God's will to be done, which is honestly a little frightening, but the next thing we pray is that God would provide for our needs. "Give us this day our daily bread" asks God to give us what we need for each day, on a daily basis. There are two things to consider as we think about this petition: what our needs are, and the daily provision of those needs.

According to Scripture, what do we <u>need</u>? Using a complete concordance, I was able to find eight things that God says we need:

food, drink, clothing, medical care, rescue from our enemies, repentance, Jesus' teaching, and fellowship with other believers. That's all. Is that enough?

I like to watch TV shows about home makeovers and home buying and selling. I really don't know why I like those, but I do. Lately I have been paying more attention to the reasons the people are remodeling their homes or buying new ones. Most of them say that they need a more modern home or they need more space. Really? One couple with two children, living in a 2000 square foot home, were desperate for more space. Think about that for a minute. They were saying that 500 square feet each is not enough.

In 1862, Congress passed the Homestead Act, giving pioneers the opportunity to obtain land by living on the land, growing crops, and building a 12 x14 foot home. That is

168 square feet. For an entire family. Yet the family on that TV show couldn't live in a home where each person in the home had almost three times that much space! And we don't even need to go to the past for such figures. The average Habitat for Humanity home built in Kenya today has 365 square feet. The average house in Sweden has 1291 square feet. The average house in the United States has 2330 square feet.

Think about your own life. Do you have food, drink, clothing, and medical care? Are you being pursued by enemies? (Real enemies, not just disagreeable people.) Have you repented of your sins? Do you have a Bible? Do you have fellowship with other believers? If you have these things, then you have what you need. Anything else that you have is just gravy. All of the other things that you think you couldn't live without are blessings—good gifts that God has given you. How much paper would you need to make a list of every single thing that you have that does not fit into the list above?

When you pray, do you pray as though you need those extra things? Or are you honest in admitting that they are things you want? I personally think it's okay to ask God for what we want; He promises to give us the desires of our heart. But we don't need to fool ourselves. Most of what we want is just that—a want. And I am as guilty, or perhaps more guilty, of that than anyone else.

Okay, so if we will admit it, we don't need nearly as much as we have. We are supremely blessed. That's not all we are asking in the fourth petition of the Lord's Prayer. We are also asking that we be given what we need on a daily basis.

Remember the Israelites as they wandered in the desert. They were given manna every morning, but it didn't last until the next day (except on the Sabbath). They were only given enough for the day.

We are not in the habit of living from day to day. We stock up food for the week, month, or even year. We are able to do that because we have technology available that will preserve the food for us. But we need to recognize that God is still providing for us day by day. The technology could fail, a natural disaster could hit, and we could lose it all.

And it's not just food. Are you stocking up money to provide for yourself in the future? There is nothing wrong with saving; in fact, I encourage it. But how much is enough? Are you failing to give to the Lord or to the needy because you are hoarding money for your own future? God tells us to give to the needy and trust Him to provide for our needs. Remember that your bank account, your job, your retirement benefits, etc. all ultimately come from the Lord—not from the government, your employer, or your 401K.

When we pray for our needs, let's make sure they really are needs. If they are wants, then let's at least be honest enough to admit it. Let us all be willing to live according to God's will and to let Him provide for us. God loved you enough to sacrifice His own Son so that you could be with Him forever. Do you think He won't provide for you now?

LESSON THIRTY-FIVE
Praying for Forgiveness and Deliverance

Question 105:

For what do we pray in the fifth petition?

Answer: In the fifth petition, which is, "Forgive us our debts, as we also have forgiven our debtors," we pray that God, for Christ's sake, would freely pardon all our sins, which we are more encouraged to ask because by His grace we are enabled from the heart to forgive others.

1. How extensive is God's forgiveness?

   Read Jeremiah 31:34; Psalm 103:12

2. How does God describe His forgiveness of sins?

   Read Isaiah 1:18

3. What did Jesus say about our forgiving other people?

   Read Matthew 6:14-15

4. How did Paul describe a mature Christian?

   Read Ephesians 4:14-15

5. What is the situation for anyone who causes a young believer to sin?

Read Matthew 18:6

6. What did Jesus say about people who cause others to sin?

Read Luke 17:1

7. How are we to use the gifts God has given us?

Read I Peter 4:10

8. How are we to treat those who have fallen into sin?

Read Galatians 6:1

Question 106:

For what do we pray in the sixth petition?

Answer: In the sixth petition, which is, "And lead us not into temptation, but deliver us from evil," we pray that God would either keep us from being tempted to sin, or support and deliver us when we are tempted.

9. What does God promise when we are tempted to sin?

Read I Corinthians 10:13

10. Why is Christ able to help us endure temptation?

Read Hebrews 4:15

11. Who is it that tempts us to sin?

Read I Thessalonians 3:5; James 1:13-14

Commentary
Lesson 35

Praying for Forgiveness and Deliverance
Catechism Questions 105 and 106

I am pretty good at doing laundry now, but that hasn't always been the case. When my husband and I were newly married, I washed a load of clothes that included all types of fabrics and colors. As I took the clothes out of the dryer, I realized that all of his white shirts were now a blotchy pale pink. There was no way he could wear them. So I tried to get the color out. I ended up using a color-remover and boiling them on the stove, which really stunk up the house. And those shirts were never 100% white again.

Our sins are not a pale pink; they are bright blood red. Think of them as blood-stained clothes. But God can remove every hint of stain and make us white as snow. That is how He describes His forgiveness. He also tells us that He will take our sins and separate them from us as far as infinity and that He will not remember them. That means that when we pray, we must remember how our Father forgives us, and then forgive those whom we need to forgive. We must pray as a forgiven sinner who forgives others. So let's talk about forgiveness. What does it mean to forgive? In the study at the beginning of this lesson, I asked a lot of questions about this phrase, and you may have wondered where I was going. I want us to truly understand what forgiveness is and what it isn't.

We know that when someone wrongs us, we are supposed to forgive them. Does that mean that we are to cast their sins away and remember them no more? Jesus told Peter that we are to forgive our brother the same offense seventy-seven times (or seventy times seven). Does that mean that on that seventy-eighth (or four hundred ninety-first) offense, we can hold as much of a grudge as we want to? Does it mean that we must continue to allow someone to sin against us?

Let's apply a hypothetical example. Susan has a brother Larry, who is a drug addict. Larry has borrowed money from Susan on several occasions, only to use it to pay for his habit. He has been evicted from his home three times, and each time Susan has let him stay with her. Each time he has stolen items from her home to pawn, again to feed his habit. What does the Bible say about Susan's forgiveness of Larry?

First, the Bible says she must forgive. Does that mean she must promise never to remember what he has done? As my pastor, John Reeves, pointed out to me, that is an impossible promise. We do not have that kind of control over our memories. When the Bible says that God does not remember our sins, it does not mean that He has a cosmic memory lapse. He knows what we have done and He will always know it. It does mean that He will not dwell on it or bring it up to us ever again. That is something that we can promise.

Now back to Susan and her dilemma. She can promise never to bring up Larry's sins again. Does that mean that she must continue to "loan" him money and to let him "crash" at her place? What else does the Bible have to say about how we treat others? Paul tells us that if a brother is caught in sin, we are to restore him gently. That means that we are to lovingly confront the sinner about his/her sin. So Susan needs to confront Larry about his actions.

Some people's interpretation of the concept of forgiveness is that when you forgive, you are in effect saying, "It's all right. It doesn't matter. It's no big deal." Think of forgiveness from God's perspective. Do we really think that when God forgives our sin, He is telling us that it's all right—it's no big deal? Of course not. Our sins are a huge deal. Jesus Christ lowered Himself to take on human flesh and to be tortured and crucified because that was the price of our forgiveness. Forgiveness does not mean that the offense is not important. It means that we will not continue to dwell on the offense.

We are also told that we should never be the cause of someone else's sin. The psychological word for this is "enabling." An enabler is a person who helps, or enables, another to continue a negative behavior, or a sin. For Susan to continue to provide Larry with money, or even a place to stay, she would be acting as his enabler. She would be assisting him in his sinfulness.

Susan is also told to be a faithful steward of what God has given her. To allow her gifts from God to be used to further Larry's sin would be dishonoring to God. She is also told in Ephesians that a mature Christian is not misled by the cunning and craftiness of deceivers. I have had quite a bit of experience with addictive personalities, and I can attest to the fact that there are probably no more deceitful, cunning, and crafty people on the planet.

So my conclusion is that forgiveness does not mean that we are to be doormats, or enablers. Forgiveness is largely for our own benefit. Grudges can be very heavy things to carry around; forgiveness transfers that weight to Christ. There is amazing freedom in forgiveness.

To those of you who are dealing with an addict, an alcoholic, an adulterer, or anyone else caught up in sin, I want to admonish you to stop enabling. It can be painful to stop, but it can be more painful not to. Please remember that no one will stop his sinful, selfish behavior unless he decides to stop. Nothing you can say or do will make him or her change. It's like talking to air. Say what you have to say once or twice, then allow the addict, etc., in your life to live with the consequences of his own actions. Live your own life. Separate yourself from him them if you need to do that for your own mental health. I've been there and I know what you are going through. It will be hard, but you will be better in the long run.

It is interesting that when Paul tells us to restore those who are sinful, he also tells us to take care that we are not tempted. I have always understood that to mean that we should be careful that we do not begin to indulge in the same sinful lifestyle. Perhaps he also meant that we should not fall into the sin of enabling. Regardless of his meaning, though, we are to pray that we would not fall into temptation.

Where does temptation come from? Only two sources—the devil and our own desires. But how does the devil tempt us? Does he bring up things we never even wanted to do and try to tempt us to do them? He is much smarter than that. Satan and his legions are very observant of those who follow Christ. They know what sins we have committed in the past, and which ones are the hardest for us to resist.

Those are the sins they will tempt us with.

So really, it's just us. Our own desires are where the temptations come from. Whether we are encouraged by the evil one, or just by our own thoughts and feelings, we ourselves are to blame. Do you remember the comedian Flip Wilson? He had a variety show in the 1970's on which he played a number of characters. His most famous was a woman named Geraldine, whose most famous line was, "The devil made me do it!" Flip Wilson was really funny, but this excuse is really not. The devil can't make us do anything. We do things because we want to do them. And even Geraldine knew that.

So what do we do when we find temptation almost impossible to bear? When we really, really want to give in? We run as fast as we can to our Savior. He understands, because He endured every temptation that we will ever face. But He never succumbed; He resisted them all. So He can help us to resist. He knows exactly what you are going through, and he knows exactly how to beat it. Let him show you.

The problem is that much of the time, we don't really want to resist. We don't go to Jesus because we don't want His help. We want to use Geraldine's excuse. Give it up. Jesus knows better and so do you. Pray for the strength to fight temptation, and pray that you would not be tempted in the first place. Forgive others when they give in, but don't be the one who helps them continue to fall. Jesus told us to pray for these things because He promises to give them to those who ask.

LESSON THIRTY-SIX
The Kingdom, the Power, and the Glory

Question 107: What does the conclusion of the Lord's Prayer teach us?

Answer: The conclusion of the Lord's Prayer, which is, "For yours is the kingdom and the power and the glory, forever. Amen," teaches us to take our encouragement in prayer from God only, and in our prayers to praise Him, ascribing kingdom, power, and glory to Him, and in testimony of our desire and assurance to be heard, we say, "Amen."

1. To which people will God give His kingdom?

   Read Matthew 5:3, 10

2. Who will be called least and greatest in the kingdom of heaven?

   Read Matthew 5:19

3. Who will not enter the kingdom of heaven?

   Read Matthew 5:20

4. Who will enter the kingdom of heaven?

   Read Matthew 7:21

5. Where is the kingdom of God?

    Read John 18:36

6. How did Jesus show His power to those around Him?

    Read Luke 4:36, 6:19

7. What kind of power did Jesus give His disciples?

    Read Luke 9:1-3; 10:19

8. What kinds of things are under the power of Christ?

    Read John 13:3; Philippians 3:21

9. How was Pilate able to have power over Jesus?

    Read John 19:10-11

10. How did Paul describe the power of God?

    Read Ephesians 1:19-20

Commentary

Lesson 36

The Kingdom, the Power, and the Glory

Catechism Question 107

Where is your home? My answer to that would depend on the context. My current residence is in Mississippi; I have also lived in Oklahoma, California, Missouri, and South Dakota. But I consider Louisiana to be my home. However, none of those places is my real home. I am a citizen of Mississippi and of the United States, but more importantly, I am a citizen of the kingdom of God. My home, my real home, is in His kingdom.

So where is that exactly? In one sense, it's all around you. The kingdom of God is here on earth; the church is made up of its citizens. Have you ever met another American when in a foreign country? You instantly feel at home—here is someone from my home country. He or she will understand me and the way I think and behave.

Have you ever met a Christian in another country or city? You may dress differently and speak different languages, but there is a common bond and an uncommon affinity that draws you together. Again, he or she will understand how you think and behave—because again, you are citizens of the same kingdom.

God's Kingdom is not of this world, but it is in this world. We know we will enter His Kingdom when we die or when Jesus comes again. But we also live in the Kingdom now. Members of different cultures have different values and different ways of doing things. Have you noticed that the values of Christians are different from those who do not believe? Are there things that we do that others do not? There should be a difference. Our faith is to be lived out as we go through this life, because our culture is the culture of the Kingdom of God. We live here, but we are living in a foreign land. We can adapt to the culture of the country in which we live, but our true values and morals come from our "home country." And our home country will last forever. Nations come and go on earth. (If I ever manage to figure out all the countries in Africa, they change the next week!) But our Kingdom is here to stay because it is ruled and held together by the power of God Himself.

When we are confronted with the awe-inspiring majesty of creation, we become more truly aware of the power of God. Have you ever seen the Grand Canyon, the Rocky Mountains, or the Pacific Ocean? Were you awed by the splendor and power? We realize that there must be a powerful God to create such powerful scenery. How about a tornado, hurricane, tsunami, or other fierce storm? A friend of mine who is blind told me that he cannot see God's power in creation, but he can hear the thunder, and when he does, he feels the power of God.

Little children sing a song which goes, "My God is so big, so strong and so mighty, there's nothing that He cannot do." They have no doubts that God can do anything. But as adults we sometimes let the cares and worries of life overtake that knowledge. We seem to forget the power our God possesses. But remember the things Jesus did when He was on earth. He walked on water. Try that in your nearest puddle.

He told a storm to stop, and it stopped. The storm was so fierce that His disciples feared for their lives, but Jesus was sleeping. When they woke Him, He simply told the storm to stop. And it stopped instantly. Jesus fed thousands of people with five rolls and two fish. He healed people who had been sick, lame or blind for many years. He even raised people from the dead. Why do we doubt His power? Do we think that now that He is in Heaven, He has less power?! The majestic King of the Universe has lost His touch?!

But it's not Jesus alone who has power; He promised to give that power to us. Luke tells us that He gave power to the disciples to overcome all the power of the enemy. We know that Satan has power; the disciples were given more power. And we also have access to that same power. 2 Corinthians 10:3-4 tells us, "For though we live in the world, we do not wage war as the world does. The weapons we fight with are not the weapons of the world. On the contrary, they have divine power to demolish strongholds." In ourselves, we are powerless; but in God we have all the power of the Almighty because He works in us, through us, and beside us.

The kingdom and power belong to God alone, as does all the glory--forever. In a sense, God's power is manifested in His glory. Remember the story of Moses? He had been in close communion with God for forty days, and when he came down from the mountain, his face glowed with the reflected glory of God. It was so bright that he had to wear a veil or people could not bear to look at him. Imagine the brightest light you have ever seen. Now magnify that about a thousand times. Maybe that's close to the light of the glory of God. Remember that when Moses asked to see God, he was only allowed to see God's "back" because no one can live who sees the full unveiled glory of God. We are told in Revelation that the new earth will not need the sun, because the glory of God will provide our light forever.

Forever is a really long time. Think of what it means. We will live in perfect happiness, perfect unity, with no sadness, no hunger, no pain, no loneliness, forever. It will never stop. We will never be asked to give up the ones we love. There will be nothing that we need that is not provided. There will be no need to fear because there will be no sin. We will live in true joy—forever.

Suppose you were marooned on an island with a ship load of other people. Some of the people you like, but many you don't. There is a scarcity of resources, and some folks begin to hoard what they have, meaning that some people don't have enough. In an effort to survive, people begin to build shelters; some are hurt and even killed in the process. Fights break out. People steal from each other.

Then a small plastic raft lands on shore. The guy manning the raft tells you that he is there to take you to a ship that will take you home. The surf is rough and you will very likely be tossed around and get seasick, but you will eventually arrive at home. How would you feel? Would you be happy to see him? Would you get in that raft? Would you be excited to be going home?

That is exactly how we should feel about going to our eternal home. But many of us don't. Why not? We have willingly given our lives to Christ, but we don't want to go home. Maybe there is a fear of the unknown. But it is not really unknown; the best moments in our lives, those times that we want to remember and re-live over and over, are mere shadows of what our life will be when we go to our home that Jesus has prepared for us in His kingdom.

Our lives are meant to give glory to God. That is one of the two purposes for which we were created. Our chief end, our goal in life, our purpose, is to glorify God and enjoy Him forever. So it all fits together. Here we are, back at Catechism Question 1. Our lives can give God glory in His kingdom forever. God gives us His power to live those lives. We are His people, living in His kingdom. Let's enjoy Him.

Notes for Study Leaders

Introduction for Study Leaders

The Westminster Confession of Faith and the Shorter Catechism which grew out of it are statements of doctrine believed and preached by many. We believe that they contain the best summary of what God has revealed to us through His Word. But we do not believe that understanding all of this doctrine is necessary to salvation.

The truths contained in the Shorter Catechism cannot be understood unless a person first has come to a saving knowledge of Jesus Christ. These truths are spiritually understood; they do not make sense to the human mind without the guidance of the Holy Spirit. If your group contains members who have not yet come to know the Lord, this might not be the right time for this study. If you choose to continue with it, please remember that salvation comes first, then very slowly, the understanding of the knowledge of God.

The Shorter Catechism, or the Westminster Confession of Faith, is NOT the gospel. The Gospel is very simple. "Believe in the Lord Jesus Christ, and you will be saved." This means that we must understand that we are sinners and have broken the law of God, and that therefore we deserve to be punished. But Christ, in His mercy, took on our sins and died in our place. If we accept His death as punishment for our sins, and agree to live in obedience to Him, out of our love and gratitude to Him, we will live forever with Him in eternity. That is the Gospel. The Shorter Catechism seeks to teach believers the doctrine of what we call the Reformed faith.

If your group contains members who are Christians, but who are new to the some of these teachings, you may encounter opposition.. Be patient with these fellow believers. One of the essential and basic understandings of the Westminster Confession and Shorter Catechism is the sovereignty of God, the control of God over all things. I encourage leaders of this study to approach the study with this understanding. There are some doctrines in the Shorter Catechism that are difficult, if not impossible, for our human minds to understand.

We plead with you not to try to argue anyone into acceptance of these doctrines. Let God be God. He will lead each person into understanding at the perfect time for that person. Simply present the truth, with the Biblical evidence, and let the God who created us do the rest.

It is our prayer that this study may be used to glorify God, and to help us all enjoy Him forever.

Answers to Study Questions

Please do not rely solely on these answers. You may find more in the verses than I did. Also, please use the study questions to emphasize to your group that the doctrines in the Shorter Catechism all come from Scripture and not merely from the mind of man. Finally, some questions are of a personal nature, and it might be best not to ask group members to answer those questions out loud.

LESSON ONE

1. *This is our purpose, the reason for our creation. If we are believers in Christ, then we have two main purposes in life—to glorify God and to enjoy Him, and to do both of these things forever.*

2. *Always, in everything we do. There should be no part of life in which God is not considered and glorified.*

3. *When we obey God, we glorify Him, because we are giving Him first priority in our lives.*

4. *Obviously, we should glorify God forever.*

5. *Answers are personal and will vary.*

6. *First of all, to thoroughly enjoy God, He must be first in our hearts; He must take first place on our priority list. Second, we need to rejoice in what God has for us.*

7. *Jesus came to give us abundant life forever. He tells us in His Sermon on the Mount (Matthew 6) that He will provide all that we need. The book of Revelation describes heaven as a place where God also will provide for everything we could possibly need or want; even the very light in heaven comes from God Himself.*

8. *Answers will vary.*

9. *Answers will vary.*

10. *Scripture is "God breathed," or inspired by God. God used the*

personalities of the individual writers, but the Holy Spirit guided and directed what they were to write.

11. *Even before all of those other books were written, God knew about them and warned us against them.*

12. *This is one of many, many examples of instances where an Old Testament passage is quoted in the New Testament. In this case, it is quoted by Christ Himself.*

13. *We can learn about God and how we can best serve and glorify Him [teaching]. We can also learn what we are doing that does not glorify Him [reproof], and how we can change that [correction]. And we can learn how to be the person that God has intended us to be [training in righteousness].*

14. *Answers will vary.*

LESSON TWO

1. *God cannot be measured; He cannot be contained in earth or in heaven.*

2. *God is everlasting. He has been and will be forever.*

3. *God does not change. He is the same yesterday, today, and forever.*

4. *God's being is everywhere. He is the beginning and the end. He is the same always.*

5. *God made the earth by His power and wisdom. He is abundant in power; His understanding is beyond measure. He has sovereign power that will never pass away.*

6. *He has ordained His covenant forever; He is holy and awesome. The earth is full of His glory; the heavens declare the glory of God. The Lord is Holy, who was and is and is to come.*

7. *God loves justice; His love extends to the whole earth and the heavens above. God will reign forever and He will govern with justice. The Lord dispenses justice day after day without fail.*

8. *God is good to all He has made, and His love endures forever. No one is good except God; He is the very definition of goodness.*

9. *Jesus is the truth, and also the Holy Spirit. They will be with us forever. God's Word is truth. It judges all of creation. God's Word cannot be destroyed. It lives and endures forever.*

10. *God is alive. He lives and walks with us.*

11. *God is the only true God. Man-made gods cannot see or hear or eat or smell.*

12. *At Jesus' baptism, the Holy Spirit descended like a dove, and God the Father spoke. Jesus commanded us to go and make disciples of all nations, baptizing them in the name of the Father and of the Son and of the Holy Spirit.*

LESSON THREE

1. *His dominion is everlasting; his kingdom endures forever; he does according to His will. He has total control*

2. *God has a purpose for His word. He has a purpose for everything.*

3. *He had a purpose for Pharaoh. He has a purpose for believers.*

4. *His purpose for His Word will be accomplished.*

He had a purpose for Jeremiah before He was created.

He has purposes for things before they are created.

5. *The Lord has made <u>everything</u> for a purpose.*

6. *Answers will vary.*

7. *The earth, the waters, the mountains, the plants, the animals*

In other words, God created everything.

8. *By the word of the Lord. He spoke and it came to be.*

9. *The heavens declare the glory of God. The birds sing, the earth is satisfied, everything looks to God for their provision; God rejoices in His works*

10. *He guides us with His counsel.*

11. *He guides us by the Holy Spirit, who glorifies Him by taking what is Christ's and giving it to us.*

12. *Answers will vary.*

LESSON FOUR

1. *Absolutely nothing existed before God created it. There was no matter or energy or anything else before Creation.*

2. *God spoke everything into being. His power, made manifest through His spoken Word, is strong enough to create the entire universe.*

3. *"There was evening and there was morning." This would imply a literal twenty-four hour day. However, there is a possibility that this could be taken figuratively and not literally.*

4. *God created the light; the expanse; the land; the vegetation; the sun, moon, and stars; the sea creatures and birds; the creatures on earth; and man.*

5. *I Samuel 12:24 defines doing good as fearing the Lord and serving Him faithfully. At the time of Creation, everything that God created was obeying His commands and doing what it had been created to do.*

6. *The Spirit moved over the waters. The Holy Spirit was actively involved in Creation.*

7. *All things were made by Him (or through Him). Nothing was made without Him.*

8. *God exists in three persons—Father, Son, and Spirit. All three persons were actively involved in Creation, and discussed making man "in our image."*

9. *God formed man from the dust, and breathed into Him the breath of life. We do not know if this involved only the spoken word of God, or a more physical act, but the fact that the creation of man was different from the creation of all other creatures implies a special relationship between man and God.*

10. *Woman was formed from a rib of man. She also is part of the unique creation and relationship with God. Her creation is unlike any other creature that God made.*

11. *Answers will vary.*

LESSON FIVE

1. *God made both male and female in His own image. There is no difference in His eyes.*

2. *She is well known for her good deeds, such as bringing up children, showing hospitality, washing the feet of the saints, helping those in trouble and devoting herself to all kinds of good deeds.*

3. *She selects wool and flax and works with eager hands. She bring food from afar. She provides food for her family. She buys a field and from her earnings, she plants a vineyard. She sees that her trading is profitable. She opens her arms to the poor and extends her hands to the needy. Her household is clothed in scarlet; she is clothed in fine linen and purple. She makes linen garments and sells them, and supplies the merchants with sashes. She is clothed with strength and dignity; she can laugh at the days to come.*

4. *God is our help in times of trouble. He cares for those who trust in Him. He has clothed us with garments of salvation and arrayed us in robes of righteousness. He makes grass grow for the cattle, and plants for man to cultivate—bringing forth food from the earth.*

5. *We are to treat animals kindly and not abusively, as God does. We are to care for those that are entrusted to us. However, we are allowed to eat animals; God has given us every good thing for good.*

6. *Answers will vary.*

7. *God sustains the entire universe by the word of His power. He provides for each of His creatures so that they have what they need to survive.*

8. *God commands everything in His creation, and it obeys. From the sea to the weather to the wild animals—all of creation is under the control of God. Christ demonstrated His ultimate control of all of nature when He calmed the storm.*

9. *God watches over and protects His people in everything they do. As they remain and continue in His Word, He establishes them firmly and helps them to prosper.*

10. *God preserves all people in some ways, but He has special blessings for His people.*

11. *God has given us laws to obey for our own good. He establishes nations, and brings them down. He guides and directs His chosen people, and executes judgment on His enemies.*

12. *Answers will vary.*

LESSON SIX

1. *If they did not eat of the tree of the knowledge of good and evil, they would not die.*

2. *Not to eat of the tree of the knowledge of good and evil.*

3. *Eating of the tree of the knowledge of good and evil.*

4. *If we know what we should do, but don't do it, that is a sin.*

5. *To transgress is to disobey the law, to do something which you know is contrary to the law of God.*

6. *Answers will vary.*

7. *Answers will vary.*

8. *Eve added the phrase, "neither shall you touch it." She was not perfectly clear about what the law was.*

9. *He told her she would be like God.*

10. *We have no idea. The apple legend is just that, a legend.*

11. *Apparently it was easy. She gave it to him and he ate it.*

12. *They realized that they were naked, and felt shameful about it, so they made loincloths to cover themselves*

LESSON SEVEN

1. *All mankind was included. Through their disobedience, Adam and Eve brought sin and death into the world.*

2. *Mankind now had the knowledge of good and evil. Each new generation would also have that knowledge. Since sin and death had now entered the world, all mankind were now sinful and would die.*

3. *All mankind is now sinful and will die. Our lives will be difficult on earth.*

4. *Everyone is sinful. There is no one who obeys God perfectly.*

5. *We all continue to live in sin until we are changed by the Holy Spirit. We are dead in our sins, children of God's wrath.*

6. *To be cast away from God, for God's face to be hidden, to be in terror, to be totally alone with our fears.*

7. *Those without God receive His wrath; he has given them over to become the perpetrators and victims of all types of sin, leading ultimately to death. Those with God can call on Him, who cares for them, and will guard their hearts and minds and give them peace.*

8. *The believer will inherit a share in the kingdom of God; the unbeliever will be cast into the everlasting fire.*

9. *A place where the worm does not die and the fire is not quenched.*

10. *Hell was created to punish the devil and his angels. Satan will be a prisoner in hell, not a ruler. Satan is on earth, prowling around, looking for someone to devour.*

LESSON EIGHT

1. *God's plan was established before the foundation of the world.*

2. *He predestined us in love, according to His own purposes.*

3. *Everyone is sinful. No one is righteous in God's eyes. No one seeks God; no one does good.*

4. *Answers will vary.*

5. *Since everyone is sinful, then no one can save himself or herself. So Christ died to pay for the sins of those who believe in Him, and was raised from the dead.*

6. *Christ has always existed.*

7. *Christ is a part of the Trinity, one of the three persons of the Godhead. He is called the Son. He is the same as God. He is the only person who has ever lived who can claim that distinction.*

8. *Christ's conception was miraculous. He had no human father.*

9. *First, this was a sign of the birth of the Messiah, the Christ. Second, in order for him to be completely holy, the Son of God, he had to have no human father.*

10. *People touched him, from his birth to his death. He did things that men do, he walked around, talked, ate, and even died.*

11. *Christ gave much evidence of His deity; He healed the paralyzed man to affirm that He had the authority to forgive sins; he calmed the storm; He raised Jairus' daughter from the dead; He walked on water; and most importantly, He rose from the dead, conquering death itself.*

12. *Christ was fully man, and was tempted to sin in every way that we are tempted. However, He was also fully God, and therefore was able to live a sinless life. When we receive Christ as Lord and Savior, His righteousness is counted as ours, thus allowing us to become a part of God's kingdom.*

LESSON NINE

1. *A prophet speaks to the people and tells them what God has commanded him to say.*

2. *Through His Word, Christ teaches us, among many things, how not to sin and how to answer others; He gives us hope, good judgment,*

knowledge, and understanding.

3. Jesus has sent the Holy Spirit to teach us and to help us remember the things we have learned in God's Word. There may be times when we have to depend on the Spirit alone for guidance when we are placed in difficult positions.

4. The priests were to sacrifice offerings to make atonement for the sins of the people, and the high priest was to enter the Holy of Holies once a year to intercede for the people. They also were to pray for the people.

5. People were to bring offerings and sacrifices to the Lord for a number of reasons, primarily for forgiveness. Once a year, an offering of atonement was made, which paid for the sins of the people for the previous year.

6. The animals offered were to be without blemish.

7. Christ gave Himself as a sacrifice for our sins, just as the animals were sacrificed in the Old Testament system. He was without sin, or without blemish, so only He was a worthy sacrifice.

8. Christ always lives to intercede for His followers. His prayer in John is an example of how He prays for us.

9. Kings should go out before us and fight our battles; decree what is just; punish the wicked.

10. We are controlled by the Holy Spirit, if we are believers in Christ.

11. He defends those who cannot defend themselves. More importantly, through His shed blood, He defends us against the wrath of God.

12. The Lord will exact vengeance. We are to repay evil with good. He will repay the faithless with their reward here on earth, and their punishment in eternity.

LESSON TEN

1. He gave up equality with God and took on human form. He was born in a stable.

2. Christ was tempted in all the ways we are. He lived a hard life, and died on the cross.

3. As He was crucified, Jesus endured the wrath of God, suffering for our sins. God had forsaken Him. There were signs such as darkness, earthquake, the rocks were broken and the curtain of the temple was torn in two.

4. It was done hurriedly, in secret.

5. Through the resurrection, Christ has destroyed death and the devil himself. Because He was raised from the dead, we will be raised as well.

6. Jesus was lifted up until He disappeared into the clouds.

7. The right hand is a place of honor, and Christ now once again is in authority over all of creation.

8. The sun, moon, and stars will grow dark; everyone will see Christ coming on the clouds with power and glory. There will be the sound of a trumpet, and the dead in Christ will rise, followed by those who are still alive.

9. No one seeks God. Everyone has sinned and fallen short of the glory of God.

10. We receive salvation by confessing that Jesus is Lord and by believing in Him.

11. Our faith to believe is the gift of God.

LESSON ELEVEN

1. The Holy Spirit comes from Christ to convict us of our sin and His righteousness, using the law of God.

2. The Holy Spirit changes us. He makes us into a new creation through a new birth.

3. The things of God are foolishness to those without the Holy Spirit, because they are spiritually discerned.

4. No one can come to Christ unless he or she is first drawn to Christ by God, so the only people who are saved are the people who are effectually called.

5. *Anyone who comes to God will be received by God. Wanting to be saved is an indication that a person is effectually called.*

6. *A person may receive Christ at any point in his or her life until death.*

7. *Salvation is the work of God. He makes us alive in Christ.*

8. *God chose us before the beginning of the world.*

9. *He called us because of His own purpose and grace that we should be holy and blameless before Him.*

10. *Because what can be known about God has been shown to them through creation; but even though they know these things about God, they have refused to honor Him or give thanks to Him.*

11. *God uses people to carry His message. In order for others to believe in Christ, they must hear the Gospel, and in order for them to hear the Gospel, it must be preached.*

LESSON TWELVE

1. *Christ lived in perfect obedience to God, then died to pay the penalty for the sins of others.*

2. *He chose to adopt us in accordance with His pleasure and will.*

3. *God chose us in our weakness, lowliness, and foolishness; and it is because of Him that we are in Christ.*

4. *The Holy Spirit does the work of sanctification.*

5. *Suffering produces perseverance, perseverance produces character, character produces hope.*

6. *God sent Jesus Christ to die for our sins; He made us alive in Christ when we were dead in our sins; He calls us His own children.*

7. *God created us for heaven and has given us the Holy Spirit as a guarantee of our eternity in heaven. God keeps us in His hand, and no one can snatch us away.*

8. *Immediately at their death.*

9. *The dead in Christ will rise first, then those who are still alive will rise.*

10. *Jesus will acknowledge us because we believe in Him. We will inherit the kingdom prepared for us before the foundation of the world.*

LESSON THIRTEEN

1. *They would be strong and able to possess the land. They would have rain for their harvest—grain, new wine, and oil—and grass for their livestock.*

2. *Obedience is more pleasing to God than sacrifice. Sacrifice can be done even in disobedience to God.*

3. *Acting justly, loving mercy, and walking humbly with God; caring for widows and orphans; keeping ourselves undefiled from the world.*

4. *The requirements of the law are written on our hearts, or in our conscience.*

5. *The moral law teaches us what is right and wrong in the eyes of God.*

6. *God met Moses at the top of Mt. Sinai. God Himself spoke the words of the Ten Commandments.*

7. *God Himself engraved the commandments on two stone tablets.*

8. *Moses was on the mountain for forty days and nights. While he was gone, the people grew impatient and afraid and demanded an idol, so Aaron made them a golden calf. When Moses came down and saw them worshiping the calf, he threw the tablets down and broke them.*

9. *God made Moses carve out new tablets and bring them up the mountain, then God wrote the commandments on the new tablets.*

10. *Jesus Christ Himself gave us the summary of the Ten Commandments. Moses also summarized the first four commandments.*

11. *Answers will vary.*

12. *Answers will vary.*

LESSON FOURTEEN

1. *The Egyptians worked them ruthlessly, working with bricks and mortar and in the fields.*

2. *Even though they were ordered to kill the baby boys, the midwives did not do so. Therefore the Israelites increased in number.*

3. *We are slaves to sin and to fear.*

4. *We are full of envy, murder, strife, deceit and malice. We are gossips, slanderers, God-haters, insolent, arrogant, boastful; disobedient to our parents, senseless, faithless, heartless, and ruthless. Temptation leads to sin and sin eventually leads to death. And we are afraid of death.*

5. *The Son (Christ) sets us free by his death. We do not need to live in fear because we can rest in His love and care for us.*

6. *The Lord made heaven and earth and He reigns forever. He created each of us, and He redeemed us to be His children.*

7. *No one will be declared righteous by observing the law. Our salvation is by grace, not by works.*

8. *The law makes us conscious of sin.*

9. *Answers will vary.*

10. *We are told to be holy in everything we do, because God is holy. We show that we love God by obeying His commands. God knows what is best for us.*

11. *He is our Creator, and His understanding is unfathomable.*

12. *If we pay attention to His guidance, we will have abundant peace and righteousness.*

LESSON FIFTEEN

1. *We are obligated to walk in his ways, to keep his decrees, commands and laws, and to obey him.*

2. *The Lord searches every heart and understands every motive behind the thoughts. He knows whatever we do and whatever we think.*

3. *Give Him the glory He is due; worship Him in gladness with joyful songs. Worship Him in spirit and truth. Live in a way that is glorifying to God. Worship Him in reverence and awe.*

4. *We glorify God when we are joyful, when we pray, when we give thanks, when we examine the Scriptures, and when we show love to others. When we obey God, we glorify Him, because we are giving Him first priority in our lives.*

5. *The fool says in his heart, "There is no God."*

6. *The wrath of God is revealed against them; their thinking becomes futile and their hearts are darkened; they become fools. God gives them over to all kinds of sin and depravity.*

7. *We can still engage in sexual immorality, impurity, lust, evil desires and greed, which Scripture says is idolatry.*

8. *Answers will vary*

9. *It is detestable, abominable, evil*

10. *God is angry and jealous when other gods are worshiped.*

11. *God is jealous for what belongs to Him; He wants to protect and preserve what is rightfully His.*

LESSON SIXTEEN

1. *Because God is Spirit.*

2. *They made an idol in the shape of a calf, and bowed down to it and sacrificed to it.*

3. *He said they were celebrating a festival to the Lord.*

4. *We must worship in spirit and in truth.*

5. *We should have teaching, fellowship, breaking of bread, and prayer. Sing psalms, hymns, and spiritual songs. Bring our tithe.*

6. *For everyone, including those in authority over us.*

7. *Bowing down to the image, crying out to the image, treating the image as though it had the power of God.*

8. *We can say the right words, but our hearts are not right with God; we can create our own rules that we require others to follow.*

9. *He created us and gives us our being. It is for His pleasure that all things exist*

10. *Offer our bodies as living sacrifices as our spiritual act of worship.*

LESSON SEVENTEEN

1. *God told Moses, "I am who I am." He also said to Moses, "Say to the Israelites, 'The LORD, [c] the God of your fathers—the God of Abraham, the God of Isaac and the God of Jacob—has sent me to you.' This is my name forever, the name by which I am to be remembered from generation to generation.'*

2. **The LORD** *is his name.*

*The LORD, whose name is **Jealous**, is a jealous God.*

*It is good to praise the LORD and make music to your name, O **Most High**,*

*The **LORD Almighty** is his name.*

*"Therefore this is what the **Sovereign LORD** says...*

*the LORD, whose name is **God Almighty**.*

*She will give birth to a son, and you are to give him the name **Jesus,** because he will save his people from their sins."*

*Simon Peter answered, "You are the **Christ,** the Son of the living God."*

*But the Counselor, the **Holy Spirit,** whom the Father will send in my name*

3. *Cry out, "Save us, O God our **Savior.**"*

*He who is the **Portion of Jacob** is not like these, for he is the **Maker of all things,***

*This is the name by which he will be called: **The LORD Our Righteousness.***

*Yet their **Redeemer** is strong; the LORD Almighty is his name.*

*But the **Counselor,** the Holy Spirit, whom the Father will send in my name*

By Him we cry, "**Abba, Father.**"

4. *Answers will vary.*

5. *To call on the name of the Lord means to acknowledge that Jesus is Lord and to accept Him as Lord and Savior. It can also mean to call on God for help in times of trouble.*

6. *People began to call on the name of the Lord in the time of Seth, at the beginning of human history.*

7. *Revere His glorious and awesome name; sing to His name, rejoice before Him; praise His name; bring offerings to His name; fear His name; honor His name*

8. *Cursing God's name; misusing God's name; failing to obey God's laws; not giving God His proper offering; failing to listen to God; serving God for our own selfish purposes*

9. *God says that He will punish the guilty and their children, to the third and fourth generation.*

10. *Answers will vary.*

LESSON EIGHTEEN

1. *We are to work on those six days.*

2. *To bring a profit; to enjoy; to have something to share with others; to earn the respect of others and to provide for our own needs*

3. *If a man will not work, he shall not eat.*

4. *We are working for the Lord.*

5. *The Sabbath was created for man to rest and to worship the Lord.*

6. *Jesus rose from the dead on the first day of the week.*

7. *Works of mercy; resting; reading the Scripture; preaching and teaching*

8. *Stop meeting together; normal work*

9. *The first person to observe the Sabbath day was God Himself.*

10. *Answers will vary.*

11. *Answers will vary.*

LESSON NINETEEN

1. *Children are to obey their parents.*

2. *Giving them respect; listening to their instruction and teaching; providing for their needs when they are older.*

3. *Attack them or curse them; despise them; rob them.*

4. *It is the first commandment with a promise.*

5. *We leave our father and mother and are united to our husband or wife.*

6. *If we need to leave them for the sake of Christ.*

7. *They should be less important to us than Christ.*

8. *Do not despise them; do not treat them harshly; treat them with purity.*

9. *We are to treat all older people as though they were our fathers and mothers*

10. *Answers will vary.*

LESSON TWENTY

1. *Murder is intentionally taking the life of another person.*

2. *Accidentally killing someone is not murder.*

3. *Killing someone during a righteous war is not murder.*

4. *Capital punishment is not murder.*

5. *Before we are born.*

6. *He or she should feed and care for it.*

7. *Provide food, water, clothing, shelter, and medical care for the needy. Speak for those who cannot speak for themselves. Protect the innocent from evil men.*

8. *Your body is a Temple of the Holy Spirit. It is not your own; it belongs to God.*

9. *Anyone who is angry with his brother is subject to judgment.*

10. *We should treat them with respect and care for their needs.*

11. *Take care of their needs. Treat them with honor.*

12. *Answers will vary.*

LESSON TWENTY-ONE

1. *Sleeping with another man's wife; defiling the marriage bed, being sexually impure.*

2. *If a man divorces his wife and marries someone else, unless his wife has been unfaithful, he has committed adultery. The same is true for wives.*

3. *The husband and wife are to leave their parents and become one flesh.*

4. *One.*

5. *Marital unfaithfulness.*

6. *If a person has an unbelieving spouse and the spouse leaves the marriage, the believing spouse is freed from the marriage.*

7. *If you look at someone lustfully, you have committed adultery in your heart.*

8. *Obscene talk, coarse jokes, vulgar references are all forms of sexual impurity.*

9. *It is better to marry than to be immoral or to burn with passion. There should not be even a hint of sexual immorality.*

10. *Sex is an important part of marriage, and each spouse's body belongs to the other. Neither spouse should deny the other.*

11. *Answers will vary.*

LESSON TWENTY-TWO

1. *We can defraud our neighbor or rob him; we can hold back wages from those we hire; we can move boundary lines and steal property.*

2. *Not trying to please them; not being trustworthy.*

3. *We can fail to pay them on time; we can deprive them of justice;*

we can deprive them of their rights.

4. By failing to give Him the tithes He is due; by giving Him less than the best.

5. Through diligent work; through fear of the Lord; through wisdom.

6. Riches do not endure; wealth is uncertain; it can be destroyed or stolen.

7. We should trust God to provide for our needs.

8. We just ask for just enough to satisfy our needs

9. Stop stealing and work, share with those in need.

10. Our treasure should be in heaven.

11. Answers will vary.

LESSON TWENTY-THREE

1. They will not go free; they will perish.

2. Helping an evil man by being a malicious witness; participating in a false charge; putting an innocent person to death.

3. Put off falsehood and speak truthfully. Encourage one another and build each other up. Warn those who are idle. Help the weak. Be patient with everyone.

4. He destroys those who tell lies; He hates them; they are detestable to Him.

5. The devil is the father of lies.

6. Insincere flattery; false words and lying visions; dishonest scales [dishonest business practices.

7. All of his officials become wicked. He may lose his position.

8. We like the lies. [They tell us what we want to hear.]

9. They flatter God, but they lie, because they are not faithful to Him. They appear as wolves in sheep's clothing. Their outward appearance is deceiving. They are conceited and understand nothing.

10. *She hid the Israelite spies, then lied to the soldiers who were looking for them by telling them that the spies had gone a different way. Then she helped the spies escape and told them how to avoid getting caught.*

11. *She was given a place in the ancestry of Christ, she was not killed; she was considered righteous.*

12. *Answers will vary.*

LESSON TWENTY-FOUR

1. *It means to want something that belongs to someone else.*

2. *To be content in every circumstance, in plenty and in want; being content with food and clothing.*

3. *Keep yourself free from the love of money and remember that God is always with you.*

4. *They plot evil; they covet property and take it, defrauding neighbors of their homes and their inheritance.*

5. *God knows what we need even before we ask; if we seek His kingdom and His righteousness, He will provide everything we need.*

6. *He gives good gifts, more than we can ask or imagine.*

7. *It can lead to murder and quarrels. God will not answer our prayers because we are asking for the wrong reasons. It destroys us inwardly. It makes us hate our neighbors.*

8. *Our work is meaningless.*

9. *We should consider them as better than ourselves.*

10. *We should ask God, but we must ask according to His will.*

11. *Answers will vary.*

LESSON TWENTY-FIVE

1. *Commit our hearts fully to the Lord, live by His decrees, and obey His commands.*

2. *There is no one who does what is right and never sins. No one does good.*

3. *We are not righteous before God.*

4. *We are deceiving ourselves and calling God a liar.*

5. *Those who committed murder or kidnapping were to be put to death.*

6. *A thief was to make restitution for what he had stolen.*

7. *Adam and Eve ate the forbidden fruit.*

8. *The serpent told her she would be like God, knowing good and evil.*

9. *We have sinned against God. Rejecting the truth and following evil. Gratifying the desires of our sinful nature.*

10. *Disobeying the commands of God, failing to honor God's name, not doing everything written in the Law.*

11. *We can be foolish, our ways can lead to death, we cannot see the heart.*

LESSSON TWENTY-SIX

1. *The wrath of God.*

2. *There is no one who does what is right and never sins. No one does good.*

3. *God requires a blood sacrifice as payment for sins.*

4. *The sacrifices of animals were not enough to pay for all of our sins. Therefore Christ Himself took on a body and paid the ultimate sacrifice, which was enough to pay for all sin for all time.*

5. *They must suffer the "second death" in the lake of fire.*

6. *Confess that Jesus is Lord and believe that God raised Him from the dead.*

7. *We repent of our sins.*

8. *To repent means to have a change of heart; to admit that we have sinned and acted wickedly.*

9. *No one can come to Christ unless the Father has made him able to come.*

10. *No one can say Jesus is Lord except by the Holy Spirit.*

11. *Be doers of the word and not hearers only; humble ourselves and be obedient.*

LESSON TWENTY-SEVEN

1. *True repentance leads us to eternal life and abundant, full life here on earth.*

2. *We were dead in our transgressions, but God made us alive in Christ by giving us the gift of faith. Before the beginning of time, God saved us and called us to a holy life, but not because of anything we had done. God did not have to do this, but He did it anyway.*

3. *We sin if we do not follow God's ways or obey His laws; we sin if we fall short of His glory.*

4. *We become conscious of sin through the law of God. The Holy Spirit convicts us of sin.*

As we meditate on the Word of God, we become conscious of our own sin.

5. *First, we must understand that Christ died for us when we did not deserve it, when we were still sinners.*

6. *The Holy Spirit is given to us to help us to turn from our sins and live according to the laws of God.*

7. *No one can obey the entire law of God by his own human effort. We are weakened by our sinful nature and our minds are set on what that nature desires.*

8. *We should obey His commands; obey the Word of God.*

9. *If we claim that we do not sin, we are deceiving ourselves and calling God a liar.*

10. *We should confess our sins, and He will forgive them and cleanse us from our unrighteousness.*

LESSON TWENTY-EIGHT

1. *The Word is the Scripture, which men received from God the Holy Spirit.*

2. *Baptism and the Lord's Supper*

3. *Jesus taught us how to pray in the Lord's Prayer.*

4. *The elect are those who have been chosen by God for salvation.*

5. *Jesus, John the Baptist, the disciples, Peter and John, Phillip, Paul*

6. *Devote himself to the public reading of Scripture, to preaching and teaching.*

7. *People cannot believe in Jesus if they have not heard of Him, and they cannot hear about Him if no one preaches about Him.*

8. *We must pay attention to the Word, as we would to a light shining in a dark place. We should seek out opportunities to read and hear the Word.*

9. *We should ask God to open our eyes so that we can understand His Word.*

10. *Receive the Word with a noble and good heart, remember it, obey it, and trust it.*

11. *Remembering the Word will help us not to sin and will encourage us in difficult times.*

12. *We are not to merely listen or read, but to do what it says*

LESSON TWENTY-NINE

1. *He will teach us what to say to those who oppose us; help us to remember what we have learned about Christ; give us power; pours God's love into our hearts*

2. *Christ told us to make disciples from all nations, baptizing them in the name of the Father and of the Son and of the Holy Spirit.*

3. *At His last Passover supper, Jesus told His disciples that the bread was His body and the wine was the blood of the covenant which would be poured out for many for the forgiveness of sins.*

4. *Jesus Himself told us to do this before He ascended into Heaven.*

5. *The dying thief believed and was saved even though he had no chance to be baptized.*

6. *An adult must believe in the Lord Jesus Christ in order to be baptized.*

7. *In the Old Testament, the sign of the covenant was circumcision.*

8. *All males 8 days of age or older were to be circumcised.*

9. *Men are no longer required to be circumcised to represent their covenant with God.*

10. *The sign that we believe in Jesus is baptism.*

11. *Everyone in the households of Lydia and the Philippian jailer was baptized. We may assume that those households included young children.*

12. *Both the eunuch and Phillip went down into the water.*

13. *They heard the sound of a rushing wind, then tongues of fire came down and touched each of them.*

14. *Personal answers. Do not ask group members to share.*

LESSON THIRTY

1. *The Lord's Supper was instituted by Jesus Christ the night before He was crucified.*

2. *The bread represents the body of Christ.*

3. *The wine represents the blood of Christ.*

4. *They were eating too much, getting drunk and not regarding others.*

5. *That they despised the church of God and those who have nothing.*

6. *We are to examine ourselves.*

7. *Wait for one another; eat at home if you are hungry.*

8. *We proclaim the Lord's death.*

9. *We are given no specific instructions about how often we should observe the Lord's Supper.*

10. *He received these instructions from the Lord.*

11. *Personal answers.*

LESSON THIRTY-ONE

1. *Supplication, blessing of others; confession; thanksgiving*

2. *Help, mercy, guidance, relief from afflictions and pains, healing, avoiding temptation, provision for our daily needs*

3. *To be able to go and preach; to be rescued from unbelievers; for the perfection of other believers; for strength and understanding for other believers; for boldness to preach the Gospel*

4. *God is near to us when we pray to Him; if we humble ourselves and pray and seek His face and turn from our wicked ways, He will hear.*

5. *Jesus told us to continue to pray.*

6. *We should pray in secret, and not with lots of repetitious words.*

7. *We can pray in general, and the Holy Spirit will pray for us.*

8. *We can expect a peace that can only come from God.*

9. *Scripture tells us that the prayers of the righteous are powerful and effective*

LESSON THIRTY-TWO

1. *He was teaching in Galilee.*

2. *Jesus was praying, and one of the disciples asked Him to teach them to pray.*

3. *No, because Jesus instructed us not to keep babbling like the pagans.*

4. *We are to pray with our minds focused on what we are saying.*

5. *We must receive Christ and believe in His name.*

6. *He said that He was the Son of God.*

7. *Everyone who does the will of our Father in Heaven.*

8. *A brother is someone who believes in Jesus Christ and follows His teaching.*

9. *Love him, pray for him, feed him, give him something to drink*

LESSON THIRTY-THREE

1. *Hallowed means holy.*

2. *To be completely righteous, blameless.*

3. *The Sabbath, A field, a tithe, the offerings, a mountain*

4. *His holy people.*

5. *No. They judged one another and quarreled.*

6. *They were chosen by God and set apart for Him, His special possession.*

7. *Acknowledge the holiness of God, stand in awe of Him; do not worship idols; do not misuse His name.*

8. *The kingdom of God is not in this world; it is from another place.*

9. *Righteousness, peace, and joy in the Holy Spirit.*

10. *We must be born again.*

LESSON THIRTY-FOUR

1. *Be sanctified, avoid sexual immorality, learn to control our body, and not wrong or take advantage of a brother, be joyful always, pray continually, give thanks in all circumstances.*

2. *Submit to authorities so that by doing good we will silence foolish men; sometimes to suffer for doing good.*

3. *To do good works.*

4. *To be conformed to the likeness of Christ.*

5. *Food, drink, clothing, medical care. rescue from our enemies*

6. *Not too much, not too little (Just enough)*

7. *Jesus' teaching, repentance, fellowship with other believers*

LESSON THIRTY-FIVE

1. *He will remember our sins no more; He will remove them as far as the east is from the west.*

2. *Our sins are scarlet red, but He makes them white as snow.*

3. *If we forgive others, God will forgive us. If we do not forgive others, God will not forgive us.*

4. *Not deceived by the cunning and craftiness of others, but speaking the truth in love, we will grow to be a mature body.*

5. *It would be better for him to drown.*

6. *Woe to those who cause others to sin.*

7. *We should serve others as faithful stewards of God's gifts.*

8. We should restore them gently, taking care that we are not tempted.

9. *He will provide a way out, so that we will not sin.*

10. *He has been tempted in every way that we are tempted.*

11. *We are tempted by the devil, and by our own desires.*

LESSON THIRTY-SIX

1. *The poor in spirit, those who are persecuted because of righteousness.*

2. *The least will be those who teach others to disregard God's commands; the greatest will be those who practice and teach His commands.*

3. *Those whose righteousness does not surpass that of the Pharisees and teachers of the law.*

4. *The one who does the will of the Father in heaven.*

5. *It is not of this world. It is from another place.*

6. *He gave orders to impure spirits and they obeyed; power came out from Him and healed everyone who touched Him.*

7. *Power to drive out demons, to cure diseases, to trample on snakes and scorpions, and overcome all the power of the enemy.*

8. *All things are under His power.*

9. *Pilate only had power over Jesus because he was given that power by God.*

10. *Incomparably great power, the same as the mighty strength by which He raised Christ from the dead.*

Notes

Books about Creation and Creation Science

Ashton, John F. *In Six Days: Why Fifty Scientists Choose to Believe in Creation*. Master Books, 2001.

Behe, Michael. *Darwin's Black Box: The Biochemical Challenge to Evolution*. Free Press, 2006.

Denton, Michael. *Evolution: A Theory in Crisis*. Adler and Adler, 1986.

Dembski, William, ed. *Uncommon Dissent: Intellectuals Who Find Darwinism Unconvincing*. Intercollegiate Studies Institute, 2004.

Ham, Ken. *The Lie: Evolution*. Master Books, 1987.

Johnson, Philip E. *Darwin on Trial*. Intervarsity Press, 1993.

Morris, Henry M. *Scientific Creationism*. Master Books, 1974.

Sarfati, Jonathan. *Refuting Evolution*. Creation Book Publishers, 2008.

Strobel, Lee. The *Case for a Creator: A Journalist Investigates Scientific Evidence that Points Toward God*. Zondervan, 2005.

Whitcomb, John. *The Genesis Flood*. P & R Publishing, 1960.

Additional Scriptures on Election / Effectual Calling

John 6:38-39

John 10:28-29

John 17:1-3

Romans 1:6

Romans 8:30

I Corinthians 1:9

I Corinthians 1:23-24

Ephesians 1:11

I Thessalonians 1:4-5

I Peter 1:1-2

I Peter 5:10

I Peter 2:9

Hebrews 9:15

Jude 1:1

(Endnotes)

1   "Grace." Dictionary.com. 2010.

2   "The Wit and Wisdom of Benjamin Franklin." *Saturday Evening Post.*
p. 19. Nov/Dec 2007.

3   *Saturday Evening Post.*

4   Ron Kurtus. "Benjamin Franklin's Thirteen Virtues." School for Champions.
7 Feb. 2005. www.school-for-champions.com.

5   Benjamin Franklin. "Letter to Ezra Stiles." 9 March 1790, in John Bigelow,
ed., *The Works of Benjamin Franklin*, at 12:185-86 (New York: Putnam's, 1904)

6   Richard Pratt. *Pray With Your Eyes Open.* P & R. 1999

7   Manford G. Gutzke. *Plain Talk on Prayer.* Baker Book House. 1973.

8   R.C. Sproul. *The Prayer of the Lord.* Reformation Trust Publishing. 2009.

9   David Platt. *Radical.* Multnomah Books. 2010.

About the Author

Paula Rodriguez was born in Arkansas and spent her formative years in Louisiana, but she has also lived and worked in Oklahoma, California, Missouri, South Dakota, and Mississippi. She and her husband Charlie are the parents of three daughters who, in addition to the states listed above, have lived and worked in Tennessee, Georgia, Belize, Chile, Ireland, and Sweden.

Although raised in the United Methodist church, Paula was led to a saving faith in Christ by a Presbyterian pastor, and she soon after became a founding member of a fledging PCA church. Paula has a strong background in Reformed theology; however, in her moves around the country, she has also worshipped at churches in other denominations, such as Mennonite Brethren, Baptist, and the Evangelical Free Church. She has served as a Sunday School teacher, Children's Catechism instructor, Bible study leader, and President of her local Women in the Church.

Paula has had the privilege of studying under several seminary professors including John Currid, George Knight, Robert Rayburn, Robert Reymond, Palmer Robertson, and R.C. Sproul. Professionally, Paula is the Chair of the Department of Speech, Theatre, and Dance at Hinds Community College in Mississippi. She holds a Master of Arts degree from Louisiana Tech University and has done post-graduate study at the University of Oklahoma, Covenant Seminary, and Reformed Theological Seminary. In her teaching career, she has taught every grade from kindergarten to college, including a brief stint as a home-school mom.

Paula is a gifted writer and speaker, and would love to discuss theology, Reformed or otherwise, with anyone who is interested.

www.ingramcontent.com/pod-product-compliance
Lightning Source LLC
Chambersburg PA
CBHW070018100426
42740CB00013B/2549